ABOUT THE AUTHORS

Peter Whitehead was born in Shanghai in 1923 then relocated to the UK as a child. At the age of 14 he made his own way by sea to Australia, where he worked on farms as a labourer and horse breaker. He served in the Australian army and air force during the Second World War and then went on to live a richly varied life in Africa as a colonial officer, game ranger, big game hunter, rancher and animal wrangler for films. Peter now lives in New Zealand.

Tony Park is the author of 21 bestselling thriller novels set in Africa and several non-fiction biographies. A former journalist, government press secretary and PR consultant, he also served 34 years in the Australian Army Reserve, including six months in Afghanistan. He and his wife, Nicola, divide their time between Australia and southern Africa.

For behind the scenes stories and pictures of Peter Whitehead's amazing life please see the 'Bwana, There's a Body in the Bath!' page on Tony Park's website, www.tonypark.net and you can follow Tony on social media as @tonyparkauthor

ALSO BY TONY PARK

Far Horizon

Zambezi

African Sky

Safari

Silent Predator

Ivory

The Delta

African Dawn

Dark Heart

The Prey

The Hunter

An Empty Coast

Red Earth

The Cull

Captive

Scent of Fear

Ghosts of the Past

Last Survivor

Blood Trail

The Pride

Vendetta

Part of the Pride, with Kevin Richardson

The Grey Man, with John Curtis

Bush Vet, with Dr Clay Wilson

War Dogs, with Shane Bryant

Courage Under Fire, with Daniel Keighran VC

No One Left Behind, with Keith Payne VC

Rhino War, with Major General (Ret.) Johan Jooste

BWANA, THERE'S A BODY IN THE BATH!

PETER WHITEHEAD

TONY PARK

Hardcover edition published in 2023 by Ingwe Publishing
First published in 2022 by Ingwe Publishing

Copyright © 2022 by Peter Whitehead with Tony Park
All rights reserved
www.ingwepublishing.com

The moral right of the authors has been asserted.

All rights reserved. No part of this publication may be reproduced, stored in or introduced into a retrieval system, or transmitted, in any form, or by any means electronic, mechanical, photocopying, recording or otherwise, without the prior permission of the publisher. Any person who commits any unauthorised act in relation to this publication may be liable to criminal prosecution and civil claims for damages.

Bwana, There's a Body in the Bath!

Hardback Print ISBN: 978-1-922825-20-9

Cover design by Leandra Wicks
Illustrations by Charley Swynnerton and Paul Toschi
Map by Laurie Whiddon
Tiger Moth picture courtesy of Brett Martin
B24 Liberator picture AC0074 courtesy of Australian War Memorial

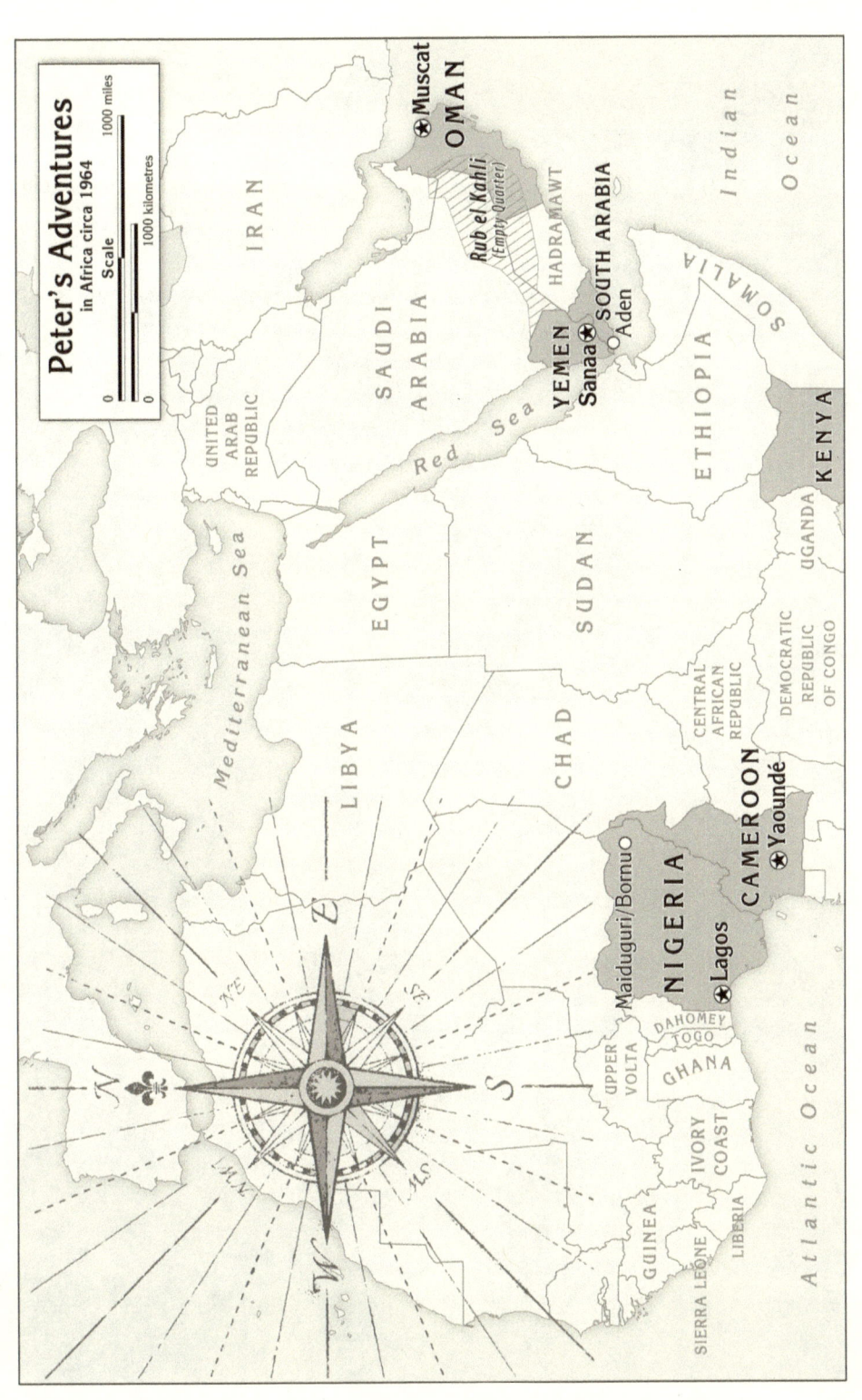

FOREWORD

It is a great honour to be invited to write the preface to the story of such a remarkable man. As you will read, my Uncle Peter has led an action-packed and colourful life. I am so delighted that he has finally managed to get his story written, after much nagging.

He first came into my life in England, when I was about seven. I was 'born on the back of a horse', and we instantly hit it off. We share a lifelong passion for horses, dogs, parrots and Africa.

For a time, I lost track of him, during his wanderings in Africa, but I never forgot him. I managed to track him down there with the help of my husband, who had heard tales of Peter Whitehead in Kenya, and was very keen to meet him.

After my mother, Wendy, Peter's little sister, died, Uncle Peter became my rock. He is now my 'go-to' for wise advice on so many different problems in life. Although we live at opposite ends of the world, he calls me on FaceTime (sometimes catching me in the shower, causing a mad dash to turn the camera off) and between us we are able to put the world right.

At times in his life, as you will read, Peter has overcome real hardships, and shown great resilience and true grit to survive. His philosophy has always been 'just get on with it', and he has.

I hope you enjoy this amazing story of the life and times of Peter Whitehead.

Anita Harrington
    The Countess of Harrington

PROLOGUE
KAFUE NATIONAL PARK, NORTHERN RHODESIA, 1957

It had been a good flight, apart from the severe turbulence, and crash landing in man-eating lion country.

The pilot, Ted Lenton, and Gerry Taylor, the provincial game officer, were in the front two seats of the Auster, a fragile little single-engine relic of the Second World War that had been designed for artillery spotting. As the youngest and least important I'd been relegated to the rear seat.

At the end of the dry season the hot, late afternoon air was rising up off Africa, baking below us. Soon the rains would come, spectacularly violent thunderstorms heralding a green revolution for the thirsty brown lands below.

The bumps got bumpier and my head was threatening to punch a hole in the roof. I'd flown during the war and had seen what Mother Nature could do to aircraft far larger and more robust than this one. I reached down and wrenched the seatbelt tighter.

All of us had our eyes peeled for likely places where the Kafue River could be crossed easily. I was watching as best as I could, out of my tiny side window and between the two men up front – after all, this little diversion from the flight plan had been my idea.

Gerry had arranged this weekend 'jolly' that we were on, a mix of business and pleasure at my permanent camp near the Kafue Hook, a bend in the river, to welcome a new member to the Northern Rhodesia Game Department to our province. Ted was giving his services for free, in return for the promise of some fabulous fishing; the charter of the aircraft was another of Gerry's fiddles.

The new appointee, together with all the staff and gear we needed for a weekend's fishing had been sent on ahead by land, leaving Mumbwa early in the morning for the 120-plus kilometre journey to the camp. Our original flight plan called for us to leave Mumbwa airstrip just after lunch and fly directly up to my camp at Myukweukwe, close to the pontoon crossing at the Hook.

I was 34-years-old by this time, the game ranger in charge of the central section of the Kafue National Park in Northern Rhodesia, which would, some years later, become Zambia. It was during our lunch that I proposed we revise our flight plan, unofficially, in order to look for a suitable site to put a pontoon in to cross the Kafue River between my central section of the park and the northern section under the control of my opposite number, Barry Shenton.

At that time, a meeting between Barry and myself entailed an arduous overland journey in the order of some 300 kilometres, whether we attempted the Mumba-to-Mankoya Road route, or the northerly one from Mumbwa to Kasempa. Both entailed long sections of bush-bashing. If we could find a suitable site for a pontoon crossing, we could cut at least 200 kilometres off the journey.

I spread out the map and showed them my revised flightpath.

'Let's head a few points west of north and cut the river here,' I pointed to a point about 30 kilometres upstream of the area I considered most likely to afford a crossing, 'then let's fly as slowly as we can downstream, and have a look at any possible sites. We should still get to Myukweukwe around 4.30 or 5pm – plenty of time for a quick hook or two in the water.'

After that it would be fresh fish for dinner, followed by a convivial evening of drinking and tall stories.

My base at Mumbwa was a cluster of about a dozen houses in varying degrees of decrepitude ranging from the game ranger's allotted accommodation, which had been condemned as unfit for human accommodation some 20 years earlier, to the District Commissioner's house, which had been updated by the Public Works Department a few years earlier to include such up-market luxuries as running water, a flush toilet and a small generator to provide electricity.

The 'boma', the collective name for our settlement, believed to be an old acronym for British Officers' Mess Area, was home to a fluctuating population of about eight men, including the District Commissioner (DC); a couple of District Officers (DOs); a medic; a police officer; and representatives of technical departments, including agriculture, veterinary, public works and game and tsetse fly control. Apart from the DC, medic and one of the DOs, who were married, the rest of us were young and single, with all that entails.

Our houses were located just west of the district administration buildings, where the road divided, the left fork curling round the east end of the airstrip through three seedy little trading stores – one run by a South African, Jukes Curtis, and the other two by Indians. The road then carried on to Mankoya, via the Kafue Hook, some 250 kilometres to the west in Barotseland.

After lunch, we headed out to the Auster, squeezed in and took off. Besides making it easier for me to liaise with Barry there was another, less urgent benefit that could possibly arise from a more efficient crossing of the river, namely tourist development.

If the park had more roads and easier access, visitors might come, but that was a long way off as the area was literally in the middle of nowhere and plagued by the most ferocious and liberal quantities of tsetse flies, many of which carried human trypanosomiasis – also known as sleeping sickness.

To further discourage humans and habitation, the area we were now flying over was home to a particularly unpleasant race of lions, addicted to human flesh. So dangerous had these man-eaters become that the colonial administration in the early 1930s had relocated the indigenous population, a whole tribe under Chief Kabulwebulwe, further west to the safer areas of Barotseland. This, coincidentally, suited the management of the newly-designated National Park.

Having arrived at the river approximately where we intended, Ted turned the nose to the west, reduced altitude to about 200 feet, and we set about looking for a likely spot for a river crossing.

The Kafue National Park is about the same size as South Africa's flagship game reserve, the Kruger National Park, itself often compared in area to Israel or Wales, and by that time already establishing itself as a tourist destination of note. The major difference was that Kafue was in the middle of nowhere, a remote, inaccessible tract of virgin bushland and sweeping plains. It boasted large herds of waterbuck and impala, as well as lesser-seen antelopes such as Lichtenstein's hartebeest and the majestic sable and roan.

'Looks like a good spot down there,' Gerry said after about 45 minutes of flying, pointing ahead through the cockpit windscreen.

Ted pushed the stick forward into a gentle dive and only levelled off when were so low that the wheels of the fixed undercarriage were almost skimming the glittering surface of the Kafue River below us.

The river was about five hundred metres wide at this point, punctuated here and there with the rounded backs of hippos. A herd of puku, a shaggy-coated, yellow-brown antelope, bounded away as our shadow passed over them. Ted tracked along the northern bank of the river while he and Gerry searched for signs of shallow water and approach paths, eroded areas where game came and went to drink and where access by motor car might one day be possible.

The spot Gerry had indicated looked promising, but we would

need to check the southern bank so Ted pulled back on the stick, turned and circled about. He dropped down again and just as we levelled out the engine coughed.

'Shit,' Ted said.

Next came a hiccup and the engine stopped. A moment later it started again, providing us all a moment's relief, but then it coughed again and began running erratically, vibrating and juddering in front of us.

Ted's spare hand flew over the controls like a one-armed paper hanger but nothing seemed to be happening. Before he lost too much more momentum, Ted pulled back on the stick, pushed on full-left rudder and just managed to clear the top of the trees running along the side of the river.

As worrying as the situation was, Ted was thinking, and he was doing the right thing. If we had put down in the Kafue River the crocodiles would have feasted on anything that was left of us after the fiercely territorial and aggressive hippos had finished chomping the aircraft and what was left of us in their massive jaws.

Give me lions, any day, I thought.

Just as it looked as though we might gain enough altitude to search for a smooth, open vlei to land, we stalled. The Auster hung, nose up, for a heartbeat, then dived for the ground, nose-first.

Luckily, Ted had only been able to climb about fifty feet before the engine finally conked out, but we still hit the ground with an almighty bang. Gerry and Ted, unlike me, had not been affected as badly by the turbulence and so had not had time to tighten their safety straps, resulting in both being a little bent on impact. They were conscious, however, and staggered out of the Auster.

I smelled fuel and, unscathed thanks to my safety straps, clambered between the front seats and was out of the aircraft like an eel swimming upstream. Looking out for each other, we all hobbled or ran as far as we could from the Auster, expecting it to burst into a ball of flames at any second. We threw ourselves down on the ground and waited.

Nothing happened. A dove cooed nearby; Gerry slapped at the first of a promised aerial armada of tsetse flies.

'Let me go see what I can find,' I said, as the other two slumped in the shade of a tree, assessing their injuries. As the least battered of the three of us it was up to me to do what I could for the common good. I went to the aircraft, swatting at flies as I walked.

The Auster had buried its nose deep into the dirt; the airscrew had shattered into a thousand pieces. The wings were askew, but it was clear from the ease we had exited that getting back in was not going to be a problem, once I was sure it was not about to explode in a ball of flame.

Sitting vertical as it was, the wreck would be no use to us as shelter and too small for all of us to sleep in, anyway, so I began rummaging about for anything that might be of use to us. We hadn't brought a firearm with us - they had all gone up in the road convoy. Our plan, had we stuck to it, was to fly as light as possible into a fully equipped camp.

From the battered aircraft I took the first aid kit, a small crash axe, designed for getting out of tight spots, such as a broken aeroplane, some tinned bully beef – to be consumed only in the direst of emergencies, a tin of powdered milk and, most importantly of all, some tea.

'Here you go, fellas,' I said as I handed my scavengings to Ted and Gerry, who set about patching themselves up as best as they could. I then opened the can of milk powder and took the bagged contents out. This gave me a handy container for water, so I went down to the banks of the river. On arrival I saw the furrowed tracks in the sand where a crocodile had eased itself back into the water, perhaps, on hearing my footsteps. Keeping a wary eye on the water I went to the edge and filled the can.

When I came back, I got a fire going and put the billy on, deciding that a cup of tea was the first priority before we did anything else. While we waited for the billy – the empty milk tin – to boil, I helped the other two dress their wounds.

We had a council of war and took stock of our supplies. Our 'emergency supplies' kit included, amongst other useful bits and pieces, some fishing line and hooks, but no tea cups. Once it had boiled, I brewed up some tea. We passed the billy between us, sipping from the hot can. I must say, the tea helped raise our spirits.

Ted looked at the sun, half way down to the horizon. 'Won't be long until it's dark.'

It had been about three in the afternoon when we crashed and light would not be long with us. While the other two rested I put on another can of water, took the axe and began organising us some shelter.

Near to where we were was a big *Kigelia africana*, a sausage tree. Lush and shady, the tree was named after the long bulbous, hard-shelled fruits it bore, which, shaped like a sausage, averaged the size of a grown man's forearm. They were no use to us as food, though baboons ate them. Had it been the wrong time of year they would have been quite a threat – a hit from a falling 'sausage' could do quite a bit of damage.

Next to the tree, and of more interest, was a large termite mound with a rich thicket of masakasaka bush filling the space between the two. Using the axe, I started hacking into the foliage, carving out a little cave in the dense vegetation.

I kept the branches and foliage I cut out of the hollow and arranged them into a spikey palisade around the front of the opening, creating a boma large enough for us to stretch out in and light a fire. I then scoured the bush around us for wood and stacked enough to last through the night, inside the enclosure.

Once all was ready, I called the other two, and showed them their new home, then got another fire going. It was now nearly dark. I sat on a log in front of the flames, thinking.

'I've got a pretty fair idea where we are,' I said, 'and no one's going to get to us for at least three or four days - and that is if they do find us.'

'We need a plan for that long,' Gerry said.

'Do we stay here?' Ted asked. Conventional wisdom had it that staying near the site of a wreck was the best course of action. 'Anyone searching for us is more likely to see the wreckage than one of us.'

I slapped at a late-flying tsetse fly. At least they would disappear with the sun. 'I reckon the Mumbwa-to-Mankoya road's between thirty and forty miles south of us, as the crow flies. I'm OK. I could walk it.'

There was some debate about that. It was fiercely hot during the day and easy to get lost in the bush, the others pointed out. The trees to our west were swallowing the last of the sun, tinged red through the dry season's dust.

'I'd walk at night – starting tonight.' I pointed up at the heavens. 'All I've got to do is follow the Souhern Cross; I can navigate by that.'

While we discussed our fate an orange full moon was starting to climb in the sky. It was a good sign, I thought, and would be bright enough to allow me to watch out for danger. I dragged some more logs on to the fire, readying myself to set off.

I turned my back on the flames, so as to prepare my night vision, and from the comparative safety of our flimsy natural fence of foliage I stared out at the bush.

'Movement,' I hissed.

'What is it?' Ted asked, from the cave in the vegetation on the other side of the fire, where he and Gerry were lying.

By the light of the moon, which I thought would keep me safe, I saw the silhouettes of three animals moving, their bodies slightly paler than the backdrop of vegetation.

'Hyenas?' I said, 'Three of them.'

The spotted hyena is a brazen animal; it'll sneak up and steal the chop off a braai, but by the same token, if confronted by an angry yell or a hurled rock it will slink away. A number of them together, however, might be a different proposition.

The animals were no doubt attracted by the firelight, perhaps the first they'd ever seen in this remote part of the park. They started coming closer, looming in size.

'We've got visitors, I called to the other two.'

As they came closer my heart skipped a beat. These animals, I now realised, were not hyenas after all.

'Shit, man,' I said, as the largest of the trio, a male, gave a growl, broke ranks and charged at our flimsy boma.

'Lion!'

1

SHANGHAI, 1929

Chinese servants screamed with a mixture of amusement and annoyance as I hurtled down the laneway on my Fairy tricycle.

The milkman, caught unawares, had to jump out of the way to avoid himself and his bottles being cleaned up by a five-year-old.

My kingdom, before school attempted the impossible task of civilising me, was the back alley. Behind the genteel, westernised suburban street on which we lived, I tried the patience of whichever servant had drawn the short straw to supervise me that day and reigned like a tiny, tyrannical emperor. I mixed with the amahs and delivery boys, played with their children, and learned to speak Chinese, badly.

Here, people gossiped and spat and took their meals crouched together. A sewage drain ran along one side of the lane and on this day of play the concrete cover outside the kitchen door of our house had been removed, where workmen were engaged in the unenviable task of clearing a blockage. A grimy place at the best of times, the alley was positively ripe in the sticky July heat.

'Out of my way, out of my way,' I called as I pedalled down the laneway.

The Fairy tricycle was not made for little people at the end of the garden, but, rather, for short humans. Following on from the success of the Penny Farthing in the 1880s, Fred Colson of the Colson Corporation in the United States had the bright idea that children might quite like to ride cycles; without a ladder the Farthing was way out of reach to someone my size, and a death trap. His 'Fairy' line was low to the ground with a cross bar almost down at road level – perfect for a little terror like me.

As I screamed along, I might have evaded the milkman, but the baker's delivery man, sick of my antics and determined to teach me a lesson, reached down as I swerved past him and grabbed my little trike by the rear and lifted it into the air.

'Let me go, let me go!' I wailed, my little legs pumping furiously but impotently as various hawkers, staff and delivery folk laughed uproariously and pointed at the white boy squealing like a piglet.

The baker's man simply did as I had commanded and dropped

me, but my back wheels were spinning at such a furious rate that I shot off like a Chinese firecracker, straight into the open sewage drain.

'Aieee!' our Amah shrieked as others covered their mouths with their hands, agog at the sight of me landing, cycle and all, with an almighty splash and going down like a submarine in crash dive mode

One of our servants, probably the unfortunate charged with babysitting me, sounded 'panic stations' as workers, passers-by and even those who found the whole thing hilarious, crowded around.

I looked up at them, white eyes peering out from a mask of effluent resulting from the lavatorial waste of the area.

I was fished out and stripped naked on the spot, amidst the cooing, chuckling, screeching denizens of the alley world. A tap was turned on and the next thing I knew I was being hosed down, pummelled from head to foot with cold water.

All of our house staff had now been alerted and had gone into full damage-control mode.

'Inside, inside!' someone hissed.

My filthy, sodden clothes were gathered and I was furtively sneaked into the house via the servants' entrance to the staff bathroom where hot water was drawn and every inch of me was again scrubbed vigorously and repeatedly until the last evidence, either visual or olfactory was eliminated from my, by now, pink skin.

A servant was dispatched to my room to get fresh clothes. There was more tutting and fussing by the high-speed pit-crew of maids and assorted other servants as my hair was combed, my buttons done up and shoes laced. Meanwhile someone, presumably one of the male staff members, had been delegated to the unenviable job of fishing my Fairy cycle out of the cesspit, hosing, scrubbing and cleaning it, then sneakily wheeling it around to its normal resting place at the front of the house.

When I was judged to be pristine, I was shepherded quietly downstairs from the servants' quarters and propelled with a gentle shove in my back into the drawing room, where my mother sat, reading and taking tea.

'Hello, Peter,' she said, looking up from her magazine, 'are you alright, dear? Have you not been out playing? You're looking unusually clean for this time of day.'

As the precursor of any future material benefits I might receive from the hands of lady Luck, I was born on Christmas Eve, 1923, in a nursing home in Shanghai's French concession. My parents were doing well and could easily have afforded to give me a double helping of presents each December 24, to make up for my lack of enterprise in choosing such an inauspicious day to enter the world, but it was never to be. Father was far too serious for that sort of thing.

Charles Whitehead was 37-years-old by the time I, the third of four children, came along. He was a partner and the managing director of a company importing and installing cotton manufacturing machinery into the developing cotton industry of a growing China.

Shanghai was booming. On the city's bustling streets white men in winged collars and bow ties marched to and from business meetings or lunch, slyly eyeing elegant Chinese women sporting short, wavy, western hairdos and wearing tight-fitting cheongsams, demurely covering their necks, but split to the thigh at each leg. The pampered wives of Europeans, clad in the latest flapper fashions, perambulated idly along the Bund, the wide walkway and office-lined road running alongside the broad Huangpu River, or made their way to a game of bridge or a bar.

Vessels of all sizes from local junks to passenger ships and Naval Dreadnoughts lined the docks. Gleaming limousines driven by chauffeurs in hats hooted past modern trams and ancient rickshaws in a city that prided itself on being a mix of the Paris of the East and the New York of the West.

It was a good life for the residents of the International Settlement, and I have memories of my father in a dinner suit, my mother in the latest frock, setting off for functions and coming in long after my bedtime.

The worst that had come of my spectacular immersion in the

sewer was a case of conjunctivitis, or Chinese Pinkeye, as it was known; this kept me confined to the dark interior of the house for a while, but I was busting to get out. The only other childhood disaster I recall was contracting scarlet fever in 1931 and being locked up in the hospital for infectious diseases.

'Hello, Peter!' my family – mother, father and little Wendy – called from the hospital grounds below as I leaned out of an open window on the upper floor, looking down at them and waving. That was as close as I got to a visit while I recovered.

Horses have always loomed large in my life and my love and fascination for them go back as far as I can remember. The Shanghai police force included mounted Sikh troopers and I recall a gigantic, magnificently bearded and moustachioed gentleman, replete with turban, colourful uniform and glittering finery which included a sword and a big pouch containing a revolver strapped to his waist. From his Olympian height astride his horse, he would reach down and hoist my little sister, Wendy, or me up on to the pommel of his saddle and parade us down the street, to the envy of the other neighbourhood children and the chagrin of their more conservative parents who didn't approve of such goings-on.

My parents had been married shortly after the end of the First World War. My mother, Mabel, was the youngest daughter of a successful farmer/horse dealer and as an accomplished horse-woman herself, encouraged her two younger children to emulate her with the help of a riding stable owner, Miss Perrin, who operated her business not far away from our house.

When I was younger mother had taken my elder siblings, Glen and Mary, and my younger sister, Wendy, and me back to the UK for a while. Glen and Mary were enrolled in their respective schools and left in the care of mother's older spinster sister, while mother, Wendy and I returned to China.

Back in Shanghai both Wendy and I were introduced to the educational process via a primary school located in Bubbling Well Road, later renamed Nanjing Road. The tree-lined, agreeable thoroughfare had been described as the most beautiful in Shanghai and led to the impressive Jing'an Temple. Among the many other children at the school was a little girl called Mary Hayley Bell, who I would meet again several decades later, when she and her subsequent family had become household names in Britain.

One clear memory I have of that time is of being obsessed with a game played with glass marbles, which entailed flicking the marbles through little holes cut in a cardboard box, though what happened to the marbles after they went through the little holes escapes my memory.

Another vivid memory is of diving for coins thrown into the water at the Municipal Swimming Pool which was located in, or very near, the Racecourse.

IN 1931 JAPAN INVADED MANCHURIA, the first step in what would be a protracted onslaught against China and, later, the South Pacific. In January 1932, Japan created an excuse to attack Shanghai.

Ultra-nationalist Japanese monks started riots in Shanghai, shouting pro-Japanese, anti-Chinese slogans. This prompted retaliation by Chinese mobs, leading to the killing of a monk. The Japanese used this and further street fighting as an excuse to attack the Chinese parts of Shanghai – not the foreign settlement where we lived – with carrier-borne bombers and later, ground troops.

Fighting raged between the Japanese and Chinese armies outside of our enclave, but the western powers, wanting to protect their business interests in China, and not keen on a war with Japan, helped negotiate a ceasefire and peace by May. It was, however, only a matter of time before the Japanese came back.

I am not sure what prompted the decision - perhaps the turbulent relations between China and Japan, the developing financial depression or the fact that I was now reaching the age when a move up from primary school was due – but Wendy, mother and I were shipped off back to the UK.

We boarded a vessel of the German Norddeutscher Lloyd shipping service, our mission to set up house and attend to the educational requirements of the now consolidated family. My father remained in Shanghai to attend to his business.

As I waved goodbye to my father, I had no idea it would be the last time I would ever see him.

I TOOK aim down the barrel of the 16-gauge shotgun, lining up a fat pigeon in the green hedgerow.

There was a chill in the air, the sky leaden and threatening rain yet again. I had thought England would be a prison, but I had managed to find an escape – the country. The weapon wavered in my skinny arms, then I squeezed the trigger.

Boom.

The butt of the shotgun slammed into my shoulder, nearly knocking me over. The pigeon flew away. I had missed, but I was having the time of my life. Not every bird I aimed at was as lucky.

From Shanghai we had gone to live in the small town of Royston, in Hertfordshire, where both sides of my father's family were part of the local community. Glen, Mary and I commuted to school in Cambridge, in the neighbouring county, each day by train, while Wendy, my partner in crime in Shanghai, was now attending primary school locally.

I can't remember much of my time at the Lower School other than playing soccer rather than rugby and being enrolled as a very reluctant member of the Cub Scouts. Scholastically, I must have done something right as I actually won a prize – a book called 'Gods, Heroes and Men of Ancient Greece' by Dr. A.L. Rowse, who, in his earlier days had apparently been a pupil at the school.

The pleasant atmosphere of lower school changed dramatically on my graduation to the upper or 'Big School'

At the Big School, as a student, I was an unmitigated disaster and a total waste of the fat fees they charged for not doing anything more than providing me with a place to spend the day during term time

Somehow, I had incurred the antipathy of a number of the masters, especially the headmaster who missed no opportunity to humiliate me publicly, admonishing me for some real or imagined misdemeanour at assembly.

The headmaster looked down his beaklike nose at me. 'Whitehead, my study, Thursday at noon.'

He took every opportunity to administer corporal punishment in the form of a length of a six-millimetre bamboo cane, with a curved handle, taped for a better grip, which he applied with great enthusiasm to my nether region. The canings were a regular feature every Thursday, designed to improve my ability to absorb the wisdom dispensed in the classrooms. From my point of view, the only tangible effect was to make eating my lunch uncomfortable.

I understand that sometime after I had left the headmaster's care, he was hospitalised for gastric ulcers, which may have accounted for his behaviour, but it certainly didn't help me, or change my view of him. As a form of encouragement for me to apply myself to my studies it was a total failure, a conclusion he hadn't come to even after more than a year's trial.

Generally, my view of the school and its staff was that they were a bunch of myopic, self-righteous sadists, happy to extort money from my parents in return for a licence to inflict corporal punishment as and when they felt like it.

My escape, as always, was the countryside.

When Wendy reached the age to attend her sister's Lower School the family moved from Royston, briefly, to the village of Shelford, before moving on to the more rural village of Fulbourn. There, we took over a delightful old wing of what was once quite a grand house called Old Shardelowes.

For me, this was a dream home, situated as it was on the very outskirts of the village, surrounded by open fields and woods with quite a big farmyard between us and the village. Needless to say, my mother was dragooned once again in to making representations to the farm owner to allow me to 'assist' on his farm whenever I had time away from school. He must have been a very kindly man, as he agreed and for the next two years I toiled away quite happily under his 'supervision'.

To make Fulbourn an even more acceptable place, the father of one of my friends from school, Bob Lacy, also farmed there, as well as training a few race horses. Bob rode in the mornings before leaving for school, an activity I would have given my soul to join him in, but alas it was not to be. Bob, a year older than I was, stood just over five-feet tall and all up dripping wet barely tilted the scales at six-and-a-half stone, whereas, I, a year younger, was already approaching six feet and weighed just over 10 stone.

YET ANOTHER BENEFIT of life in Fulbourn was that across the road from our house, in what had once been a labourer's cottage, lived the local handyman and reputed poacher, Jim Plum.

Jim and I became great friends, with him assuming the mantle of mentor in the field arts of rural England, as defined by those with very little money. Under Jim's tutelage, I learned to shoot, snare and trap, pluck, skin and prepare all manner of legal and illegal game in and out of season.

In doing so I helped mother stock the table, even if she was a little embarrassed to learn where the bounty had come from. Guilt by association does not seem to have been too evident, as my farmer mentor, who worked all the fields around our house, often used to loan me his 12-gauge shotgun.

Ostensibly, I was to wander about the fields during autumn and winter to shoot wood pigeons, rooks, rabbits and other vermin. However, when no one was in sight, if something more tasty wandered into my sights the offer would be accepted, and the resulting victim stuffed down the back of my coat, or hidden in the hedgerow for retrieval later, a-la-Jim's teaching.

'Watch him, boy,' Jim said, standing close by me as we watched a pheasant, 'and don't forget to lead him. Now!'

As the bird, deliberately spooked, took off, madly flapping its wings, I did as Jim had taught me and aimed slightly ahead of it, allowing for the time it would take the pellets to reach it. I squeezed the trigger, ready for the recoil.

'Good shot, boy!'

Surrounded by farmland and remnant woods, I began to find something of my true calling. I was a willing farm labourer – anything was preferable to the classroom. I had decided that the two things in life I wanted to pursue were rugby and farming. Animals, in particular, intrigued me.

The farmer wasn't complaining. I was more than happy to muck out stables, cow byres, and pig sties. For me it was bliss – give me the smell of manure and a bit of physical labour over the scratching of a pen nib on paper, or the swish and *thwack* of the headmaster's cane, any day, I thought.

In time, I graduated to leading horses here and there, and driving cattle to and from the fields. Eventually, as I got older, I was given more responsible jobs, such as harrowing fields with a team of two or three horses on my own, or taking the horses into the village to get shod. In the summertime during hay-making and grain harvesting, I would lead the horse and cart whilst the men built huge loads onto the cart which were then roped down. The horse and cart would then be driven to the farmyard for unloading onto the stack or tipped into the barn.

For me it was an idyllic existence, and no doubt kept me out of mischief from my mother's point of view. The farmer seemed more than happy to have an unpaid hand around to do some of the less technical work.

Altogether, life at Old Shardelowes couldn't be bettered. During the season, I was able to play rugby to my heart's content at school; the sport became, and still is, an abiding passion.

I also learned the art of cutting school, escaping whenever the opportunity occurred. Out of school I had all the work and entertainment a boy could dream of; the only fly in the ointment was the attentions of the headmaster at regular intervals

BY THE AGE OF 13, I felt as though school would never end; however, ironically, my salvation from the crushing boredom of the classroom and the sadistic ministrations of the headmaster came at the hands of the Imperial Japanese Army.

I was upstairs in my bedroom when the phone rang. I heard my mother answering the call, talking away, but then something about her tone of voice changed.

'No!' she yelled down the line.

When I got to her she was sobbing.

'What's wrong, mum?'

'Your father... the Japanese have invaded Shanghai and he's been captured. Whatever are we going to do, Peter?'

My mother was no doubt worried about my father, and the fate that awaited him as a civilian internee of the Japanese, but she was also, quite rightly, worried about us. Father had been our source of money as he had continued to work, but now we were suddenly without means.

While this latest conflict between Japan and China had been sparked by another seemingly trivial incident – a missing Japanese soldier, this time, and an exchange of gunfire over him at the Marco Polo Bridge in Wanping – it led to all-out war. Unlike the relatively short conflict between Japan and China on the outskirts of the international zone in 1932, the attacks of July, 1937, led to bloody street-by-street fighting throughout Shanghai in a battle later compared to the epic struggle for the Russian city of Stalingrad.

Somehow, my father had been caught up in all that, although we'd had no word from him.

Both my older siblings had left home - Glen had gone to sea as an officer cadet on a passenger line, and Mary was a nurse in training at Great Ormond Street Hospital in London. However, mother still had to clothe, feed and school Wendy and me.

Wendy and I continued our schooling or, rather, I should say, Wendy carried on learning, while I continued my less than acceptable conduct, ducking school whenever I could.

One afternoon, I ducked off to one of the local cinemas. I can't remember what the film was that I went to see, but I'll never forget the newsreel that came before it. In the days before television our only visual source of news, other than the newspapers, was short snippets of documentary footage before the main feature.

As I sat in the mostly empty cinema, dressed in my school uniform, an item came on the screen about Australia. It was about the Royal Easter Show, in Sydney, New South Wales, an annual event when the rural people from all over the State and indeed the whole country came to the city to exhibit their livestock and produce.

Included in the arena entertainments was a 'Bushman's Carnival', what is now known as a rodeo. There was film of bucking horses, bull riding, steer wrestling, camp drafting and other exciting pursuits that the stockmen of Australia indulged in.

I watched, enthralled, as a man with a hat who looked like an American cowboy from the pictures, held on for grim life as the horse he was trying to ride did its level best to catapult him into the air.

'Hell,' I whispered to myself, 'that's for me.'

I rushed home. I had come up with a plan to save my family from the poorhouse.

I was going to become an Australian stockman.

2

AUSTRALIA, 1938

It was still dark when, shivering under a thin blanket, I roused myself from my bed, an old wool bag strung between two crossed sticks of wood at my head and two at my feet.

Other than where I slept, there was no other furniture in the cold, old shearer's hut made of rusty corrugated iron. Outside was a bucket of water, with a layer of ice beginning to form on the surface. I plunged my hands in, to wash my face and give my body a quick sluice.

No one had told me Australia would be cold, but here, at Cowra, about 400 kilometres west of Sydney, across the Great Dividing Range, it could get awful chilly in winter.

The moon was going down and the sun not yet up as I finished dressing and walked, feet crunching on frost, towards another day of back-breaking labour.

How the hell had I ended up here?

It had not been easy to convince my mother of the merits of my scheme, that I should emigrate to Australia, aged 13, to save her from the burden of having to feed, clothe and educate me.

It was even harder to get the headmaster and the school's board of governors to let me out of their sadistic clutches – every child was an earner for them and I was, literally, and figuratively, their favourite whipping boy.

Somehow, perhaps given the fact my father had been captured by the Japanese, feared dead, I wangled it. My mother and I had done our research and had been in touch with the Big Brother Movement, one of a number of dodgy schemes running at the time to ship orphans and children of poor families out to the erstwhile colonies. Supposedly, we would be taken care of by families or kind-hearted Samaritans and enjoy a healthy, well-fed life in the sunshine and open air of the great outback.

The reality was that we were slave labour for farms, or worse.

Some of the unfortunate children dragooned into these schemes suffered physical, emotional and even sexual abuse. Some little boys and girls were lied to, being told by their new masters that they were orphans, so no one would care what happened to them or what was done to them, when in reality they had parents back in the United Kingdom who had been assured their offspring were going to a better place.

At the age of 14 I found myself on a ship, bound for Australia. I was mostly in the company of adults, so growing up fast. Many of the passengers were Australians who'd been visiting the Old Dart and were returning home. I remember sitting on deck with a group of men who had befriended me, all of us talking about our plans for the future and how we might make our fortunes.

'Don't worry about money, ever,' I remember one philosopher saying to me, as our ship approached the port of Fremantle, near Perth, Western Australia. 'If you ever want it, it'll be there. Don't worry about it.'

I don't know whether this was his optimistic view on life, or if he saw something special or unusual in me, but, as it happened, he was dead right. All my life, whenever I needed it, somewhere, out of the blue, a windfall would arrive. It was nothing ever great, but enough to see me through, and after all, what more does one want?

My arrival in Sydney did not get off to an auspicious start. When our ship docked, there were 11 'Big Brothers' waiting on the docks at Circular Quay, but 12 little brothers on board. All were paired off, except for me.

I would have been alone in a strange country had the local secretary of the Big Brother movement not taken pity on me. She stood in for my absentee Big Brother, doing what was necessary until I was moved on to Scheyville Farm on the outskirts of the city to await 'distribution'.

Scheyville, under the sponsorship of the Dreadnought Scheme, a similar organisation to Big Brother Movement, trained city boys and immigrants in basic farm work for service on the land. The whole place, a rundown collection of curved corrugated iron Nissen huts, had more of a feel of a Borstal, or juvenile prison, to me. In the past it had, actually, been a prison camp, for interned German civilians and enemy POWs during the First World War, and subsequently served as a drying out tank for alcoholics and deadbeats.

FROM SCHEYVILLE I was palmed off to a sheep and wheat farmer at Cowra. It was there that I was dropped into the punishing, almost medieval routine of life as a 'wood and water joey'.

Rising before dawn, the air at its coldest, I walked across to the stable to put out the feed, before saddling-up the night pony and going out to the horse paddock to muster up the draft horses, which would be needed for the day's work on the farm.

Once having shut them in the stable for their morning feed, I left the pony tied up outside while I went over each horse with a dandy brush to knock the sweat off their shoulders from the previous day's work. That finished, it was off again to get the milk cows into the yard, before going up to the dairy for the buckets and other bits and pieces that attended each days' milking.

Having milked the six or eight cows, I would let their calves join them before letting them out into their paddock, after which I would take the milk up to the dairy for separating. Having separated the milk, I took the house milk and the cream to the kitchen before taking the skim milk to the pig sties, where I added it to their feed.

Next, I washed down everything concerned with the milking, and chopped wood for the house fire and stacked it in the house ready for use. The 'water' part of my job description started with filling two fountains, large tubs with taps on them that stood on the woodstove and provided hot water for the kitchen. After that, I cleaned and scalded the separator and milking utensils and scrubbed out the dairy before going into the kitchen for breakfast.

Finally, it was time to go to work! I would put in a day's labour on the farm, doing whatever the season required and then at four in the afternoon it was time to start reversing my morning chores. I caught up the night pony to go out and bring the milk cows with their calves in and separate them for the night, before filling the mangers in the stables for the draught horses coming in from their day's work.

My last job at night, after having had dinner, and just before going to bed, was to let all the draft horses out of the stables and turn them into the horse paddock to graze until I picked them up again at about 4.30 am the next morning.

So my time passed, for five and a half days of the week. On Saturday afternoons I just had to bring the cows in, while on Sundays I did my normal before-breakfast chores, combined with getting the horses in, fed, let out, and their mangers filled ready for Monday morning. Then, the whole weekly cycle was repeated again.

So much for being an 'Australian stockman'. My princely stipend for all this effort was five shillings a week, plus my keep. Somebody was getting a bargain out of this deal and it sure as hell wasn't me.

THE DAYTIME WORK on the farm moved with the seasons.

When the harvest was being brought in, it was bloody hard work. My young body ached in the evenings, but started growing muscle from carrying 100-kilogram wheat bags on my back. In all it was tough, thankless, hard and miserable work.

There were some compensations, though. I spent a good deal of time riding horses, which I did bareback, or at least with an empty chaff bag instead of a saddle. I thought this would improve my balance and 'stickability', in preparation for my ultimate ambition to be a buck-jump rider. I learned a little bit about sheep, and quickly decided I was not interested in them. It was a pretty rough introduction to rural Australian life, but it helped me develop a sense of independence that I didn't know I possessed.

On Sundays, after the morning chores were over, I had a weekly bath in an old zinc tub I had found under the tank-stand. I filled it with a couple of kerosene buckets heated over an open fire. Having scrubbed as much dirt off as possible, dried and dressed myself, I then washed my dirty clothes and other odd bits and pieces in the now cold water, and hung them on the fence in front of the hut to dry.

On the odd occasion, if nothing else could be found for me to do, I could sit on the veranda of the hut and just do nothing but enjoy the sunshine. This didn't happen very often as the old man would use Sunday as an opportunity to walk round the garden, orchard and buildings of the homestead. If he found anything not to his liking, I would be called out to fix it.

Twice in six months, I managed to get a Saturday morning off and hitched a ride into Cowra. My so-called Big Brother, the one who was supposed to collect me off the ship, lived in Cowra, which I understand was the reason I was sent there from Scheyville. However, each time I tried to contact him in the town, he was either busy with a domestic problem, or a business issue. He was a small-time businessman and evidently not a successful one.

Often, I might have been somewhat disenchanted with my work, but I found I loved Australia. I revelled in the eucalyptus smell of the bush, the wildness of the countryside, and being around the animals and the playful, but hard-working sheep and cattle dogs.

While the bloke on the ship had been right, on one hand, that I wouldn't have to look far for money, I was never going to be very independent on five shillings a week. Money aside, I had not come to Australia to chop wood and feed pigs and draft horses; I had come in search of what I had seen on that newsreel clip in Cambridge, a life as back country stockman and buck-jump rider.

I stuck it for a bit more than half a year, then told my boss I was off.

STILL WELL SHY of my 15th birthday, I hopped a train to Sydney and got off at Central Station, in the seedier southern end of the central business district.

With limited finances I found myself a bed in one of the cheaper dives around, the People's Palace, in Pitt Street, not far from the station. Despite its grand name, this collection of dorms and dank rooms was the flophouse of all flophouses, run by the Salvation Army and catering to the city's down and out denizens, winos, and hobos.

Fortunately, I'd stayed in touch with the secretary of the Big Brother organisation and she helped me find another job, this time near Moree, in the far north-west of New South Wales, in the Gwydir Valley. It was about twice as far from Sydney as Cowra, but the farmer, Frank, ran sheep and cattle. Where there were cattle, I knew, there would be horses.

Though I was once again taken on as the wood and water joey, Frank was a kindlier soul than my ex-employer at Cowra, plus my duties included a lot of work with his horses. Frank had a club foot and although it didn't inhibit him in any way from normal riding, he was at a distinct disadvantage in riding the less disciplined of the horses on his property. As a result, he was quite happy to let me take on that chore once he found out that was all I was really interested in.

'Looks like you're happier working with horses than doing chores around the house,' Frank noted one day.

'You're right. It's what I want to really do, work with horses,' I told him.

After I'd done a couple of months working as the wood and water joey-cum-roustabout, Frank hired another young man from the city. He'd been taken on as a station hand, but it soon became obvious he knew nothing about the bush, let alone the work of a stockman.

Frank gave him the duties I was performing and promoted me to station hand.

'Same money, though,' he said to me. I would be stuck on seven shillings a week, plus keep.

I couldn't say no, because I was finally going to get a chance to do what I had set out to do. Frank, being a keen horseman himself, was breeding far more horses on his property than he could ever use in the course of his day-to-day operations on the station, but as he owned the station and it was about his only pleasure, what did it matter if a bit of grass was eaten by horses and not cattle or sheep?

The horses he bred were good, either three-quarter, or seven-eighths thoroughbred with a few true thoroughbred mares amongst the breeding stock as, amongst other things, he was a keen follower of bush race meetings.

Most of the general station stock were what used to be called Walers, named after the state of New South Wales. These hardy horses had already carved themselves a place in history, not only on the wide brown lands of their homeland, but also as mounts for Australian soldiers on the South African veld during the Anglo-Boer War of 1899-1901, and in the desert columns that rode triumphant through Egypt and Palestine in the First World War. There were also a few likely looking gallopers in the mob, who would eventually turn up at the local race tracks, and possibly go even further if they turned out to be any good.

I think we made quite a good team, Frank and I. Whenever there was a lull in general station work, or actually any other excuse he could find, Frank was more than happy to ride out with me to the distant paddocks on the station where he ran his horses, and run a suitable mob into the yards he had set up at his outstation, Karaba.

He would then sit on the fence and instruct me in the art of dealing with rough horses. On his better days, one of his favourite pastimes was to select a particularly stroppy looking horse, get me to rope it and pull it up to the fence. Between us, we would saddle it and then I would climb on it and he would let it go.

Off I went, with Frank keeping count of how many bucks I stayed on before being dumped. We would repeat the process until he was happy - either the horse gave in, or I got hurt.

If I had a secret as a horse breaker, it was developing a sense and an understanding of a horse's temperament from the moment I laid eyes on it, or first touched it. Towards the end of my training period, over the course of about year, I really felt confident that I could run my hand over a line of horses in the race or crush and tell, just by touch and sight, which horse was going to be stroppy and which was going to be easy to break.

With Frank watching, I learned to go about my business with a new horse in the yard. The procedure, if there was no crush, was to put a rope around its neck and choke it down. Once down, an old chaff bag was wrapped over its eyes, the choke rope loosened, and, if I was quick enough, get a front leg tied up.

A halter was then put over its head and the blindfold removed. Once the blindfold was off, the horse would struggle to its feet and hop round the yard a bit with some encouragement from me on the end of the halter shank. As soon as it settled down a bit, I approached it with the old chaff bag, flapping it round until it realised it wasn't going to get hurt. After that, I rubbed my hand over its face and body and this was generally enough to allow me to let the near-side leg down and go around to repeat the process on the off- side.

I strapped a bridle and saddle into place and the horse was then encouraged to hop around a bit more, which it generally did with a lot more enthusiasm. Once it showed signs of settling down, the offside leg would be freed and I would climb aboard.

The whole process took about an hour, and if all went well, the horse could be ridden out of the yard, wheeled around the paddock, then steered back into the yard where I dismounted, stripped the gear off, and declared the horse broken.

By today's standards my methods may sound barbarous, but one must remember times were different then. Horses were the mainstay in operating those large stations; there were plenty of them and, most of all, they were cheap.

Horses today are something special, out of the ordinary and

generally for people with money. They're bred for the track, or shows, or as pampered mounts of the landed gentry. Back in the 1930s a horse was a beast of burden, a working animal, like a dog.

Then, a horse was the alternative to a farm implement or a machine. Unlike today, where a foal comes into contact with its owner the moment it arrives, the horses on Frank's property, and others, were born out in the paddock or the bush and left to run wild with their mothers until they matured. Their only contact with humans would be when they were branded and, where necessary, castrated – a brief, painful and unpleasant experience.

Frank was a very good horseman and was willing to spend endless time patiently passing his skills and knowledge on to me. In a year or so I evolved into quite a competent back-country horse-breaker. It is incredible how quickly one can pick up the techniques, if not the experience, if one is passionate about something.

Frank must have thought so as well. 'You should start going around and breaking in horses for people on some of the other stations around here, if you like,' he said to me.

I saved the wages I received from Frank and with his encouragement and a small loan to top me up, I invested in a couple of horses of my own, some tack and some camping gear and set myself up as a contract horse breaker.

I moved from station to station, wherever work was available. I had no doubt Frank was recommending me to the other property owners in the region, as I certainly had plenty of work.

It was also financially rewarding. If the horses were easy, I could do four or five a week which at a rate of either 30 shillings a head, and keep, or 50 shillings if I fed myself, even if I only broke one horse per week I was still streets ahead of where I had been eighteen months earlier as a 14-year-old slave on the farm in Cowra.

Within six months I had paid off my horses and gear and had a nice little sum in the bank – enough for me to take some time off and go down to Sydney to see the Easter Show. Where it all started, I thought, as I sat by the ring, watching the bucking horses, the bull riding and all the other features of an Australian Bushman's Carnival

Sydney, itself, held little attraction for me. It was far too big and noisy, with too many people. I'd left the crowds behind me in England and had no desire to go back to what some people called 'civilisation'. I ordered a new saddle, a real beaut, and when that was ready, happily headed back up north to the Gwydir Valley.

It was good to get back to the country. *This* was what I had signed up for. I had gone from living a life of privilege in Shanghai and England to working as a wood and water joey, and now I was, if not a true stockman, at least a specialised rural worker. I was as happy as a pig in shit and fancied I could live this life for a very long time.

Then, the world went to war.

3

Although far distant from where I was, the clash of nations had already touched my family.

In September, 1939, Hitler had invaded Poland, and Britain and many other nations declared war on Germany. Australia, loyal to the mother country, followed suit. Japan had launched a full-scale invasion of China in 1937 and my father had disappeared, apparently off the face of the earth as far as the British Red Cross could ascertain.

My brother Glen had gone to sea as crew on a passenger liner and the ship he was sailing in was sunk off the coast of West Africa by a German U-Boat early in the war. He survived and eventually returned to the UK with only the clothes he'd been wearing at the time of the sinking. He immediately joined the RAF and my elder sister, Mary, abandoned her children's nursing training to join the Women's Auxiliary Air Force, or WAAFs. Hearing all this news from the old country, it seemed high time for me stick my finger in the pie.

I certainly wasn't homesick, but with a war on, I naively thought the only chance I'd have of seeing my mother again any time soon was to volunteer to go to sea. In 1940 I was still only 16, but I offered my services to the Royal Australian Navy via the mail and, in a reply, was told to report to the Public School at the small village of Weemelah, south east of Mungindi, where I sat down to complete a fairly basic literacy and numeracy test.

When the results came in, I was shattered to find I was deemed to be 'illiterate' and of no use to a modern navy. Who'd have thought I would have needed to be well versed in Shakespeare and the classics to swab the deck of a destroyer?

Having made the initial decision to join up, I was now more determined than ever to serve in some capacity or other. I let my horses loose – with a war on, no one seemed interested in buying them – and put all my gear in the hands of the local stock and station agent for safe keeping, and caught the train to Sydney.

I once more found myself at Moore Park, site of the Sydney showgrounds, in the city's east, and home of the Easter Show. Now, it had been turned into a giant recruitment centre for the Australian Army and, judging by the collection of no hopers and ruffians – like myself – who were waiting in line, there would be no literacy or numeracy test required here!

'Fill in this form,' a sergeant said to me, pushing a bit of paper my way.

In my best handwriting I inked in my name, pushed my age up by more than a year to 18, and under the heading 'occupation', proudly printed 'Contract Horse Breaker'.

'Horse breaker, eh?' the corporal said.

No one bothered to check my age, my standard of education or anything else. I was prodded by medics and doctors, and measured and inspected like some farm animal in the auction yards. I had thought I would be enlisted into the 2nd Australian Imperial Force – the 1st AIF had served with distinction in the First World War, and battalions were being raised and re-raised for service overseas. The 2nd AIF would go on to serve in North Africa, Greece and Crete, before being shipped home to Australia a couple of years later to deal with a new threat, Japan.

For now, though, it turned out my occupation, rather than my vital statistics, was of most interest to the recruiters. I was given my orders: 'Report to the 2nd Remount Section, Australian Army Service Corps, for a trade test.'

BEFORE THE INK was dry on my attestation form, I was on my way to Holsworthy Barracks.

Although now overtaken by urban sprawl, Holsworthy, in south-western Sydney, was on the city's fringe in 1940, near the town of Liverpool. It's still an Australian Army base today, home to the 2nd Commando Regiment, support units, rifle ranges and training areas.

In order to best employ the army's limited stocks of motor vehicles and fuel for training and other frontline services, those in charge of the military machine had decided that horses should be pressed into service to take up the slack when it came to transportation, particularly in rear areas, such as internment and Prisoner of War Camps and remote training areas. Mounted troops were also to be employed patrolling Australia's eastern seaboard coastline and the far north of the country, particularly after Japan entered the war.

The army's veterinary services and remount units, which were charged with providing horses, had been pared back to their bare bones after the First World War, but now they were in the process of being ramped up. The army had saddles and harnesses and a good number of sturdy General Service (GS) four-wheel wagons capable of carrying troops and supplies, but it lacked horses.

The 2nd Remount unit consisted of about 24 horsemen, eight farriers, a saddler and around eight regular army soldiers who made up a ceremonial troop, to take part in parades and other such formal occasions. The officer commanding was a veterinarian, Captain Victor Cole.

The horsemen were divided into drivers, for horse-drawn transport, and rough riders, whose job it was to break in the many horses the army now found itself in need of. This was the mob I was going to join, assuming I could prove myself.

On arrival at Liverpool station I was met by the daily gig from the

Remounts, which ferried in their supplies, and taken out to the camp where I was told to report to the RSM, or regimental sergeant major.

The RSM, who was down at the yards, was the senior non-commissioned officer of this unruly bunch. He managed the day-to-day operation of the unit and was generally known amongst the troops as 'Jaz'. I found him leaning against the rails of one of the yards, chewing on a stalk of grass. After looking me up and down, and apparently disappointed in what he saw, he stirred himself sufficiently to point to one of a dozen horses, rank, wild looking things, that circled about the yard.

'That one,' Jaz growled, 'catch it and ride it around the yard.'

I got into the yard, and separated the horse he indicated from the rest. Just by looking at him I could tell, already, he was going to give me a hard time, but this was my 'trade test'. If I caught him and rode him, I was in, otherwise it was back to Moore Park.

I eventually trapped him in a corner and got hold of him, got a halter over his head and pulled him over to where the saddle and bridle were lying over a rail of the yard. I got the bridle on and after a bit of to-ing and fro-ing managed to get the saddle on and girthed up tight enough to ensure it stayed in place, I then pulled him round to face the centre of the yard, grabbed his tongue and pulled it out of his mouth up alongside the cheek piece of the bridle.

I pulled his head right round, until it was just about touching my hip – a trick Frank had taught me. This ensured he wasn't going to move an inch until I was fairly and squarely in the saddle.

By holding him this way I made sure I was in the driving seat when the action started. Once I was on him, I let go. The horse tried a couple of perfunctory bucks, which I managed to ride, then I was able to pull his head up and get him moving about, without much trouble.

I took him around the yard a couple of times and brought him back to where the Sergeant Major was, still leaning against the railing.

'OK,' Jaz said. 'You'll do, boy. You're now a Rough Rider – First Class. Now get to work.'

Without a lick of military training, or even a uniform, I got stuck straight into the work at hand, breaking horses, for the princely 'specialist' pay rate of six shillings and sixpence, a day.

There was no shortage of four-legged recruits for the army. They arrived off properties all around the state, even a whole train load of real roughies, genuine wild Brumbies from the Kosciusko-Monaro high country region in the south of New South Wales.

We rough riders worked from sun-up to sun down and slept in makeshift tents. It wasn't much different from the life I'd lived on the land, just more horses and less money. There was no army bullshit and for the first six weeks of my service I wasn't even issued a uniform, though some time later I was issued with a complete outfit, sans boots. Mostly, I still wore my civilian moleskin trousers and riding boots to work each day and nobody seemed to mind.

Breaking yet another horse at the 2nd Remounts yard

Strangely enough, on the very few days we were allowed time off, the main form of amusement for us Rough Riders was to test our skills at little rodeos and bushman's carnivals within striking distance of Sydney. Now and again we went further afield.

'Just be back after the weekend,' Captain Cole said to five of us, as we left camp and headed for Liverpool Railway Station and the night train to Queanbeyan, about 250 kilometres south and not far from the national capital, Canberra. There, the Red Cross had organised a morale-boosting carnival for the troops and locals.

A full program of events had been scheduled for the weekend, including bucking horses under saddle and bareback bullock riding, bulldogging (leaping off a horse and wrestling a steer to the ground), steer decorating (taking a ribbon off a running steer), and camp drafting (separating a beast from a mob of cattle and then working it around an obstacle course).

We arrived at the showgrounds early, and drew lots to see which horses we'd be allocated for the various events. I signed up for two rides. My first horse was called the 'The Gunner' for some reason, not a pretty horse to look at being a big, ungainly, bay/brown, hairy lump with a very ugly head.

He didn't play up much being saddled in the chute, and when he came out I really thought I had his measure. His bucking was high enough to look good, but mainly straight forward and reasonably easy to ride. I was already counting my placing and feeling a trifle self-satisfied, when just before the whip cracked The Gunner changed tactics and threw himself over backwards.

Not expecting this wild manoeuvre, I, too, started a reverse somersault, but caught my left foot under the saddle just as The Gunner hit the dirt. My body rolled, but my foot stayed stuck, wrenching and twisting my knee to its limits.

As the dust settled and the crowd flagged, I struggled to my feet, brushed myself down and limped away. My knee was sore, but the real damage was to my dignity – to add insult to injury I received no marks, having hit the deck before the whip cracked. Nor was a replacement ride offered for the same reason.

My second engagement, in the afternoon, was to be on a mare

with the promising name of 'Easy Molly', though what she promised was anyone's guess.

'She's a Brumby,' one of the saddling crew told me, as I inspected her. 'Brought her in from the hills especially for this weekend.'

Saddling her in the chute was quite a problem, as she had never even been yarded before, let alone confined in a little, narrow high-sided enclosure with men climbing up and down and forcing things on her head and on her back. She put up quite a struggle, but eventually all was in place and, I climbed up on the fence then eased myself down on her.

Getting thrown from a horse at a bushman's carnival

Molly came out of the chute bucking like a beauty, putting on quite a show, when, unlike The Gunner, she began spinning and bucking in circles. She caught me completely unawares, and inexperienced as I was, instead of just letting go and taking what came, I tried to hook my right spur into the girth in order to anchor myself and hang on for the last second or two until the whip sounded, and make the ride.

Instead, by moving my leg, together with Molly's unpredictable momentum as she bucked, I slid off her back, under her belly, and on to the ground. I landed hard in a cloud of dust. Molly bellowed with rage and decided to finish me off.

She reared up and came crashing down, smashing into me with her hooves. Choking on dust and trying to roll away, I felt shockwaves through my body as she drove hammer blows into my back, my shoulder and my face.

Arthur Winter, one of Australia's top buck-jump riders and also an acting corporal in the Remounts, was at the Carnival for the same reason the rest of us, and was also acting as pick up man for the contest. It was part of his job to pick up fallen riders. As soon as he saw what was going on, Arthur drove his mount into Molly, shouldering her off me. He and his horse then fought hard to keep Molly away from me. She was determined to kill me, and nothing was going to stop her.

In desperation Arthur pulled one of his stirrups off his saddle and used it as a makeshift whip to flog Molly off, and try and dampen her rage. She charged again and again, but he managed to keep his horse between Molly and me until I could be picked up and carted off.

If it hadn't been for Arthur's quick thinking and action, I might easily have departed this mortal coil at my first major buck-jumping contest! As it was, I have to admit, it was a less than glorious debut.

I WAS TAKEN to the hospital in Queanbeyan and treated for a dislocated jaw and a fractured shoulder.

'Plus, you've got three cracked vertebrae,' the doctor told me. 'We're keeping you in for a few days.'

So much for getting back to camp by Monday morning, as per Captain Cole's orders. From Queanbeyan I was transferred to the military casualty clearing station at Liverpool, and spent the next two months recovering in the main camp hospital before, somewhat sheepishly, I returned to duty.

Back at the 2nd Remount Section it was business as usual, with trainloads of horses coming in to feed the army's still almost insatiable demand. Some of our horses were to be used by members of the Volunteer Defence Corps – old soldiers who had served in the First World War, like members of Britain's Home Guard or 'Dad's Army' – to patrol the coast. When Japan entered the war, bombing Pearl Harbour in December 1941, then Darwin the following February, a call went out for more mounted troops to patrol Australia's remote northern coastline. Many people feared a Japanese invasion was imminent.

Not long after I returned to work, a trainload of horses came in from the Snowy River country and being in the party detailed off to unload them I went along to the depot siding to see what the new intake looked like.

Newly caught horses tied to their picket lines

What an unprepossessing bunch of back country scrubbers they were. There were all shapes, sizes and colours, and generally they were the type of animal that in any other context would probably have gone straight to the meat works. However, the army still needed horses, and for want of any better, this lot had been dredged up.

I moved down the line shaking my head and tutting, then stopped, dead in my tracks.

It was Molly.

Inevitably, there had to be a reckoning. Once they were over their journey, the mob was brought in for processing and sorted out into groups for breaking.

'That's Easy Molly,' I said, pointing her out, and for the benefit of the blokes who hadn't scraped what was left of me off the dirt at Queanbeyan, I added: 'She's mine.'

Looking at her I mentally said 'You and I have got some unfinished business my girl and the sooner we get down to it, the better.'

When her mob finally made it to the yards, I made a bee line for her in the crush, haltered her and was on the front of the line when she came out to be pulled around. I wanted her to know that I'd be with her all the way, for as long as it took. I wasn't seeking revenge for the pain and humiliation she'd caused me – I just saw her as a challenge that needed to be met, for me and now for the army.

Like every other member of any service organisation, horses were subject to a fair amount of 'hurry-up-and-wait', long periods of doing nothing interspersed between periods of work or training. The first thing these wild horses needed to become accustomed to was being tied to a picket line.

The world's cavalry, with its vast experience over the ages in keeping a great many horses in one place at any one time, had developed many variations of picket lines; the system we used consisted of a series of stout rails set on hefty posts, planted firmly in the ground. About five metres behind these rails, a two-inch cable was set firmly into the ground as a heel line. In effect, our set up was really a stouter, permanent version of the old British cavalry temporary rope picket line, used when the unit was on manoeuvres or in action.

The Remounts' procedure for breaking-in horses was, in general, pretty much the same as I'd used on the stations. I took over Molly's introduction to the army's way of doing things. I pulled her around a bit, tied up each of her legs one at a time to take a bit of the sting out of her, and generally got her used to odd things happening to her.

She protested a bit, but no more than any of the other unbroken stock that came our way. After her session of having her legs pulled up and handled, I tied a split chaff bag around her neck and passed a rope around the two free ends of the bag tying them firmly together. I then passed the rope through the jowl piece of the halter before looping it around the tie rail, securing it with a special knot that could be easily and readily released if things got out of hand. The bag around the neck, although not a regular bit of equipment, took the pressure off the halter, should the horse pull back, and ensured that the horse couldn't hurt its head nor rub itself raw on the poll.

Once the head was tied up, leather shackles were fastened to the hind legs and tied to the cable on the ground behind the horse. Secured like this, it was easy, and safe, to handle the horse while getting it used to the routine of the picket line.

Gear could be put on and taken off and the horse could be groomed, washed, and inoculated with ease. The handler could jump on and off at will and, in general, de-sensitise the horse and get it accustomed to things happening around it without any harm coming to either horse or handler. At times we might have as many as sixty or seventy horses picketed out in this manner, waiting to be worked on in the next stages of their breaking process.

After a couple of days going through all the various softening up gimmicks and the 'sting' having, hopefully, been drastically reduced, the big moment arrived.

The working yards were normally organised chaos, with several horses at once undergoing their first ride. Others were being harnessed for driving work while yet more might be having pack-saddles fitted. However, when it was time for Molly's first ride, all was as quiet as an empty street in a Wild West movie gunfight.

The word had, indeed, got around. Riders, drivers, yard hands and hangers-on gathered, spilling from tents, the company offices, and even the cookhouse, and began lining the fence. I walked Molly, already saddled, out into the yard. The pair of us, like a couple of gladiators, nodded to the crowd.

'Right-o, Molly.' I grabbed one of her ears and, despite her snorting protests, she got down low enough for me to slip up into the saddle. Once there, I let go of her ear and hung on.

A cheer rose up from the audience on the rails as I was shot off Molly like a 25-pounder high-explosive artillery shell leaving the barrel. Determined and mad, I brushed myself off, went after her, and grabbed her ear again.

Half an hour later, although it seemed a lot longer to me, I was stumbling around the yard, bleeding from a flattened nose and myriad other cuts to my arms and face. My head was ringing; much of my exposed skin was already turning purple with bruises.

Once again, we squared off. Molly, too, was showing signs of the battle. She had blood coming from her nostrils from banging her head on the ground each time she threw herself down in temper. She even tried to roll on top of me one time. Time and time again I would grab her, screw her down by her ear and get back up into the saddle. Sometimes I succeeded, and managed to hold on for a few seconds here, a minute there. At other times I could not even get on her, having to pause and take a breather, much to the amusement of the gallery on the sideline, who hadn't seen such a show since, well, Queanbeyan.

Our blood and sweat was intermingled in the powdery dust and on each of our bodies; the sun beat down, the crowd quietened.

I wiped the back of a filthy hand over chapped, cut lips, and tasted the coppery tang of my own pride on my tongue. Aching all over, I took hold of one ear yet again and brought her down. She resisted, but, like me, was on her last legs.

I hauled myself into the saddle and Molly, reluctantly, walked around the yard a couple of times, to the muted applause of those spectators who had lasted as long as we had.

Apart from the odd flare-up every now and again Molly settled into the routine of army life well. I saw her through her basic riding course as a matter of pride, then turned her over to the drivers and other handlers who completed her training by introducing her to the pack saddle and being driven, both as a pair in a GS wagon and as a single in a long shafted breaking jinker, before she was ready to be issued out to a unit.

From Holsworthy, Molly was sent to the POW camp at Hay in the far south west of New South Wales, which was home to the Japanese people who had been interned after their parent country entered the war, and to a growing number of prisoners of war.

She had come to us a wild bush Brumby, full of fight and spirit. While I had been the largest factor in putting her on the straight and narrow path to redemption, she too had her revenge, or maybe it was The Gunner. Either way, to this day, some eighty years later, I still have a number of physical souvenirs of our meetings at Queanbeyan and Holsworthy.

Over a period of nearly two years, from when I first joined the 2nd Remount, in 1940, we broke in something like six thousand horses.

One day, when we were all going about our apparently chaotic duties and the dust was billowing out of most of the yards like a desert dust storm, a group of strangers turned up - Americans.

American soldiers, sailors and airmen were invading Australia in vast numbers, all part of a massive build up for the operations to come against the Japanese in the Pacific and this group was our introduction to the joint effort.

They arrived in jeeps and trucks, and emerged at our dusty little camp dressed as if they'd just stepped onto a parade ground, or from the silver screen itself.

Their commanding officer, dressed like his troopers, wore a Smokey-the-bear hat with a starched brim and crossed swords, shirt, tie and a tailored uniform jacket already bedecked with medals, riding britches and a pair of cavalry boots that gleamed so bright I could have used them as a shaving mirror.

We, in our mismatched uniforms and bushman's clothes and battered riding boots, lounged against the yard railings, smoking or chewing grass stems while we watched the show come to town.

The American officer exchanged a snappy salute with our Captain Cole, and introduced himself and his unit. 'We're the 112th Cavalry Regiment, part of the 56th Cavalry Brigade, Texas National Guard. We're shipping out to Noumea, New Caledonia, and we need some horses.'

'Good-Oh,' said Captain Cole. 'I'm sure we can help. How many horses would you like?'

'Two hundred,' said the American officer, showing perfect teeth as he smiled.

'Two *hundred*? How soon do you need them?'

'Right away, Captain.'

We all overheard the conversation and looked at each other. It was a tall order, but certainly do-able. We set to, upped our work ethic a trifle, and did their 200 horses in record time. When the Americans came back for their horses, we had their mob of newly-broken remounts all ready for them to do whatever they wanted them for in the South Pacific.

For what it was worth, I personally had no idea what was happening on the French island of New Caledonia, much less why the Americans would want to take horses there but then I wasn't even a minor cog in the mighty war machine. It turned out the Americans were only going there to act as garrison security and probably had to find some use for their cavalry troops. It was probably a first – a US Army cavalry unit mounted on Australian horses – but, sadly, things didn't go as well as planned. It turned out that the Australian horses had no immunity to Malaria and suffered badly from the disease on the island.

Somewhere, a decision had been made that our Aussie horses in New Caledonia would be better employed in India. The Japanese had conquered Burma and their advance had stopped on the Imphal Plain in north-west India. An offensive was launched later in the war by the Allies to retake Burma.

Sadly, one of the two troopships carrying the horses was sunk, by a Japanese submarine, and the former cavalry mounts, like so many other animals, became casualties of war.

. . .

AFTER 20 MONTHS of hard work the flow of horses arriving at Holsworthy and the pressing need to have them broken and trained ready for service, was finally easing.

The tide of the war had not yet turned, but the Allies had held the line in places such as Milne Bay and Kokoda, in Papua New Guinea; Stalingrad in Russia; and El Alamein in the Western Desert of Egypt. Factories in Australia, the US and the UK were churning out vehicles, tanks, guns and aircraft by the day.

Word came down to the 2nd Remount Unit that those of us who had been brought into the unit on a 'hostilities-only' basis, like myself, should start looking for other employment.

The horse yards, once a scene of daily dust clouds generated by men and horses, were all but deserted. Most of the men in the unit seemed to be away on some other business or, more likely, like Jack Delahunt and myself, engaging in the time-honoured soldier's pastime of keeping out of sight.

Jack, a likeable bushman of Irish origin, and I were skulking in the tack shed situated in the centre of the yards, keeping a low profile, Jack was entertaining me with sensational, technicoloured stories of his early life, living with old 'Hop-along-Harry'. Hop-along was an eccentric old bush horse breaker, whose party piece, when drunk, was to grab the tail of an unbroken horse and jump astride its hocks, cooeeing and shrieking like a banshee as it went cart-wheeling around, or until he got dumped (and no doubt kicked for his impertinence).

His jaw was permanently bent to one side as a result of one such ride. Jack was also a font of lurid tales of his time with Thorpe McConville's travelling rodeo show to pass on to his willing audience of one.

My entertainment was interrupted by the sound of galloping hooves, coming down the road from the Veterinary Hospital and the Artillery Camp, some way beyond our establishment,

'Who the bloody hell is that, in such a rush now?' Jack asked.

We took a peep outside and, to our surprise saw a GS wagon

being drawn by two horses, hurtling down the road at breakneck speed, lurching and bouncing about all over the place.

'There's no driver,' I said. The wagon was empty.

'They'll be from the artillery,' Jack shot back.

We had just delivered a consignment of newly-broken horses to the artillery training unit, located up the hill from us, past the veterinary hospital. It seemed that the horses, finding themselves unattended and far from what they had known as home, had got away and decided to return to our depot and the yards where they had done their training drives with the wagons.

Luckily, the gate leading off the road into our working yards happened to be open, allowing the horses to turn into our main collecting yard, without clipping either post.

A First World War-era GS wagon, pressed back into service

'I'll get the gates,' I said to Jack, referring to the entry into the large driving paddock that was used for new horses. It was purpose-built, large enough to allow for a bit of tear-away action and stoutly fenced.

I raced out of the shed to the gates and flung them open. After a wild round of the collecting yard, the horses saw the gates they knew were open. They bolted straight through, without touching either post. Once they were in, I closed the gates. I was quite happy to let them run themselves down, but Jack had other ideas – he wanted to stop them before they hurt themselves, or smashed the wagon to pieces.

As they checked momentarily for a corner, before starting on their next circuit, Jack was able to get hold of the near-side horse's bridle and rein. Digging his heels in and hanging on for grim death he managed to slow the pair down a bit. It was enough to allow me to get the off-side horse and shake some sense into his head.

With a man at each horse's head, it wasn't long before we had them stopped. Although they were still pretty steamed up, it seemed an unnecessary waste of energy to lead them up to the tie rails to unhitch them, so I gathered up the loose reins and climbed into the driving seat. Once I had kicked the brake on as hard as it would go, and taken a strong hold of the horses' heads, Jack got up into the offsider's seat and I released the brake. I started them off for what I thought would be quiet, settling walk round the paddock, before taking them up to the rails to unhitch them.

Whether it was the sound of me kicking the brake off, or they were still too agitated to be reasoned with, I am not sure, but what I do know is that the minute I let them have their heads, they were off again.

With the horses now contained in the paddock, which they knew well, and knowing they couldn't come to much harm, the only sensible thing to do was to try to gain control, by keeping them going in a wide circle round the paddock until they ran out of steam.

We hadn't completed a single circuit of the paddock, when suddenly the panic flag went up a couple of notches, and the wagon was at full tilt again.

We were lurching and bouncing about in a most unusual and

totally disturbing manner, with the horses being thrown out of their stride and becoming completely uncoordinated as the wagon bumped into their hindquarters and bounced back again.

One didn't have to be the brightest star in the firmament to realise a very serious situation was developing. Jack, who had a reputation for making snap judgements in times of trouble, did the sensible thing and bailed out.

I was about to do the same thing, but first I took the precaution of tying the reins to the back of the seat and kicking the brake full-on before I jumped overboard, right over the offside front wheel.

When I hit the ground, I stumbled. The horse on my side blindly turned into me. I put up my hands to ward him off and found myself with a bunch of the horse's mane in my left hand and the cheek piece of his bridle in my right. I held on frantically with both hands, knowing that if I relaxed, even for a fraction of a second, it would be curtains, especially as I lost my footing and was lifted away by the runaways.

On we thundered, in a cloud of dust. As the horses continued to turn into me, I somehow managed to get my feet on the ground again and into running mode. This allowed me to put some weight onto the head of the horse I was engaged with. Gradually, I managed to pull the whole outfit round and slow it down a bit.

Jack was back in the game and managed to get up to the near side horse and grab hold of its bridle. For the second time, the pair of us managed to bring them to a halt and hold them steady.

'Shirts!' I said. Taking it in turns, one holding the horses whilst the other stripped, we took our shirts off and wrapped them around the horses' heads as makeshift blindfolds, to help steady them.

In their highly agitated state, the slightest thing could have set the horses off again. Neither of us wanted to get involved in that nonsense a second time. Until the traces were uncoupled and the collar straps undone, they were still attached to the wagon, constituting a seriously dangerous set-up.

'Settle, boy, settle,' we were saying, each of us trying to distract and soothe our horse while carefully, we began the dangerous business of unhitching them.

In turns, one of us stood in front of them holding their heads, while the other went behind each horse to release the traces from the swingle-trees, join them together, ease them up over each horse's back, then go around the front and unbuckle the collar straps. The final task was to unbuckle the two sets of reins off the bits, which I had tied to the back of the seat before bailing out.

All this had to be done with extreme care, as even with the blindfolds on there was no guarantee that the horses would not blow up again. Finally, we got them unhitched and were able to take the two badly distressed horses to the tie rails and anchor them firmly before stripping off their harness.

Having made sure the horses were safe, Jack and I then walked back to see what had caused the problem. We had noticed, when releasing the traces, that the pole joining them to the wagon was no longer attached. The lynch-pin attaching the pole to the turntable had sheared, dropping the rear end onto the ground, but leaving the front end attached to the cross bar, which was strapped to each horse's breast collar.

Consequently, the pole had been dragged along between the two horses, bouncing and beating their legs and thighs as they raced round the paddock while the wagon, with no pole to stabilise it, performed feats it was neither designed nor constructed for, rattling along behind them.

I might add here that army procedures, very sensibly, precluded the use of blinkers being attached to bridles under normal circumstances, so horses in training were not fitted with them. So, besides all the other frightening things happening, those two poor unfortunate horses were able to see this terrifying monstrosity leaping and jumping behind them, beating them mercilessly on the flanks and legs, apparently catching up to them no matter how much they tried to evade it. One can't really blame them for losing their composure.

How lucky we all were – Jack, the horses and me – that none of us got badly hurt and that the stricken wagon didn't roll.

A soldier with a dog came across the paddock to us. He was a dog handler, one of the guards from the Holsworthy Military Prison located near the remount yards, and had been exercising his canine comrade. He had witnessed the whole thing.

'How the hell did you two manage to stop that wagon?' he asked, wide-eyed. 'That was bloody amazing.'

Jack and I looked at each other; he was probably still shaking – I know I was.

'Ah, she was nothing, mate,' I said, with all the insufferable cockiness of youth, 'happens every day around here.'

After he left, Jack muttered quietly: 'Sure, and somebody up there must have been looking down on us today.'

4

The writing was on the stable wall for most of us at the 2nd Remount Section. If we wanted to stay in the armed forces then we would have to re-muster – that is, find another job.

Word had filtered through to us that horses might be needed for a hush-hush operation in New Guinea. The plan, bizarrely, was to drop horses by parachute into the jungle, along with pack howitzers – artillery guns which would could be broken down into loads manageable by a horse – and gunners. I volunteered.

I reported to the relevant army camp at Randwick Race Course in Sydney's eastern suburbs and started learning what I could about this operation. In true army style, it wasn't going exactly to plan. It appeared that some bright spark somewhere in the army had sourced some pack saddles in New Zealand, without checking any of the details. When they were unpacked it was pretty obvious that they were designed for mules, not horses, and there was no way they could be adapted. One wonders if there were any red faces in the planning department.

Nevertheless, I was a keen volunteer for this novel undertaking. One thing I was sure of was that having been rejected by the Navy, and stuck in Australia breaking horses while others served and fought overseas, that I did not want to come through the war without having seen any action.

As a volunteer for parachute training, we had to pass certain physical tests.

'Today, we will simulate the impact of landing on the ground, under a parachute,' a sergeant told us. 'When you hit the ground, you have to roll.'

I'd taken more than my share of falls as a rough rider, so I was game.

'You lot, on the truck,' the sergeant barked at half a dozen of us recruits.

We climbed aboard the 30 CWT (hundredweight) truck, which then proceeded to trundle around the turf track of the race course. Where once thoroughbreds ran before crowds of well-to-do and aspiring gentry, now soldiers were being dispatched, one at a time, off the tailgate of a moving automobile.

'Number three,' the sergeant said, pointing to me, 'go!'

I jumped off the truck, tried to land with both feet together, as instructed, and rolled.

Bugger this, I thought. This was about as much fun as Easy Molly, though perhaps not quite as dangerous. A few bones did go by the end of the day, though fortunately none of them mine.

My next step to becoming an airborne artilleryman was to undergo a medical check.

The doctor, a white dust coat over his khaki uniform, looked up, aghast, as he flicked through my army medical record. 'Broken back, broken shoulder, dislocated jaw. What happened to you?'

'A horse fell on me, sir.' Several, and several times, in fact.

The quack shook his head. 'No, no, no. I'm afraid you're not fit to jump out of an aeroplane.'

I was fit enough, it seemed, to jump off the back of moving trucks and to be bucked off horses at the army's discretion. What was one more fall going to do to me? I tried to argue to the toss with him.

'No,' he made a note in my file, then looked up. 'The best we can offer you is something like a medical orderly.'

I recoiled from him. 'A po-juggler? Not on your life.' A po-juggler was slang from the First World War for an orderly or officer's servant who had to dispose of the contents of a chamber pot, or 'pot (pronounced '*po*') de chambre' in French.

'Well, then, as you're a volunteer and have been injured in the course of your service, you'll get an honourable discharge, Whitehead.'

'No bloody fear,' I growled to myself as I saluted and left.

The navy didn't want me, and the army was washing its hands of me. There was only one option left.

From Randwick I made my way by tram and bus across Sydney to the seedy dockside suburb of Woolloomooloo, near the Garden Island naval base. US and Australian warships were tied to the wharfs. American sailors in white and Australians in dark navy blue strolled or staggered along grubby footpaths, gaudily-dressed floozies on their arms. Shady spivs in suits and hats loitered in the alleyways, offering black market food, and other illicit substances.

I hadn't come to drink, but rather to find the Royal Australian Air Force's 2nd Recruitment Depot, in Palmer Street, between Bourke and Crown streets. Many military units in New South Wales were designated with the number 'two', as each Australian state was also designated as a military district - NSW was the 2nd Military District.

I joined a line of air force hopefuls and when it was my turn to front the blue-uniformed corporal he told me that as a member of the army I could only transfer across to the RAAF if I was joining as air crew.

'That sounds fair enough to me,' I said. Many Australians who joined the air force were being shipped to the UK, to serve in Bomber Command. At the time, in late 1942, aerial bombing was the only weapon the allies had to hit the Germans in Western Europe. As with my failed plans to join the navy, I also thought that joining the air force might get me a ticket back to England to catch up with my mother, whom I had last seen in 1938.

'Fill out this paperwork,' the corporal said, sliding the obligatory forms across the counter to me. 'You might be suitable for pilot training, but you'll need a good standard of education.'

Uh-oh, I thought to myself.

'Here are some pamphlets outlining the sorts of subjects you'll be tested on,' the corporal said, handing me a sheaf of paperwork. 'The next intake's in three months' time. You can come back then for your exams.'

BLOODY HELL, I thought to myself on the train ride back to Holsworthy. *What have I let myself in for?*

I went to the company offices and asked to see the OC, Captain Cole.

'Come in, Whitehead,' he said. 'How did it go in Sydney?'

I told him of my failure to join the airborne horse artillery unit, and that I had approached the RAAF about transferring across as aircrew, perhaps even as a pilot.

He frowned. 'I tried for pilot training, myself. My brothers are both Spitfire pilots, based in England, but I was told I couldn't transfer. Apparently, the army doesn't have enough veterinarians.'

'I don't know how I'm going to pass the tests, sir,' I said, sharing his misery for a moment. 'I was a failure at school and left before I turned 14.'

Cole looked up at me, his face suddenly a bit brighter. 'You can be my batman.'

'Sir?' As an officer, Cole was entitled to a batman, the army's term for a servant – another po-juggler job. My military career was going from bad to worse.

'No, no,' he said, reading my look, 'you'll just be attached to my quarters, no other duties involved. I'll use the time to teach you what you need to pass the entrance test.'

We weren't given to shows of sentimentality in those days, not like today, but I was touched. This man, out of the goodness of his heart, was going to take time out of his day to help someone else fulfil the dream that he'd seen snatched away from him.

If I thought breaking in horses was hard work, I had no idea what was in store for me.

Every morning, straight after breakfast, I'd report to Cole's quarters and we would sit at his little kitchen table, he as the teacher and me as the pupil. We went at it from morning to night.

Mathematics was very important for would-be fliers, and was needed to give students the basic knowledge they would require for navigation and other flying skills.

'We'll concentrate on that first,' Captain Cole said. He took me through the basics of arithmetic and algebra, day after day. I could read and write to a certain standard, but to me, mathematics was like trying to learn Ancient Greek from scratch.

In the sheaf of paperwork the RAAF corporal had given me was a sample list of 20 questions of the type I would be asked in the examination. Cole and I went over these, and similar questions that he made up, over and over and over again.

In school it had been easy – I would just blank-out in class when it all became too or hard, or bunk off and go to the cinema, or go shooting birds with old Jim the poacher, and then pay the ritual price every Thursday in the sadistic headmaster's office

This was different. Captain Cole was giving me his time and we both had a goal at the end, to get me accepted for pilot training and to get into the war in an active role. It was bloody hard yakka, as the Aussies called hard, grinding work, and tougher than anything I'd done as a wood and water joey. Basically, Cole was trying to drum the entire syllabus of the last two years of high school into my head in the space of three months. It was relentless.

Captain Cole started to draw in the pages of an exercise book. 'The square on the hypotenuse is equal to the...' I stared at the drawing of the triangle. 'The sum...'

He waited, then let out: 'The sum of the squares on the other two sides, Whitehead.'

The brain, they say, is a muscle, and mine was throbbing from too much exercise and not enough rest. Would I be able to soak up and retain enough knowledge to pass the entry exam?

Not since I'd been pounded by Easy Molly had I felt like I had been through such a wringer. On the morning before the exam I dressed in my best collection of uniform gear – I had still not even done an army recruit course – and Captain Cole saw me off.

He handed me an envelope. 'Give this to the assessors and the selection board.'

'Thank you, sir.'

More scared than I'd ever been, I set off on the train for Sydney, and the RAAF recruiting depot at Woolloomooloo. There, in a drill hall full of rich farmer's sons, accountants, articled clerks, university types and the sons of Sydney's social elite I sat down at a table and took out my pencil.'

An air force officer in blue serge told us to turn over our first paper, as he pressed the button on a stopwatch. 'Your time starts now.'

As I read through the first few questions, I felt the panic rising up in me. Those wasted days in England all came flooding back to me, but so, too, did the odd nugget that kindly Captain Cole had drilled into my head. I reckoned I had the answers to some of the questions, but others just left me foundering and baffled. I scratched and scrawled away as the clock on the wall ticked its way towards impending disaster and the instructor checked his watch.

'Time's up, pencils down,' barked the officer, who must have been a schoolmaster in civilian life. Our papers were collected.

I waited outside the hall with the others, most of whom, as was the custom in those days, were smoking. I was pleased to see some of them looked nervous, but others were already cock-a-hoop. The funny thing was that even though my mother and father and older siblings smoked cigarettes, as did pretty well everyone I met on farms or in the army, never in my life did I feel the urge to put one of those things in my mouth and light it.

'Whitehead?' an officer called.

I marched in, to the best of my ability. I was a Rough Rider, and while I had been 'first class' at breaking in horses, I was clearly out of my league with this mob. I was told to sit down in front of a panel of three RAAF officers.

The one in the middle, who looked to be the senior, cleared his throat. 'Whitehead, the results of your test papers are, quite frankly, awful.'

My heart sank. Was I to be confined to a life of cleaning bedpans in an army hospital?

'However,' the officer added, shuffling through the papers in front of him, 'you have a first-class recommendation from your commanding officer, a Captain Cole, who speaks highly of you. On that basis, we're prepared to give you a chance.'

'Thank you,' I said, remembering to add, 'sir.'

He gave me a stern look. 'If you fail any single thing, Whitehead, you'll be out on your arse.'

I caught the train back to Holsworthy, feeling on top of the world. I thought about Captain Cole. He was a good officer, a gentleman, not a martinet, like some of them were. He had been in charge of a pack of ratbags, outback stockmen and roughneck larrikins, but he never had to read the riot act or discipline us. When the odd one or two of us got into fights he would intercede and calm things down, or, if it was one of us against an outsider, he would back us up. Never did he have to send any of us to the Military Police or the dreaded military prison, just a horseshoe-toss from our yards. As evidence of his character, he would later go on to fulfil a distinguished career as a veterinarian after the war, becoming the president of the Australian veterinary association.

I went straight to the company offices and knocked on his door.

'Come.'

I entered, then saluted as he looked up from his desk.

'I passed.'

Like I said, it was not a time when men showed emotions, and certainly not to each other. There were no 'high fives' or hugs in 1942, but I could see something there, in the slight upturn of his mouth, perhaps.

'Good luck, and away you go.'

5

'You'll be right,' said my instructor, Flying Officer (FO) Higgins, as we buckled up our leather flying helmets and pulled down goggles over our eyes, 'horsemen tend to make pretty good pilots.'

The smell of fuel and the heat of exhaust gasses were blown back over us by the Tiger Moth's wooden propellor as we taxied down the runway at Narrandera in southern New South Wales.

As we lifted off my stomach lurched and I looked down over the side of the open cockpit. Below us were the wide-open spaces and flat farmland of the Riverina region. Places like this around the world, from the prairies of Canada to the golden, grassy vleis of Rhodesia and the plains of rural Australia had been chosen to train airmen for the allied war effort in a logistically impressive endeavour known as the Empire Air Training Scheme.

I was one of tens of thousands who would learn to fly in these remote corners of the British Empire; their empty skies and open spaces had been selected for a very good reason – accidents were all too common. It was expected that around 10 per cent of us would probably not survive flight training, even before we joined an operational squadron. Once we got into action the odds of survival were even worse – more than a third of all the Australians who served in Bomber Command in Europe were killed in action. Many more were wounded or taken prisoner.

I was in the air, for now, but I was still a long way off from fulfilling my current dream, to see active service, and it was by no means certain that would ever come true.

I'd worked bloody hard, though, to get this far. After just scraping through my entrance exam I was sent to No. 2 Initial Training School (ITS) at RAAF Bradfield Park, a base in Sydney's north.

Bradfield Park was a 640-hectare site in the suburb of West Lindfield which was to have been a new suburb named in honour of John Bradfield, the public works engineer who was the chief proponent of the Sydney Harbour Bridge and the city's underground rail network. War, however, had superseded town planning, and Bradfield Park was now home to a number of RAAF units, including the Women's Australian Auxiliary Air Force (WAAF) training depot and a hospital.

At ITS we received the basic training we would need to become aircrew – everything from learning how to march up and down a parade ground, saluting, basic weapons handling, and which knife and fork to use in the mess. There was also more cerebral study – mathematics, aerodynamics and navigation.

I battled like buggery in the classroom just to stay abreast of the other 120-odd recruits in our intake. Having got this far I was absolutely determined to make the grade and move on to pilot training. I had already come to the conclusion that this was the only course open to me – my lack of maths precluded me from training either as a navigator or a wireless operator and I was too tall to be considered for training as an air gunner, so the only thing left was pilot training. That was what I wanted.

Once again defying the odds, I completed ITS and received the news that I had made the grade to move on to the next step towards becoming a pilot - I was posted No. 8 Elementary Flying Training School (EFTS) at Narrandera.

For the first four weeks of our 12-week course we underwent more classroom training and assessment together with our first 10 hours of flying lessons, to further assess our aptitude. If we passed that hurdle, we would undergo another eight weeks of intensive flight training and then move on to an SFTS – a service flying training school. There, we would learn how to be military aviators, developing the skills we would need to function either as fighter or bomber pilots. There were 12 EFTSs in Australia and eight SFTSs; over and above that there was also the possibility of being posted to an SFTS overseas, in Canada or Rhodesia.

I had made it into the air, soaring above the plains around Narrandera. I kept a watch out around me, not for enemy fighters, but for fellow trainees, who could be just as dangerous. We'd all heard the stories of the trainees before us who'd been involved in mid-air collisions with each other, or crashed on take-off or landing.

A Tiger Moth - the type of aircraft in which I learned to fly

There was little tolerance for failure or slow learners and our instructors were generally referred to as 'screaming skulls', thanks to the way we were treated. My flying instructor, FO Higgins, however, was a more gentle, patient fellow, which was just as well as it turned out I needed all the help I could get.

FO Higgins was a bush boy, the son of the owner of a large

outback cattle station, and had learned to fly before the war. It was his theory that accomplished horsemen, such as me, made good pilots. Quite where he got that idea I did not know, and, as I took control of the Tiger Moth from him, I felt he might soon be revising his theory.

Unlike riding, flying did not come naturally to me. I was learning that coordination, using one hand to control the stick, one to handle the throttle and my feet on the rudders, while keeping an eye on the various gauges, did not come naturally to me.

My only relief from the stresses of learning in the classroom and the cockpit came on the periods of leave we were given, when I would leave the base and go out to a local sheep property whose owners I had become friendly with. There I went back to what I knew best, breaking horses and riding. Even there, however, it seemed I was off my game. I was thrown by one of his horses, which then kicked me in the head, landing me in the base hospital for a while, where I was treated for concussion.

In the air, I survived my first six hours of dual control flying – just – and then had to go solo.

I took off, nerves balling in my stomach, in control of the Tiger Moth by myself for the first time. Using rudder, stick and throttle I was able to complete a couple of circuits of the runway and then had to line up for a landing. The idea was that an accomplished pilot, or even a trainee like me, should put all three wheels on the deck at the same time, a three point landing, but when I came in, I was only able to land by touching down with the front two main wheels first, before letting the tail gradually drop so that that tailwheel made a gentle contact.

The best that could be said for my effort was that I didn't crash. I taxied up to the hangar where my instructor was waiting with a clipboard. I shut down the engine and climbed out.

'Not really good enough, Whitehead,' Higgins said, frowning, 'a bit wobbly.'

The kind-hearted Higgins battled on, seeing me through another six or seven hours of solo flying, with not much sign of improvement. It was becoming clear to me that I was never going to be the next Douglas Bader, the fighter ace, although in that context, I might very well crash at some time and lose both my legs.

'What should I do?' I asked Higgins.

He shrugged. It was clear that unlike some unforgiving Screaming Skull, he was going to leave the choice to me. I could qualify, perhaps, but then would I go on to become a liability in an operational squadron, perhaps even a danger to my fellow pilots, or my crew if I ended up in a multi-engine bomber?

The other thing that was playing on my mind was that things were changing in the war, and in the air force. From not having enough pilots at the outbreak of war, the Empire Air Training Scheme was now proving incredibly successful at churning out would-be flyboys by the thousand. Word was coming down that there were long waits for freshly-minted pilots to be posted to operational squadrons,

On the other hand, air gunners were in far greater demand, to compensate for the losses in Europe and the expanding air war against the Japanese in the Pacific. My childhood friend Bob Lacy had joined the RAF as an air gunner when war broke out. Bob's parents had owned the racehorse stud near where we lived in England, and he had been apprenticed to a trainer at Newmarket. Sadly, he was killed in action in 1941.

By now it was 1943, and the tide was beginning to turn against Japan. Bombing missions were being launched from Australia's far north and New Guinea, against an enemy empire not quite in retreat, but with every indication of being on the ropes. The numbers spoke for themselves as well – in a bomber with a crew of 7 to 10, depending on the type, there were one or two pilots, a navigator and a radio operator/gunner, and the rest of the crew were straight gunners. I had a far better chance of seeing some action behind a machinegun than I did as a pilot.

I had to ask myself the question: *do I continue and run the high risk of being scrubbed, or perhaps never seeing action, or do I voluntarily step down?*

'I can get you an appointment with the CO,' Higgins said, after I had done some more soul searching.

We both fronted the Wing Commander in his office. Higgins gave a rundown of my progress, or lack thereof, and I told the commanding officer that although I was not sure I was cut out to be a pilot, I did not want to be drummed out of the air force. My fallback position was to apply to retrain as an air gunner, manning a turret or other machinegun position on a bomber.

The Wing Commander leafed through my reports and personnel file while I awaited his judgement. 'Well, there's no chance of you becoming an air gunner, because you're too tall, Whitehead. The maximum height is six foot.'

I wanted to scream. He looked up from his desk. 'Let's get another medical board done, see what they have to say about your fitness for other duties.'

I packed a bag and my service records and took the long, slow trip from Narrandera up to Sydney, back to the RAAF recruiting depot in Woolloomooloo. I went before a medical examiner and he just shook his head.

'I'm afraid there's nothing I can do,' he said. 'Leave your records here and we'll have another look. Come back after lunch.'

Dejected, I left the depot and went across the road to the nearest pub and ordered a schooner of beer, with which to drown my sorrows.

'Peter?'

I looked across the bar. Another patron came to me, and after a moment I recognised him. We shook hands. It was the medical sergeant from the base hospital at Narrandera. He had left No. 8 EFTS and been posted to the Palmer Street depot in Woolloomooloo.

'What are you doing here?' he asked me, as we drank our pre-lunch beers.

Out came my tale of woe.

'Not to worry mate,' he said, 'we can fix that.'

After lunch we went back across the road to the recruiting depot and the Sergeant spoke to an orderly, who fetched my file from a stack. The sergeant opened it and took out his pen. He struck out the 6'1'.

'There you go,' he said, printing neatly and deliberately, 'five-foot-eleven and seven-eighths of an inch!'

Beaming, I shook his hand and thanked him. I then took the long ride back to Narrandera and reported to the station CO.

The CO read my revised medical board and new height. 'I knew you'd do something clever, you young bugger!'

From Narrandera I was transferred to RAAF gunnery school at West Sale in the Gippsland region of Victoria, about 200 kilometres east of Melbourne, not far from the coast.

Just as I had applied myself to the best of my ability to qualify for pilot training, I was determined that I was going to be the best aerial gunner on my course. This, finally, was my chance to get into the war, properly.

The aim of the gunnery course was to instruct us in the operation of gun turrets and the machineguns carried on board bombers, and in enemy aircraft recognition and tactics.

While it might not have been as glamorous as being a Spitfire pilot, I was more at home with the labour-oriented business of gunnery. We were given basic firearms training on a shooting range. Concepts such as the fall of shot – the trajectory a bullet takes when fired – and deflection, aiming off to allow for a target's own forward motion, were ideas I was already familiar with from poaching pheasants in the hedges of Cambridgeshire. We learned to strip and assemble the Browning .303 calibre machinegun, the type of weapon used on most British-designed bombers, and to clear stoppages that might prevent the gun from firing when in action.

Like the pilots, the gunners were a mixed bag of civilians who had signed up for wartime service, from a variety of backgrounds. Some of the trainees had never fired a weapon in their lives and a few were quite dim, so some of what they were being taught was going over their head. This wasn't a bad thing for me, because it allowed me to take on the role of sideline teacher. I found that as well as helping my fellow trainees, this also helped me absorb all of what we were being taught – all the better for me to follow my hidden agenda of becoming top student and earning myself a passage to England.

On the ground we simulated air-to-air combat by sitting in fixed turrets behind gun cameras – these set a film camera's reels turning when we depressed the firing mechanism. Our target was a model aeroplane perched on a stick which was fixed to a dolly, a cart on wheels pulled along a narrow set of railway tracks. As the enemy 'aircraft' flashed past we practised using the ring sight on our cine guns, fired away, and the results were later played back on the big screen for all to view.

It wasn't all work.

When we had periods of leave there were dances to go to and films to watch and various organisations to look after servicemen far from home. I'm not sure that I really had a home. I had a mother in England and my saddle and tack in the stock and station agent's office in Moree, and that was about it.

I'd never had time for a girlfriend and, to be fair, I was only just reaching adulthood after nearly three years in the armed forces. At one of the service centres in Melbourne, however, while on leave from the course, I got chatting to a young woman named Marie.

'What did you do before war,' she asked.

'I was a stockman and a horse breaker. You?'

'A model and an actress,' Marie said.

It showed. She was a city filly of the highest order. About the only thing I had going for me was my uniform – there was a certain amount of glamour attached to the RAAF, even if I was no longer going to be a Brylcreemed fighter ace.

Clearly, I was in a different league to Marie and I'm fairly sure she used me as a sort of backstop until someone better came along. However, I saw her whenever I could make it to Melbourne.

BACK ON THE course at West Sale we sat in a darkened theatre on-base, a film projector whirring behind us, lighting up the screen and an instructor up on stage.

A brief few frames of a head on-view of an aircraft flashed up on the screen for less than a second.

'Come on boys, what is it?' the instructor yelled, half of his face lit up by the projector's bulb. 'Smith?'

'Um...'

'Junkers JU88, sir,' I piped up.

'Well done, Whitehead. German night fighter."

The next aircraft appeared in front us, as fleeting as it would be if it was diving past our bomber at 300 miles per hour.

'Quick, quick,' the instructor, said. 'Your life depends on this!'

And so it went on, day after day, cleaning weapons, sitting in classrooms, pretending to shoot German and Japanese airmen until we at last took to the air.

The collection of British-built aircraft at Sale were almost ready for the museum by late 1943. Several of us boarded an Avro Anson, a twin-engine reconnaissance aircraft based on a 1930s airliner. Ansons did see service during the war as coastal command aircraft, hunting for U-boats or downed aircrew, but they were pretty hopeless against enemy fighters. Nevertheless, our training aircraft had an enclosed gun turret with a single .303 machinegun.

I sandwiched myself into the turret. The height recommendations were there for a reason and I barely fitted inside the rotating cage of Plexiglass and steel.

'Target ahead,' the Anson's pilot said over the intercom.

'Roger.'

My target was a drogue, a long tubular sleeve of fabric being towed on the end of a cable by a tug aircraft, in this case a Fairey Battle. The Battle was another aircraft past its prime. Designed as a single-engine bomber between the wars, Battles had been pushed into service early on by the Royal Air Force, in the fight for France, before the British Army was evacuated from Dunkirk, and in Norway. They had been completely outclassed by the Luftwaffe and despite wave after wave of brave RAF pilots taking the fight to the Hun, hundreds of these underpowered, under-armoured aircraft had been lost to enemy action. The surplus aircraft had been shipped to Australia for this ignominious duty.

It was a beautiful day for flying and below us the Gippsland Lakes had given way to the long, narrow strip of sand known as 90 Mile beach.

A terrible accident had happened here during gunnery training in 1943. A Fairey Battle pilot, perhaps trying to impress some people on the beach, had flown so low that his target drogue had snagged a fishing rod and line. The drogue had become detached, but the towing cable started whipping about with such force that it severed a 16-year-old girl's two legs above the ankles. Another man lost a leg and four other civilians were injured.

I lined up on the drogue, aiming off, but not too much – the Battle was already underpowered and flying even slower than its optimum, thanks to the airborne anchor it was dragging behind it.

I pressed the firing lever. The .303 machinegun shuddered and the turret filled with the sharp odour of cordite. This was more like it.

'Good shooting, gunner,' the pilot radioed.

I let off another burst. It wasn't my first time on the gun and, in truth, the drudgery of training seemed as though. it might never end. The novelty had worn off and air-to-air gunnery practice was also getting boring. I fired again, popping off a few more rounds for the hell of it.

'Hey!' yelled the pilot. 'The tug pilot says you nearly shot him!'

Shooting down a Fairey Battle would not have advanced my campaign to be named student-of-merit, so I got back to doing my best on the ground – and in the air.

The course was ordered to report to the Turret Room, a hangar in which the different models of gun platforms we might find ourselves manning were laid out as static displays. The most common models were FN series of turrets, designed by Archibald Frazer-Nash of the Nash and Thompson company, for the RAF's bomber fleet.

There were different two-gun variants for the front and mid-upper positions on four engine bombers, such as the Avro Lancaster, and the four-gun rear-gunner's position. While the 'tail-end Charlie' as he was known had the added benefit of two extra Browning machineguns, this was also the most dangerous place to be, with most enemy attacks coming from the rear. Those of us posted to Bomber Command in the UK would be required to complete a tour of 30 missions over Germany and while the odds of achieving even that milestone were not good, it was whispered, over drinks, that a tail-end Charlie's life expectancy was five missions – about two weeks.

Me, centre, with two mates on the gunnery course

We'd carried out our weapons handling drills so many times we could clear stoppages blindfolded. We might very well find ourselves with a jammed gun in the smoke-filled turret at night over the Ruhr Valley, so such skills were needed. For today's lesson we were going to learn about hydraulic systems that controlled the turrets, and to practice our drills while controlling the motorised turret as well.

I wasn't the only one with my sights set on high achievement in the course. In our section of eight was a pugnacious little fellow named Wilkinson, from Darwin in the Northern Territory. He fancied himself as officer material and would grab any opportunity to show off his potential to the instructors.

'Look lively,' he said to us, his peers of the same rank, as we entered the hangar. I groaned, inwardly. He was at it again, trying to form us up in front of the instructor.

'You there, Whitehead, stand over there,' he said, pointing to a spot furthest from the assessor.

I stayed where I was. 'Fuck off, Wilkinson.'

His face went red and he took a swing at me, in front of everyone. I dodged and aimed a punch back at him, which glanced off his thick skull. I'd had enough of his bombastic ways, but I also hoped this blue would be over soon – it was said that Wilkinson had been a boxer, the middleweight champion of the Northern Territory, and had done time in jail.

Our fellow students intervened, grabbing hold of Wilkinson and me and separating us.

We were hauled, separately, before the school's senior non-commissioned officer, a Warrant Officer. The WOFF, as he was called in the air force, was the equivalent of a Warrant Officer Class 1, or regimental sergeant major in the army.

'You're staying on the course, Whitehead,' he growled at me, 'but you're bloody lucky. If you'd thrown the first punch, we would have dropped you.'

I *was* lucky, but the other man had needed to be put in his place. I'd served with real leaders already, understated, but effective men, such as Jaz, the RSM of the Remount Section, and our OC, Captain Cole.

In any case, training was over. I was off to war.

6

'You did well on your gunnery course, Whitehead,' said the RAAF officer allocating our postings to us.

'Thank you, sir.'

Despite the danger it entailed, I was sure I had my ticket back to Blighty, to play my part in the bombing offensive aimed at bringing Nazi Germany to its knees.

'We've got a special assignment for you.'

'Sir?' My expectations were rising. My brother Glen, I had learned in letters from my mother, was flying twin engine Mosquito bombers. Made of wood, the mosquito was a fast bomber used in low-level, precision raids and aerial reconnaissance. Glen would go on to be a 'pathfinder', whose members, the best of Bomber Command, flew ahead of the massed streams of aircraft to light up targets with flares.

'Yes, several of our squadrons are converting to new aircraft, American B-24 Liberator bombers. You'll be joining 24 Squadron, in New Guinea.'

This was not the outcome I had hoped for, but at least I was going to get into the fight.

First, though, I needed some more training. The B-24, manufactured by the Consolidated Aircraft company in San Diego, was armed with American-made Browning M2 .50 calibre machineguns. The gun fired a bullet half an inch in diameter, which carried a certain amount of authority with it. So far, I had only qualified on the .303-calibre machinegun.

Half a dozen of us slated to join the new squadrons were sent to New South Wales, to RAAF Rathmines, a seaplane base on Lake Macquarie, in the Hunter region, near Newcastle, about 150 kilometres north of Sydney. If nothing else, the war was giving me a good look around Australia.

At Rathmines I got into my flight gear and stepped aboard a twin-engine Catalina flying boat, another US-made product of the Consolidated corporation. The Catalina was a beautiful piece of work, used mostly in reconnaissance and anti-submarine work. With a large main wing and the ability to fly on one engine at a time, the Catalina also had a very long range. Australian Catalinas kept the only aerial link to Britain open during the war, with crews flying 27 hours non-stop from Western Australia to Ceylon (Sri Lanka), for the first leg of the trip.

Our interest, though, was in the guns. The Catalina had bulbous glass 'blisters' on each side of the fuselage, which each accommodated a .50 calibre machinegun. The gunner stood, which was far more comfortable than being squeezed into a turret.

After receiving lessons on the basic operation of the gun and how to deal with stoppages, we took off on the lake's glassy surface, sunshine glittering on the water and after a leisurely run along the coast, turned towards the firing range. We'd already done air-to-air gunnery, so there was no risk of me shooting down another target tug aircraft, and our main aim was to get used to firing the guns.

The pilot lined up on the range and I took aim at some drums in the open. I was able to correct my fall of shot by watching the tracer. The gun was fed with a belt of ammunition and one in every few rounds was a tracer round, a bullet containing phosphorescent material which glowed red. On another strafing run someone on the ground ignited a burning flare and I fired at that.

It was all very satisfying and the .50 cal, as it was known for short, proved to be a very capable weapon, firing 750-800 rounds per minute, with far fewer stoppages than the old .303. I was itching to get into the fight, but it also soon became obvious, as we languished by the lakeside for a few days, that we were marking time until our turn came to get a flight north.

We were given leave while we waited and I caught the train from Newcastle down to Sydney where a rodeo had been organised as entertainment for our American guests. I entered the draw and while I did no good in the competition, I was reunited with a quite a few old mates from the 2nd Remount Section and I survived my rides pretty-much unscathed. I had done it – riding a bucking bronco at the show-grounds, just like the rider I'd seen in the cinema as a boy. It seemed like another lifetime ago, even though it had been just a few years.

After the rodeo a bunch of us, Australians and Americans, repaired to The Burton, a sleazy hotel opposite Central Station in Sydney. While the booze was flowing, I was not too sure of its quality. What I do remember is finding myself outside the pub at 10 pm, sitting on the curb and bringing up everything I'd consumed in the previous 24 hours.

From that point, things got worse. I had vague recollections of dumping my gear in a hostel in Kings Cross, which was being used as a troop billet, before the rodeo. I felt like I was going to die, but managed to stumble and weave my way through Sydney's war-darkened streets to its main den of iniquity, the 'Cross'.

I lurched through the doors of the hostel and found my dormitory room, or, rather, I thought I had found the right place. I couldn't be sure, so I got down on all fours, to the protests of some of the half-asleep soldiers, and started crawling around, between and under beds, looking for my gear.

The next morning, I woke up, fully clothed, lying on the floor.

I'D FALLEN in love with the Catalina flying boats at Rathmines, taking off and landing on the lake, and would have loved to have landed a posting to a flying boat squadron.

The Air Force, however, was hell bent on sending me north, so a mob of us, all destined for the same squadron, boarded a Dakota, the military version of the DC-3 passenger aircraft, and set of for New Guinea.

Australian militiamen, part time soldiers from the 39th Battalion, had proved their mettle on the muddy, mountainous terrain of the Kokoda Track and the jungles of the Owen Stanley Ranges. With the help of regular units from the AIF, pulled back from British control in the Western Desert to defend our corner of the world, Australian troops halted and then turned back the until-then unbeaten troops of the Japanese empire.

Even in late 1943 and early 1944 there was still much heavy fighting to come and our party touched down on the steel planking of an instant runway which had been laid at the recently taken airstrip at Nadzab, just in from Lae, in New Guinea.

I'd come from an army and an air force that jealously husbanded its meagre resources, using wild bush horses in lieu of motor vehicles and giving air gunners just 2,000 rounds of ammunition on which to qualify. Here, in this out-of-the-way jungle clearing, however, was my first glimpse of the might and resources of the vast American war machine that had, after some initial reluctance early in hostilities, been cranked up to near full-speed.

There were mountains of stores, ammunition, food, and weapons everywhere. Seabees, US Navy engineers, were hard at work scraping back the jungle with bulldozers and rolling out dirt roads and taxiways, and buildings were going up everywhere. Aircraft of different types lined the runway.

My unit, 24 Squadron, RAAF, had been flying single-engine Vultee Vengeance dive bombers from Nadzab. The Vengeance had the ability to dive at an inclination of zero degrees – that is, straight down – allowing the pilot to drop his bombs with almost pinpoint accuracy on individual positions, but with General Macarthur's plan to recapture great swathes of the Pacific had come a need for long range, heavy bombers.

I watched as my new mount, a B-24 Liberator, came in to land. If the Catalina had been as sleek as a seabird, then this thing was more like a flying whale, a great slab-sided, burnished aluminium beast nicknamed by its American crews the 'boxcar'.

With four engines and a crew of up to 10, the Liberator had been designed to carry a bomb load of 8,000 pounds, although that decreased the further the aircraft had to fly. Those of us in 24 Squadron would be the first Australians to transition to B-24s, initially with US Air Force aircraft.

I was assigned to a crew, and we were a diverse bunch. Our captain was Ralph Wilkins, who'd been an accountant before the war, and his co-pilot was Max Chaffey, a farmer from the New South Wales north coast. The bomb aimer was an Irish publican from Sydney, and by the look of his size he'd been making a dent in his own profits by downing plenty of stock. Another gunner, who became a good mate, was Duggy Campbell – his father had been Lord Mayor of Melbourne.

A Royal Australian Air Force B-24 Liberator (AWM AC0074)

The Liberator was bristling with .50 calibre machine guns – a couple in the glasshouse nose for use by the bomb aimer when he wasn't dropping bombs; one each side of the fuselage for waist gunners, who fired standing up; a twin-gun 'ball' turret underneath, which had to be hydraulically raised back up inside the aircraft before landing, as it would have scraped the runway otherwise; and a tail-end Charlie position. Because I'd done well on my course, and we were all new to the aircraft so none of us had more experience than the others, I was put in the mid upper gun turret, a two-gun rotating dome set up behind the pilots. From this vantage point I was the gunnery controller, whose job was to call out who was to fire, and when.

After just one orientation flight around the local area, we started operational missions pretty much straight away. We learned the aircraft and our standard operating procedures on the job, as we took off from Nadzab and went into action against the Japanese.

Our first sorties were bombing raids around New Guinea, against Wewak and Rabaul, so they were fairly short flights. There was no anti-aircraft fire and by this stage the allies had air superiority over the area so other than test firing our guns we had no need to use them in anger. It was satisfying, however, to know that I had finally entered the war.

While we had not been shot at, back on terra-firma there was no mistaking the fact that we were in a dangerous business – there were wrecks of crashed aircraft bulldozed into an aeroplane graveyard at one end of the runway.

Proof that even our own second-hand aircraft was already war weary came on our third flight. Having survived our bombing run unscathed, Ralph brought us in to Nadzab, but the moment we touched down he called over the intercom: 'Brace, brace, the hydraulics have failed!'

We all grabbed on to whatever we could in our positions as the B-24 hurtled down the pre-fabricated runway, with no brakes. The trees at the end of the strip loomed closer and when the metal ran out, we bounced and ploughed our way into mud and jungle grass.

The aircraft came to a halt and we all climbed out, marvelling at our luck. None of us had been hurt, but the Liberator was a write-off.

Back on the ground I continued to be amazed at the can-do attitude of the Americans. It was a bit of a culture shock. Whereas Australians tended to be generally laid-back people, except if we were on a mission or applying ourselves to a particular job, the Americans seemed to be on the go all the time, brimming with enthusiasm and rarely complaining.

Our crew settled into something of a routine and both in the air and in between missions we became a tight-knit group. We would receive a briefing in a tent on the edge of the airstrip in the evening, with details of the next day's mission, such as the target, the approach and return routes, and likely enemy flak concentrations.

The next morning, we would take off, two aircraft at a time, and then circle while we waited for the rest of the squadron or our American friends to get off the ground and form up. Most of our missions were anti-shipping strikes, aimed at denying the Japanese the ability to resupply their increasingly isolated outposts on and around New Guinea.

The Japanese had not only been stopped at Kokoda, earlier, but had been pushed all the way to the north coast of New Guinea, where they put up a fierce defence at Buna and Gona, but were eventually defeated.

ONCE WE WERE familiar with our Liberators and had gained some operational experience, 24 Squadron was pulled back from New Guinea to Darwin, where we were equipped with new B-24s.

From a base outside of town, we began flying longer-range missions, striking at the Japanese-held islands. We would receive our briefing and then set off for Timor, an island which had been divided between Dutch and Portuguese rule before the Japanese took it, and Java in the Netherlands East Indies – now Indonesia.

Although we were back in Australia our living conditions hadn't changed all that much from Nadzab. We lived in tents in the bush, alongside our remote airstrip and rarely got into Darwin itself. In any case, the northern capital of was more like a forward military base than a town. Japanese air raids on Darwin had continued all through 1942 and into 1943, but now the enemy was no longer able to strike this far south. The Japanese were being pushed, slowly but surely, back to their home islands.

Our longest flights were to the Celebes, now known as Sulawesi, Indonesia, and Balikpapan, on the island of Borneo, which was a 16-hour round trip. Borneo had been a key strategic target for the Japanese early in their campaign, as it was home to oil fields and refineries. Our bomb loads were light on these raids, as we needed to carry extra fuel, but we sometimes supplemented our loads with empty beer bottles, which whistled through the air as they fell, hopefully causing the Japanese to scatter below, thinking they were bombs raining down on them.

While the allies had gained virtual air superiority, we still had to keep a sharp eye out. We were returning from a raid on Japanese shipping targets in Kupang, on the island of Timor and I was in my slot on top of the aircraft, scanning the sky. I had a great view, but the sun was relentless, streaming into my glassed-in turret.

Suddenly, I saw dots. 'Bandits, bandits,' I said into the intercom. 'Three single engine aircraft. Ralph, head for the clouds,' I said to the pilot.

Ralph took evasive action and aimed for the nearest cloud bank. I could see the dark spots silhouetted against the clear blue sky. This far from Australia, they had to be Japanese. We passed on the alert message to the other bombers in our formation. As much as all of us would have liked to have been blazing away at the enemy with our heavy machineguns, our best course of action was to keep out of the fighters' way.

Bombs fall from a B24, over a Japanese-held island below.

Ours was a different war to the bombing campaign being waged by the allies out of the UK, against the Nazis. We might not have faced swarms of enemy fighters, massed flak and searchlights, in the South West Pacific, but there were other dangers.

Whereas the air war in Europe was fought over densely populated areas, which could be a plus or a minus depending on where you bailed out or crash landed, our missions were conducted over thousands of kilometres and much of our flying was over empty oceans or inhospitable jungle. Our aircraft were well maintained, but the constant flying, weather, fatigue and other elements all took a toll.

One wasn't even necessarily safe when an aircraft made it back to Australia. There were crash landings in remote parts of northern Australia, including the sad case of 'Little Eva', an American B-24 that went off course and ran out of fuel over Cape York. Most of the crew bailed out and those that did were scattered wide and far. One group made for the east coast and was rescued by a hunting party of

Aboriginals. Their remaining four crew mates, however, headed west. Three died of starvation and thirst before the fourth, the ball turret gunner, was rescued.

Part of our job was maritime surveillance, not just looking for enemy shipping, which we might then have a crack at, but also on long searches for our own downed aircraft, lost at sea due to flak damage, navigation error, or mechanical problems.

Each aircraft carried a 'Gibson Girl', a crank-handled emergency survival radio copied from a German design. The name 'girl' came from the hourglass design of the radio's case, which allowed it to sit between the operator's legs, as he sat or lay in an inflatable life raft. Gripping the girl like a cello with his knees or thighs, the operator then turned the crank, which sent out a morse code SOS message, which could be picked up by aircraft overhead. Later models had a balloon, filled with compressed gas, which could be shot aloft to carry an antenna wire, increasing the range to a couple of hundred miles.

I remember hearing that signal on at least three occasions, our four-engine bomber droning over the vast, empty Pacific Ocean, everyone scanning the glittering waters below. All of us, in our headphones, could hear the tinny-sounding dots and dashes of an emergency signal. Downed crews also had fluorescent dye packs which would stain the water a bright colour to further aid their rescuers in finding them.

Backwards and forwards we flew, as long as our fuel would allow, hearing the distress calls of men somewhere out there, frantically praying or yelling for rescue or salvation, their skin burned, voices hoarse.

The term 'needle in a haystack' does not do justice to the size nor the sadness of the task. Although we heard them transmitting, and did everything possible to locate them, we never found them.

FLYING OUT OF DARWIN, we ran into bad weather. The Top End of Australia has two distinct seasons, the long, mild, 'dry', from May to

October, when the skies are clear and the days sunny and warm, and the 'wet' when it rains almost every day for the remainder of the year. The hot, rainy summer is preceded by build-up, around October-November, when temperatures soar and the air becomes heavy with the promise of rain.

The heat and the humidity take on a malevolent quality, an almost physical presence, an enemy whose onslaught can drive people mad. Not for nothing was this time of year referred to as 'Suicide Season'. Locals drink to excess, fights break out, and the rain seems as if it will never come.

It was building, though. From my turret I could see we were entering a cloud bank ahead, great towering Everests of cumulonimbus clouds forming where earlier there had been an azure blue sky. Where possible, we flew around the clouds, but with the formation of the squadron spread out as it was, inevitably the outer aircraft had to enter one cloud or another.

Our 'Lib' became separated from the rest of the squadron. We found ourselves surrounded by formations that looked like angry volcanic eruptions, and then we were in one.

Without warning, we fell.

From cruising along at our normal speed of about 170 miles per hour (a shade under 300 kph), we found ourselves plummeting straight down, not even diving, as if we'd just fallen into an enormous sinkhole.

I was thrown against my harness and the turret roof. It felt as though my stomach was trying to crash through the top of my skull. Gear was flying about, suddenly weightless, and the pilots were yelling to each other as they fought for control of the B-24. Our 55,000-pound bomber was falling, with the aerodynamic grace of a house brick being tossed off a high-rise building.

Ralph had been trying to climb above the weather, which was probably just as well, because we lost about 30,000 feet of altitude in one hit. As we bottomed out, at somewhere near 2,000 feet above ground level, my belly was now in my boots.

The drama was not over. The B-24 was, at last, flying forwards again, but our flightpath was anything but straight and level. The whole aircraft shuddered and bounced.

'Jettison anything that's not nailed down,' Ralph called through the intercom.

The crew went to work. I undid my safety harness and climbed down from my turret. The aluminium skin of the Liberator was buzzing and vibrating and the engines seemed to straining to keep us aloft.

'Bomb bay doors opening,' Ralph said.

The B-24's doors were not the kind that dropped down to open, like other bombers, such as the American B17 Flying Fortress or the British Lancaster. Instead, they rolled up and to each side of the fuselage, like a roll-top desk or garage doors. This reduced drag when flying, meaning we could get over a target and drop our bombs without losing too much speed. This arrangement also helped on the ground. As the B-24 had a tricycle undercarriage, with a nosewheel at the front and wheels under each wing, sitting low to the ground, it did not have the ground clearance for typical 'clamshell' type doors.

The doors screeched and rattled into their upwards, open position and in front of me – I was looking rearwards - I saw ocean below, as air rushed in

'Bombs gone,' Ralph said. I watched as our payload disappeared, whistling away to detonate harmlessly in the Pacific Ocean. That was some weight gone, but Ralph was clearly worried enough to want every superfluous piece of kit gone, in order to keep us in the air and help him handle the shuddering kite.

Running down the centre of the fuselage, where the bomb bay doors met when closed, was a narrow catwalk. I picked up what I could find that was lying around the front of the aircraft – our meal boxes for the flight, spare cans of ammunition, anything not bolted down, and threw it out the into the ocean. I moved to the rear of the Lib, carefully walking along the narrow walkway – if we hit another air pocket like the first I'd more than likely be involuntarily jettisoned, along with the excess stores.

Once we had offloaded as much gear as we could, the aircraft was actually back over Australia. We struggled and wobbled on until we arrived over our base, where we braced for what we thought was going to be a shaky landing - we weren't wrong.

As soon as we touched town we were bounced and thrown about, even once all landing gear was down. That in itself was a problem - the whole airframe had actually been bent and twisted by the force of being dropped by the turbulence. When Ralph eventually shut down the engines and we were able to get out and inspect the damage, we could all see that this massive aircraft had been bent so much that only two of the three sets of wheels could connect with the runway at any one time. Like a broken toy a giant child had tired of, the B-24 was a total write-off, all thanks to Mother Nature.

WE FOLLOWED the course of the war, shipping out from Darwin towards the end of 1944 for the island of Morotai, which had just been liberated, more or less, in November.

Morotai was a small island at the north end of the Halmahera group, which in turn was part of the then Netherlands East Indies, now modern-day Indonesia. It had been selected by the allies as a staging post for aircraft, troops and supplies for the subsequent re-taking of the Philippines. Our supreme commander, the flamboyant and outspoken US General, Douglas MacArthur, had been forced to leave the Philippines soon after Japan had entered the war, vowing in those immortal words 'I shall return'.

There were a few pockets of Japanese resistors still on the island, but mostly we were left to ourselves, camped, once more, in tents on the edge of a jungle airstrip. We were assigned to the US 5th Air Force. While the American aircraft and crews were plentiful and only flew once every 10 to 15 days, there was only a token flight of four RAAF Liberators attached to the main force. So, to keep up appearances and appear to shoulder our share of the load, we had to fly every two days.

From Morotai, we were closer to Balikpapan and we kept up the pressure on the oil fields and refineries. This was the target where we most often encountered flak – enemy anti-aircraft fire. The Japanese knew the storage tanks were of just as much importance to us as they were to them, so they were ringed with guns.

In order to improve our chances of survival we would climb to 30,000 feet to make our approach to Balikpapan, out of reach of most of the enemy's anti-aircraft guns. The problem was that at that altitude it was, literally, freezing. As many of our missions were at low level the RAAF had not seen fit to issue us with cold weather gear. The Americans, by contrast, had access to anything they needed.

'What do you want, boys?' the American supply Sergeant whom we nicknamed 'Trader Horn' would ask us when he pulled up at our tented camp in his deuce-and-a-half, a 2 ½ ton truck, loaded to the brim with equipment. He was named after a popular 1931 film about a trader in the wilds of Africa.

'Cold weather flying jackets and boots,' I had said to him.

'No problem,' Trader Horn said. In the back of his vehicle were leather jackets, flying helmets, overalls and boots, all lined with sheepskin. By contrast, we were expected to take to the air in our thin khaki tropical uniforms.

'Whaddya got?' Horn asked.

From my tent I brought out a crate of Australia's finest amber fluid. That brought a smile to Horn's face. Our food might have been fucking disgraceful, but the RAAF did keep us supplied with beer, which the Americans, being 'dry', always needed.

Meal time was torture for us on Morotai. Bivouacked next to us was an African-American unit – their military was segregated until the 1950s – and we were forced to endure the smells of their kitchens and mess-halls. The succulent odours of roasting chicken and barbequing pork ribs, even steak at times, had us literally drooling.

There were so few of us Australians that the RAAF had decreed we did not merit a full-blown cookhouse of our own, just a makeshift affair with a couple of men doing what they could with what was on hand. For lunch we might get a piece of stale bread with some canned butter on it – awful blue-green stuff the consistency of axle grease – topped with a watery concoction from another tin, known as 'tropical spread'. The packed lunch boxes we took on missions with us were so vile they'd often be jettisoned.

The never-ending grind of missions continued. I don't think I was ever really scared; the flak bursting over Balikpapan was more a curiosity than a source of fear. I'd watch the different coloured shells bursting, and occasionally we'd be buffeted and maybe take a sprinkling of shrapnel, but, thankfully, none of our crew was hit, nor our Liberator seriously damaged.

The worst thing that happened to me was a cold, a serious one. I had a blocked nose and ears and my head felt as though it was stuffed with liquid cotton wool; by rights I should not have flown.

'I have to fly,' I told Ralph, after the pre-mission briefing, blowing my nose as hard as I could.

He looked at me, but did not argue. None of the others did, either.

We had an unwritten rule in our crew, that we would only ever fly all together. Soldiers, airmen and sailors at war can be a superstitious lot and while our losses were not as great, say, as if we'd been flying out of England, we had all, or so we believed, noticed a worrying trend – it seemed the only time an aircraft was lost was when it was carrying a replacement crew member. None of us wanted to carry a Jonah, an odd man out, nor to be that sole survivor whose life was spared when the rest of the crew did not return from a mission.

I flew with my cold. It was agony. It felt like my head was going to explode as we climbed to altitude, and it was as bad coming back down after the mission.

Mercifully, as we had been operating out of Morotai for quite a few months and were due some rest and relaxation, we returned to Darwin. Unfortunately for me, while all my crew mates went swimming, or propped up the bar in one of Darwin's hotels, I was stuck in a RAAF hospital with doctors pumping warm water up my nostrils, trying to clear my clogged ear canals.

The treatment never really worked and my ears have continued to give me trouble. To this day, I find it very difficult to hear what is going on or follow a conversation without continually saying: 'would you repeat that please?'. It's been extremely annoying and embarrassing, but at the time there was no way I was not going to fly.

'REPORT TO BATCHELOR,' I was told, when I was discharged from the hospital.

I caught a lift in an air force vehicle heading south of Darwin to Batchelor, a large air force base. There, I was given orders to go in front of a selection board, to see if I was the right sort to be commissioned as an officer.

I'd been a Sergeant as a gunner at Sale and then been promoted to Flight Sergeant when I started flying on operations.

'Congratulations, Pilot Officer Whitehead,' an officer said to me after the selection board. I was given a new rank – pilot officer is the air force equivalent of a second lieutenant, the most junior commissioned officer in army – and a nice little officer's hat to wear.

Our crew returned to Morotai, where we kept on flying. VE Day, which marked victory in Europe over Mr Hitler's bunch, on May 8, came and went without much celebrating in the Pacific. Each day was much like the one before – we would have our briefing, take off, we'd test fire our guns, drop our bombs and then fly back to our little clearing in the jungle.

We'd clean out our rubbish and the spent brass casings from the .50 cals and then service the guns and turret, fill the ammunition bins and tidy up before heading for the tents and what passed for dinner. In what little spare time we had we went swimming on the beach or watched a film at the Americans' open air cinema near our camp, or drank beer.

For us there was no 30-mission goal on an operational tour; we were expected to just keep on flying. I lost track of how many missions I flew – certainly it was more than 70 and I know my flying log book was almost full. I think I clocked up something in excess of 2,000 flying hours, give or take a few.

It seemed at the time that the Japanese had no intention of giving up but, rather, were more inclined to fight to the bitter end. The battles to retake the islands closer to Japan became bloodier, and the enemy more fanatical in his commitment to die rather than surrender. Kamikaze aircraft were being deliberately flown into warships by Japanese pilots, and others, we heard, would ram the new B-29 Superfortress bombers that were now bombing Tokyo and other targets in Japan.

And then, one day in August, 1945, it was all over.

7

The end of the war was a total let down.

For five years I had become totally geared towards away of life that catered for virtually all of my needs. I'd even met a girl.

It was a great relief, of course, that it was all over, brought to a sudden end by the dropping of two atomic bombs on Japan, but Morotai was hardly the place for a grand celebration. Very quickly I realised that as an air gunner – even one who had now risen another notch up the promotion ladder to Flying Officer – I was now surplus to requirements.

'You and the other gunners are going home to Australia,' we were told in a briefing.

Our flight of Liberators had been assigned to the armada flying to Malaya to collect Australian prisoners of war, who had suffered so horribly at the hands of the Japanese. The survivors were considered to be in too poor a state for transport by sea. All of us who were no longer needed – gunners, bomb aimers, armourers and other personnel who had only existed in the eyes of the air force to drop bombs on the enemy or shoot him, were sent packing. Our crew, a group of men who would never fly unless it was 'one for all and all for one' was broken up. Just like that.

We were flown to Darwin and, from there, I ended up in Melbourne, where I was demobbed – demobilised. I asked to stay in the RAAF, but was told in no uncertain terms I was no longer needed. I discussed my future with the Air Force de-mob people, who had various schemes on the go to support people like me.

After some exhaustive testing and a number of interviews, I was informed that, if I wanted, they would recommend me for tertiary education. What little common sense I was possessed of reared its rarely-seen head, and I opted to study for a diploma course, rather than a university degree, selecting Agriculture as the discipline.

I'd lost contact with Marie, the actress-slash-model. With the end of the war I suspect her sights were set on someone other than an out of work gunner, but I decided to stay on in Melbourne. It was somewhere different. My friend and former crewmate Duggy Campbell's family lived in the suburb of Toorak and his brother had a farm at Broadmeadows, adjacent to the abandoned Victorian branch of the army's remount service, where I could work with horses. The cards seemed to have fallen right for me again.

With my Air Force pay – there had been little to spend it on, on Morotai – and my deferred pay I bought a three-storey terrace house not far from Toorak and set about renovating it, while I worked out what to do with my life. I decided to divide the house into separate flatettes, each with its own kitchenette and a communal bathroom on each floor. I ended up renting the rooms to Ansett Airways hostesses, as flight attendants were once known. If I'd thought this would bring an end to my bachelorhood, or provide some fun, I was wrong – they all had boyfriends, mostly pilots.

My association with luck, up until this point in my life, had been more about surviving, than coming into any great windfall. I had been lucky to escape serious injury during my time with the Remounts, and had survived unscathed during my brief exposure to the real face of the war, finishing up with nothing worse than a crook back and a heavy dose of deafness. The focus of my luck was about to change.

While I was waiting for my agricultural diploma course to start, I filled in my time between working on the renovation of the house and hanging around Flemington and various other Victorian horse racing venues. There I ran into a couple of bookmakers who came up with an interesting sideline for me.

They had just been contracted to help re-stock the racing industry in Singapore and Malaya with horses. Racing everywhere had suffered drastically during the war – in Australia due to the lack of man-power and in Malaysia due to the complete breakdown of all services after the Japanese invasion. As a result, there were dozens of poor-to-medium quality gallopers in the stables and on farms and stations in Australia which were ripe for sorting out and export to Asia. My two bookies were concerned with Victoria only, mainly Melbourne and the near vicinity.

They had the money to buy the horses and the contacts to find them, but not the expertise to check them out for suitability, which is where I came into the picture. There were plenty to choose from and between us we went through what was offered, selecting those we thought might be suitable.

Once the horses were selected and a veterinarian had run the rule over them, my job was to re-educate those that had previously been broken in, and break those which had not. As the contract was to supply sufficient horses to make up an initial two ship loads, those coming directly from the racing stables made up only a very small percentage, so my part in the exercise looked like turning into something much bigger than had previously been anticipated.

To carry out my part of the deal I had arranged to take over the old army remount yards and paddocks, which were standing idle pending their sale and were admirably suitable for my needs. With a workplace secured and sufficient tack and gear on hand, I needed a couple of good hacks to help me get started with my work.

To this end I spent what spare time I had at horse sales and farm sales looking for something to fit the bill. Although we had plenty of thoroughbred horses to choose from, in the main they were not really the sort of horse one wants as a breaker's hack, being too light and in general, too 'fizzy'.

What I needed was something with a good deal of substance. He would need a sensible temperament and the ability to use his weight as an anchor, when necessary, yet be light enough on his feet to be able to move quickly. Such horses are not easy to come by.

It was a dreadful Saturday, cold, with sleeting rain driving down in front of a bitter wind. The black clouds were just high enough to avoid being classified as mist, swirling around when I arrived at the sale yards in a small rural town in the foothills of the southern Victorian Dandenong Ranges, for the monthly horse sale.

The sale was scheduled to start at noon, so I organized my arrival for about 11 o'clock to give myself time to see what was being offered. As I didn't really expect to see anything of interest, I would also have enough time to get back to my yards, check that all was in order, and then go home for a quiet, warm afternoon off.

Looking along the lines of horses, their breath, like mine, freezing where it hung in the air, it seemed to me the main trade here was for the abattoirs. The paltry number of buyers on hand on this miserable day just confirmed my view.

'Have you had a look at Rhumba?' one of the hands, who I'd been speaking to about my needs, suddenly said.

'Nice name.' The sarcasm was heavy in my voice, as I conjured up an image to accompany the moniker - slinky South American or Creole girls shaking their shoulders, and doing whatever else one does on dimly lit dance floors in the company of men attired in frilly shirts, extravagant trousers, thin moustaches and patent-leather hair.

After a quick walk round the sale pens, and seeing nothing of any interest, I was on my way back to my car when I saw, in the gloom at the opposite end of the sale building, a big lump of a creamy/dun-coloured horse, quite on his own.

As I hadn't noticed him on my way in, I went over to have a look, and was immediately impressed by what I saw. Standing outside the pen he was in, looking thoroughly miserable and obviously in some distress, was a young woman.

'Know anything about this horse?' I asked, forcing a note of jollity into my voice to try and cut through the day's greyness and raise her spirits.

'This is Rhumba,' she said.

Aha, I thought. Not quite the sleek, dark-eyed filly I'd imagined, but, rather, a fairly solid, sensible looking fellow.

'He's mine,' she sniffed, 'but he's taken to bolting whenever I ride him. My husband's insisting that I get rid of him before I get hurt.'

'I'm sorry to hear it, but he looks like a good horse, nevertheless,' I said.

'The problem I've got, is that everyone around here knows him and his problems. That's why no one's interested in buying him, and I'm worried he's going to end up at the slaughter yard.'

I felt for her. Rhumba clearly meant a great deal to her. 'Was he broken in when you bought him?' I asked.

'I broke him myself,' she said. 'At first everything was fine, but as he grew older and stronger it got to the point where I couldn't control him any longer. That's when he took to bolting.'

I took a closer look at the recalcitrant Rhumba. Make and shape-wise, he was exactly the type of horse I was looking for. At a rough guess I would have put him down as a mix of Connemara Pony, and Clydesdale, with a large dose of thoroughbred in there somewhere.

Whatever he was, he was the best, in fact the only, option I'd seen that gloomy morning. I didn't say anything to the woman, mindful of her attachment to the animal and her distress, but I reckoned Rhumba, who looked like a smart, sharp type of horse, had simply taken advantage of his kindly mistress. In doing so, he'd done himself no favours!

'How old is he?'

'Five-years-old,' she said.

He was still young enough to take a chance on, I thought. 'How much do you want for him?'

She shrugged. 'Thirty pounds?'

I ran my hands down his flank, saying nothing, and then looked him in the eye.

'You think there's hope for him?' she pressed.

I could see the hope in her face, and hear it in her voice.

'Twenty-five?' I countered.

'Oh yes, deal!'

I could tell it was the thought Rhumba would be saved, rather than the money that had sealed the deal. I gave her the asking price and sorted the auctioneer out with his commission, glad to have done the deal before he went through the ring, as, being in really good condition, he would probably have brought a good deal more for slaughter than I had paid for him.

As I led him out of the sale yard, one old bushy nodded to me. 'Dangerous horse, that one,' he said to me. 'Only fit for the knacker's yard.'

We'll see, I thought to myself.

The following Monday morning, my new acquisition and I became acquainted.

I looked him over again, remembering my time in the remounts, when I reckoned I could tell a good horse from a bad one just from a touch and a glance. I'd had some experience with rank and unpredictable horses in my time, but Rhumba just didn't give off any dangerous vibes – clever and smart, yes, but dangerous? I was prepared to bet, no.

I went through my usual routine with new horses, checking whether there were any hidden vices, such as cow-kicking, biting, being ticklish near the girth, but in every instance, Rhumba came up trumps. He picked up his feet readily and let me clean them out; I had no trouble lifting his tail, or pulling his ears; in fact, everything about him tended to confirm my growing opinion that he was, in fact, a very nice horse.

He saddled up readily, no tension or blowing himself out when the girth was tightened, no walking on tip-toes all humped up when I moved him around, and he seemed to respond easily and willingly when I tested his mouth with the reins.

However, being well aware of his reputation for uncontrolled bolting, I took the precaution of rigging up a bit of rabbit snare wire across the front of his nose, just above the peak of the septum, and tied it in place with a piece of cord running down the front of his face, from the bridle poll piece.

The effect of this rig was somewhat similar to that of a Kineton nose band, but infinitely more drastic if used harshly. If applied with tact however, it really gets a horse's attention. It should only need to be used for a very short time in order just to get the message across, no more, unlike the Kineton, which once brought into play, had to remain so.

Loriners – makers of bits - have, over the centuries, produced all manner of bits with varying degrees of severity, designed to control hard pulling horses. Personally, I had never been a proponent of any but the mildest of bits, having always felt that hard mouths, which are often the lead-in to bolting, are nearly always the result of bad management, rather than an inherently bad horse.

Nevertheless, being faced with a situation such as I was with Rhumba, a few sensible precautions were very definitely the order of the day.

As a preliminary to giving him the opportunity to try his specialty, I rode him around the yard for a while before taking him out into a larger enclosed space, where I walked, trotted and cantered him about for an hour or two just to see what he felt like and how he handled.

As I suspected, he didn't handle very well, but he seemed willing enough to make an effort to do what I asked. All the time I was riding him I was gently putting pressure on his nose through my bit of rabbit wire, until I felt him showing signs of his nose becoming tender, such as throwing his head up when I touched the reins.

Once I was pretty certain he wasn't going to try and 'bull' his way through the wire, it was time to see if we were on the right track, or if he was a lost cause. To do that I took him out into a fairly large paddock nearby. This field had been ploughed and cultivated in preparation for sowing some crop or other. I started out riding him in circles and snake tracks, stopping and turning constantly to keep him concentrating on what I was asking for, rather than dreaming up any mischief.

To begin with, all the exercises were at the walk, gradually progressing to a trot. We then increased to a gentle, controlled canter, through all of which he responded very well - braking instantaneously whenever I touched the reins a bit heavily, causing the wire to nip his nose.

After about half an hour on the loose, ploughed ground, I felt he had done enough for one day. It was always beneficial, I found, to end up a work session on a good note. I took him back to the yard, washed him down and let him go for the day.

The next day, knowing his nose was going to be very tender indeed, I wrapped the rabbit wire in a couple of layers of rubber inner tubing, and after going through all the exercises of the day before in the vicinity of the yards, we went out into the ploughed field again.

This time, though, after a few little trots and stops, then slow canters and stops, during which he let me know in no uncertain manner that his nose was quite sore, I thought it time to see if the message had penetrated properly. I set him out along the long side of the field and almost let him have his head. At first he seemed to go very willingly but still under complete control, then gradually I started to feel him building up and beginning to want to take charge, perhaps remembering how he'd been with his previous owner.

At this point I gave him a light, but firm touch on the nose. He threw his head up and tucked his hind legs under his belly and virtually slid to a halt.

'Good boy, Rhumba, good boy.' I stroked and patted him and cooed in his ear how pleased I was with him. 'You're a sensible horse, aren't you, boy?'

We set off again and when I was ready to stop him, he obliged again, perfectly. Feeling that he was really beginning to understand what was wanted and not wishing to press my luck, I took him back to the yards, washed him down and turned him out for the rest of the day.

The next day, Wednesday, we did the whole thing again, only this time I let him get a full head of steam up before asking him to stop. He didn't quite slide to a stop as he had done the day before, but he certainly took notice of the touch on the reins and stopped relatively readily.

All this showed me that Rhumba was not, and never had been, bolting blindly but rather had been doing it out of devilment, and was quite happy, when pressed, to give up the whole idea and fall into line. From then on, although I kept the piece of wire, suitably padded, over his nose for quite a long time as insurance, I never had a moment's trouble with him.

Rhumba took to his job as a breaking horse like a duck to water.

In no time at all he had worked out where to put himself and how to brace against horses trying to get away from him. He would push them by turning into them, or pull them by turning away, and crowd them against the yard rails if they needed steadying up. In fact, whatever was needed, he seemed to do instinctively, without any cues from me.

For the next eight months Rhumba and I worked virtually from dawn to dusk, seven days a week, sorting, breaking, gentling and rehabilitating the steady stream of horses going through our hands en route to Malaya.

I did have a couple of other work horses which I used now and again, but Rhumba was such a star and such a pleasure to work with that I selfishly tended to use him much more than I should have – all I can say in my defence was that he seemed to thrive on the work and never lost an ounce of condition during the whole time we worked on the contract. He never went lame, nor showed any signs of muscular strain, no matter how much pulling and tugging about he was subjected to in the course of a day's work.

Besides his skill as a breaking horse, Rhumba developed quite a number of tricks. He learned to come when I whistled for him, and, later, when I was breaking the odd horse in as a side line to my studies, I could put him in the paddock with the unbroken horse and very shortly have it coming to the whistle too.

During that same period, I broke Rhumba to harness and many a time brought two unbroken horses home, one tied to each shaft of the sulky. Rhumba would trot along between the shafts, having earlier spent a rough hour or two pulling them around in the yards, teaching them to lead, before being put back into the shafts of the sulky for the journey home.

Another of his many other quirks was his ability to assess people. Rhumba could pick out a novice, or a poseur with unerring accuracy. With the former he would never put a foot wrong, nor do anything that would put them at risk, but with the latter it was a different story entirely. He would expose their deficiencies ruthlessly and, if I don't miss my guess, really enjoy himself doing it. Very few of these braggarts ever returned for a second ride on him, whereas novices and children could, and would, climb up onto him whenever the opportunity occurred and enjoy every minute of their ride in perfect safety.

I had been lucky with Rhumba – not because I had avoided being hurt by him, but because I had found a friend.

8

As soon as it was practical after the war, my mother sailed from England to Australia, to visit me. I hadn't seen her since I left home as a boy, and now I was a man. It was good to see her, and she hadn't changed much; she still had her very proper, Calvinistic Scottish manners.

'Sit up straight, Peter,' she chided, when I took her out to dinner, 'elbows off the table.'

She was full of news from old Blighty. Glen had survived his operational tours in Bomber Command, while Mary had ditched her nursing studies and had become a WAAF, also serving throughout the war. My younger sister, Wendy, on leaving school had joined the WRENs, becoming a limo driver, ferrying senior naval officers about. In doing so she had become engaged to a Norwegian officer, whom she subsequently married.

There was still no news of my father, however, so mother and I set about contacting the Red Cross in Australia. They proved more successful than their counterparts in the UK, but, sadly, when we received the results of their investigation it was not what we wanted to hear. Father had died in a Japanese internment camp in 1943.

Saddened, but at last having found some closure, Mother

returned home and I packed myself off to the Dookie Agricultural College, near the central Victorian town of Shepparton, which had started life as a sheep farming area, but was now better known for its fruit orchards and the SPC cannery.

The work on the course was not particularly taxing, so with time on my hands I asked the manager of the college's working farm if I could be of use.

'What can you do?' he asked me.

'I was a contract horse breaker before joining up,' I said.

'We've got plenty of young horses on the farm that were overlooked because of the war, and labour shortages. Have a go at them.'

I was given the free use of the yards and facilities and duly put what horses they had on the straight and narrow path to righteousness. Having done the farm manager a favour, I was able to make a quid pro quo deal to bring in the odd outside horse for breaking.

Through that little sideline I met an old Irishman by the name of Dinny Ryan, one of the district's great characters. Dinny ran a sheep and cattle property about three hours away from the college and given where he'd been born, it was no surprise that horses were one of his passions.

Dinny engaged me to work with a few of his horses. He had some very nice young ones running on his property, all of which I broke in for him to our mutual satisfaction. On what was just about my final visit to him, he asked if I would be interested in taking on a big, upstanding brown horse he had running in the back paddock with his mares.

'He's a bit older than the others, so he is, about five-years-old,' Dinny said, pointing to the horse. 'A couple of other breakers have had a go at him, but for some reason or other they failed. I've no idea why.'

To me the horse looked like a nice, big, useful sort of a fellow, ideal for both riding and driving. Besides, I liked a challenge, so I said I'd see what I could do.

The following weekend I headed over to Dinny's property with Rhumba trotting along happily in front of me, between the long shafts of the sulky we used for breaking horses to harness. I felt that if Dinny's horse was to be broken into harness he might as well start right from the beginning by getting used to something following on behind, making all sorts of unpleasant noises.

Dinny had the horse in the yard when I arrived, so after a cup of tea and a bit of a yarn I caught him up, and gave him a bit of a pull around to get the feel of him. However, as he had been handled quite a bit before, he was no trouble, so I put Rhumba back into the sulky, tied the new horse to the near side shaft, and set off back to the college.

The first two or three miles were fairly hectic, but by now Rhumba was fairly well used to what was going on and took it all in his stride. Eventually, Dinny's horse decided he'd had enough of misbehaving and settled down to a quiet trot. In due course, we made it back to the college and both horses were turned out in the paddock together.

The next day, after my studies were over, I headed to the yards. I caught hold of Dinny's horse and started walking him. When I gave him a rest, however, I noticed that the horse, rather than trotting off, was following me.

In fact, he was stalking me.

I turned around, distracted by something across the paddock, and the next thing I knew the air beside my face was being displaced by a pair of flying hooves. If I hadn't turned, the horse would have connected with my head. He kicked out again, as I ducked and weaved out of the way, just in time.

All through the rest of the afternoon, as we danced around each other, the horse let me know that the moment my attention was on anything other than him, he would try and flatten me. I was beginning to get an inkling of why the other breakers had given up on him – this was like no other horse I had ever come across. Not only was he mean and dirty, he also appeared to be able to think!

One of the first lessons I'd learned in horse breaking was never to get into a position where it was possible to get hurt. This was important, as most of the time I'd be working solo, in a paddock or yard away from the homestead, with no one else in sight nor earshot. If I was injured there was little chance of any help.

If this meant taking extra precautions, and sometimes being a bit tough on a horse, then so be it. Dinny's horse, if he was ever going to be broken of his bad habits, had to be made to understand that such behaviour was definitely not acceptable.

It was no use me pulling a front leg up, as I might have done a with wild horse fresh in from the bush, as that wouldn't stop Dinny's devil from kicking me with his rear hooves. Instead, my first job was to get a side-line on him, which would pull up the hind leg on the off side – the opposite to the side I was working on. This would severely restrict his chances of getting a successful kick in.

In the past, when sidelining a restive or dangerous horse I had always found it safer to have it free in the centre of the yard, rather than tie it up; it might mean that I had to move about a bit more, but at least it ensured not getting trapped against the rails if the horse decided to swing into me.

Eventually, with the aid of a long bit of wire, and much ducking and diving, I succeeded in getting a rope round his off side hind fetlock. With a hind leg up and the danger of getting kicked or run over pretty well under control, the next stage was to get him onto the ground by pulling his head up on the opposite side, and getting his chin as near to his wither as possible. This was a procedure I had read about in an American book by a man called Rarey, who had styled himself as a professor in horse breaking. He had used this method a number of times in the past with great results.

Once down, the off side front leg was strapped up, after which the horse was virtually immobile and the breaker could desensitise it in any way he saw fit. In the past I had found that after a couple of strenuous efforts to get up, a normal horse would give up and relax. Once the restraints had been released, it would get up with a completely changed attitude to life.

Dinny's horse was the exception. When I let him get up it was obvious the message had not been received, so down he had to go again. This time there was an improvement when I let him up – he appeared subdued and quite a bit more receptive to me working around him, but when I tried to pick up one of his hind legs, he reverted immediately.

I had never before had to put a horse down a third time, but this was not a normal horse, so down he went again. This time I gave him a good going over, flapping him with an old sack, rolling him over from side-to-side and generally showing him how helpless he was.

It was pretty rough stuff, but in general it was probably no more than the discipline meted out by the leader in a herd of horses, to a stroppy colt getting above himself.

The real test, however, would be putting a saddle on him and seeing if he could be ridden. Suspecting that this was going to be a fairly robust experience I enlisted the aid of another student, Johnny Cram, who fancied himself as a bit of a buck-jump rider and was willing to chance his arm. I climbed up on Rhumba, who was used to pulling and pushing young horses about on their first ride or two.

All hell broke loose. After poor Johnny had been tossed off a couple of times and Rhumba nearly jerked off his feet trying to hold Dinny's horse down, we decided to bring in plan B: no more pussy-footing or snubbing him up to Rhumba, just get on and try to ride the buck out of him.

'You want me to have a go?' I asked Johnny.

'No,' he said, with all the pride and determination of youth, 'She'll be right.'

I blindfolded the horse, grabbed him by the ear, and brought his head down while Johnny got on. I let his ear go and whipped the blindfold off.

No sooner had I done that, than I was picking Johnny up out of the dust. Undeterred, Johnny brushed himself off and got back on. I was having flashbacks to my own time with Easy Molly. Twice more we went through the same procedure, after which I decided John had had enough and it was my turn to have a go.

Using a reliable little trick I had picked up way back, I pulled the horse's tongue out of his mouth and held it, the bit and the cheek strap in my left hand, at the same time pulling the horse's head right round to my left thigh. Holding him in this manner, I was able to slip quietly onto his back, pulling his head up towards his wither as I got on, and holding it there until I was nicely settled.

Once the action started, I walloped him at every jump with a broken folded girth that I used as a 'flopper'- a substitute for a whip - which made plenty of noise, but didn't hurt the horse too much. I also used my spurs along his shoulders and his ribs as liberally as I could to keep his mind on the job.

Maybe the horse was getting tired after throwing Johnny so many times, or perhaps I was riding a bit better than normal; whatever the reason, he eventually gave up bucking and settled down to trotting around the yard. I'd been here before, though, so at this point I wasn't prepared to give him any relief; with the flopper and the spurs I hounded him round and round the yard until I thought he was exhausted.

Finally, on pulling him up, he just stood, his head hanging down, heaving and gasping for breath and literally shaking. While he was in this state, I got off and back on him a couple of times, then went around to the off side and repeated the process; if he showed any sign of resentment, I shook him and shouted at him.

The whole idea was to impress on him that he had shot his bolt and from then on, he had to front up and do the right thing, whatever that may be.

After a week of being ridden daily, both inside and out of the yard, he was ready to be driven in the long-shafted sulky. With Johnny riding shotgun, we took him to a fallow paddock that was being prepared for seeding and as such had a nice deep tilth from all the harrowing and rolling that had been going on.

We hooked him into the shafts and Johnny held him while I climbed into the driver's seat. I then took a tight hold of him, pushed the brake on as hard as I could, and Johnny clambered over the back and sat beside me. With the brake off, I gave a gentle click of my tongue and we moved off.

At first, everything seemed to be going well until suddenly the horse realised that there was something not quite right behind him.

He got into high gear almost immediately and wasn't too concerned about where he was headed, but between the brake and the tilth he didn't go too far before slowing right down. After a couple of token kicks at the shafts and traces rubbing against him, he settled down and spent the next half hour trotting round, doing figures of eight and stopping and starting in a very reasonable manner.

He spent another week or so being ridden and driven and doing everything that could be expected from a green horse and at that point I decided it was reasonable to take him back to Dinny. The day before I did so, though, I took him for a ride in the same fallow paddock that had featured in so much of his training.

Johnny came along on Rhumba and we cantered round the edges of the field, lobbing along with our collective minds in neutral, or, to be more specific, the collective minds of myself, Johnny and Rhumba. Dinny's horse had something else on *his* mind.

As we approached a large gum tree, standing a couple of metres in from the fence, I had a sudden premonition that something was going to happen, and just as I did, Dinny's horse ducked towards the gap between the fence and the tree, throwing himself straight into a sturdy strainer post, directly opposite the tree. By some instinctive, involuntary reaction, I just managed to lift my right leg up in time to avoid having it smashed into the post. The horse then launched into a couple of flying bucks, doing his best to catapult me into space, before eventually deciding to settle down again.

I was less than amused by the incident but there was nothing to do about it, as it was far too late to remonstrate with hm. It was certainly time for this bloody horse to go back to its owner. My saddle to this day carries the rake marks along the flap to show where Dinny's horse scraped against the post. The incident just confirmed what I had felt all along, this was one very dirty, evil horse who would kill someone one day if he got the chance.

THE FOLLOWING DAY, I drove him over to Dinny's place, with Rhumba tied on behind, just to prove to Dinny that his horse could be driven.

This, together with the saddle marks on him from the day before, showed he had been ridden also.

As I often did, I spent the night at Dinny's place so I could get an early start for the long drive home, before it got too hot. After dinner, with a couple of beers under my belt, I took Dinny to task over misleading me about the horse.

'You knew exactly why the other two breakers bloody-well quit, Dinny,' I said, pointing a finger at him. 'You knew that bloody horse was dirty. Also, fancy telling me he was 'around five' when you'd bred him. He's at least nine-years-old.'

I carried on a bit, effing and blinding away at him. When I'd exhausted myself he held up a hand.

'Let me tell you a story, Peter,' he said in his Irish brogue. 'That horse's mother was a beautiful creature, one of those one-in-a-million horses one so seldom comes across. She was a favourite of my late wife, right up until the time she passed away.'

Most of my ire was spent. 'Sorry to hear,' I mumbled.

He nodded. 'That mare spent all her life working for my family, but also being treated like one of us, being petted and cared for. When she grew too old to do any work we decided to get a foal from her, to keep her line going.'

'OK,' I said, intrigued at where this devil had come from.

'The foal was born just before my missus passed away, Peter, and when she saw it, she said to me: 'it's got the look of a good one, Dinny. Promise me that you'll look after him. I'm sure he'll be as good as his mother was."

Dinny was tugging at my heartstrings, but I couldn't connect the foal of a sweet family pet with the monster who'd done his best to murder Johnny and me.

Dinny took a sip of beer, his eyes far away, then carried on: 'A couple of years after my wife passed away there was a huge storm, during which a very large branch broke off a big, old red-gum tree in the horse paddock. The young horse had been sheltering under the tree and the branch fell on his head, then pinned him to the ground.

'When the storm passed, I found him, there, lying stretched out, buried under the branch. At first, I thought he was dead, but as I came closer to him I saw he was still breathing. A helper and I pulled the branch away and got him up onto his feet. He had a swelling the size of two tennis balls just above his near side eye, stretching towards his poll, and numerous cuts and bruises all over his body, but he was able to walk, just.'

The poor animal, I thought.

'Eventually,' Dinny said, 'the cuts and bruises healed, but it took nearly a year for the swelling over his eye to go down. After that experience, I must be honest with you, Peter, he changed from quite a docile, friendly two-year old to a wild 'nut case', whom nobody could do anything with.'

I let out a small chuckle at Dinny's new-found honesty.

'He remained that way until he was indeed 'around five," Dinny went on, 'when I decided to try and break him in. I tried at first, with no success, then passed him onto the local breaker, who had even less success. The horse knew by now that in a competition with humans, he could win. After a year or so, another horse breaker arrived in the district and took up the challenge. He took the horse away and came back three days' later saying: 'there isn't enough money in the world to get me to have anything to do with a horse like that again!"

I shook my head. 'So, why me?'

'You were my last chance, to make good my promise to my wife, Peter.'

My chest swelled a little, with pride. 'Thank you, I think.'

Dinny nodded, and gave me a kindly smile, 'Yes, Peter, you appeared young and trustingly stupid.'

I nearly choked on my beer.

Dinny grinned. 'Sure, and I thought that if I didn't tell you the full story you might just take it that it that this was a mildly dirty horse, and get on with breaking it in – which is, of course what happened.'

I didn't know whether to thank Dinny or to start swearing at him all over again, but he paid me a handsome tip well over my normal fee and, I must confess, I felt a certain smugness at having succeeded where others had failed.

. . .

AFTER TWO YEARS OF STUDY, during which time Rhumba and I also dealt with more horses for the racecourses of south-east Asia, I graduated from Agricultural College, with surprisingly good marks.

So good, in fact, were my marks that I enrolled in a science degree at Melbourne University. I completed a year and while it was hard going, I decided to pursue a new dream, of becoming a veterinarian. To do that I would have to pack up or dispose of my belongings and move to Sydney, where the only veterinary training college in the country was located.

When eventually the time came for me to move from Victoria to New South Wales to continue my studies, I had to face up to the prospect of finding a home for my old mate, Rhumba.

I needed to find somewhere where his talents would be put to good use and where he would be looked after and appreciated for what he was. Certainly, I would have had no trouble in selling him to a riding establishment or to a hobby rider, but knowing his background and propensity for devilment, I felt that really wasn't the sort of home where he was likely to be appreciated.

A farm or a station might have seemed the obvious place for him, but in those days people were pretty rough on their horses. I really wanted him to go somewhere special where he would be valued and prized for his character as well as for his many talents.

In actual fact, I didn't have to look very far.

During my visits to Dinny's run, either picking up, or delivering back horses, Dinny had seen Rhumba at work and been so impressed with him that many times he had asked me if I would consider selling him.

'Sure, and he's one in a million, that horse,' Dinny had said to me.

Very early on in our association I had come to realise that aside from his tendency to hold back important information, horses were Dinny's abiding passion. I strongly suspected they were more important to him than the commercial stock on his farm.

Dinny's very evident passion for his horses, and his very high standards of their management made him just about the best option I had of settling Rhumba in to a good home. I took Rhumba out to Dinny's farm as the day of my departure drew near.

'You can have him, Dinny,' I said, swallowing the lump that had found its way to my throat, 'for a good price.'

'Thank you, Peter,' he said, running his hand along Rhumba's creamy flank.

'On one condition.'

He raised his bushy eyebrows. 'And now what would that be?'

'You're not to sell him Dinny. If you do find yourself in a position where you have to get rid of him, then I want you to make every effort you can to find me and I'll take him back, no matter the cost.'

The form of that deal alone gives some idea of the measure of regard I had for Rhumba. Of the hundreds of horses I had and would end up buying and selling, all over the world, Rhumba was the only horse I have ever parted with on terms such as those.

Reluctantly, I said goodbye to my friend.

Rhumba - a special friend and a fine horse

9

Post-war Sydney, in the late 1940s, was a rough old place. I had already been lagging behind in my quantitative physics and chemistry studies in my first year at university, at Melbourne, but had been allowed to transfer to the University of Sydney's faculty of Veterinary Science on the premise that I pull my socks up, and catch up in my own time on the subjects I was failing in.

The first place I moved to in Sydney was a broken-down farm near Parramatta, about 25 kilometres west of the city and university. I had the solace of a couple of horses and a few dogs out there, but I was living in borderline poverty. The government had given me a grant, to cover my tuition and other expenses for study, but that had run out with the completion of my agricultural diploma. The next allocation of their funding was in the form of a loan.

As with most students, I needed money to fund my studies and live, so to find work I had to move into the city itself. An old mate of mine from the Remounts, Frank Ransome, had bought a city-licence taxi and he offered me a job driving at nights and weekends.

The cab was stabled in a garage just behind the fire station at King's Cross. In those days the 'Cross' was a fairly disreputable part of the city abutting Woolloomooloo and not far from the city's Botanic Gardens and the Domain, a large park.

I was lucky to find a small flat across the road from the Fire Station and swapped the rural sounds of magpies, cockatoos and barking dogs for the less pleasant clang and clamour of sirens, car horns and heavy traffic. It did nothing to improve my view of city living.

Brain-dead from study and red-eyed from driving all night I cruised around the city and suburbs looking for fares. Tucked down beside my seat was always a tyre-lever or Stillson wrench, which sometimes had to be produced to induce reluctant fare payers to meet their obligations, or discourage those who had imbibed too much from relieving themselves of their discomfort in the cab.

Sydney was going through a wartime hangover and the areas around Woolloomooloo were populated by a miscellaneous rag-tag of multinational deserters, ship-jumpers, and de-mobbed servicemen from the sharp end of the fighting who found peace lacked the excitement of war. There were others who looked on conventional living as something for others, not themselves.

The result was a fairly seedy community with little, if any, regard for the law. The situation got so bad that the police eventually formed a group of their toughest 'gentlemen' who cruised the area on motor cycles with side cars and dealt swiftly and effectively with any group greater than two found moving about after dark. Whether official or not, it worked. After a short while one could even pick up a fare in the area and expect to be paid without an argument.

I hated the job and I hated the city. I had to admit, though, that part of the problem was down to me – I was fast learning that I did not like people.

I was driving a cab to stay alive and with my weekdays consumed with lectures there was no time for me to do the study I needed to make up my failing grades. My dream of being a well-to-do equine vet, running a thoroughbred stud farm, was disappearing like mist in the morning.

Well before the results of the year's exams came out, I knew I hadn't made the grade and would have make some sort of plan for the future

Dejected, I went to the movies on one of my rare nights off. Randomly, the film I had chosen was *The Macomber Affair*, based on a short story, *The Short Happy Life of Francis Macomber*, by Ernest Hemingway.

As I sat there in the cinema, visions of East Africa flashed up in front of me on the silver screen - the wide-open plains of Kenya and the palm-fringed beaches of Malindi. The film was a sordid tale of a love triangle between an American couple, Margot and Frank Macomber, and a dashing big game hunter, played by Gregory Peck.

There were charging lions, rampaging elephants, fearless cape buffalo and intrigue and lust aplenty. Just as had happened when I was a little boy, sitting in the theatre in England, watching the bucking bronco riders of Sydney's Royal Easter Show, I had a light-bulb moment.

Africa, I thought.

'Jeez, that's for me!'

MY MIND MADE UP, I started looking for ways to get to East Africa, but soon learned there were no direct sea links from Australia to Africa.

All was not lost, though, and I worked out the way to get there was via the UK. I leaned on a university friend whose uncle was the Sydney Harbour Master, he found me a position as a utility steward on a ship leaving for the UK. Once there, I would work out how to get to my ultimate destination.

Our first stop on leaving Sydney was Melbourne. As the ship would be tied up in Melbourne for more than 24 hours, I took the opportunity to borrow a car from Duggy Campbell and scooted up to Shepparton to see old Dinny.

When I arrived, he greeted me warmly and took me to see Rhumba. He looked in fine form. Dinny's cantankerous brown horse, the offspring of his wife's favourite, had sadly passed away, but Rhumba had been a fine companion to him.

Perhaps Rhumba had become a last link to his wife, because when I reminded Dinny of our deal he spat on his hand, in time honoured fashion, and took mine. 'Peter, I'm going to make you a promise. There's not enough money in the world that would make me part with your horse – he's going to stay with me until one or the other of us is dead.'

Back on board the ship I went back to serving and washing up in the crew's mess. We had more people in the crew than was really necessary, so the work was not all that onerous. I volunteered for early shifts and once I was done, I would have most of the day to myself. Our accommodation was pretty gruesome, with four stewards per cabin, but I spent most of my free time sitting up on the fo'c's'le deck by the anchor winches, where the passengers were banned, and enjoyed the sun by myself or with a mate or two. It was money for old rope and at the end of the cruise I even had a pay packet.

We berthed at Southampton, and after paying off I walked down the gangplank with some of the other service crew, a rough, but good-hearted bunch. To my utter embarrassment, in front of my new friends, there was Mum, bless her, waiting for me on the docks with a Rolls Royce she'd hired for the day. To the jeers and cheers of the crew we were reunited and I couldn't get into the sleek, black car quick enough.

While Sydney might have been hungover from the war in 1949, London was still on its knees with two black eyes, barely recovering from the fight. The city had suffered terribly during the blitz and as I traipsed about from one company or government office to the next, looking for work abroad, I saw whole city blocks that had been bombed, then demolished. Food was still rationed and while people were no doubt pleased the war was over, the country was yet to reap the rewards of victory.

After about a month of turning over every stone I could think of, in search of a job in Africa, two offers of employment came through the post box.

The first was with a sugar company in the Caribbean, which on the surface appeared very attractive, in terms of salary and prospects for advancement, but I didn't really fancy the idea of working on a plantation.

The other was for a cattle production extension officer in Northern Nigeria, and although not my preferred East Africa, it was nevertheless on the right continent. It also sounded more like my thing.

Either I made a good impression on my interviewers, or they were desperate for someone to take up the job, because having signalled I was interested and available, within a couple of days I had a letter saying I had been accepted. Arrangements were put in place for my departure, by sea, for Lagos in a month's time.

In the meantime, I was told I should present myself at a numbered room in the Colonial Office on a given date to sign my contract and receive my outfit allowance, plus all the other necessary information I would need before embarking.

In the month prior to boarding the ship for Lagos I set about learning what I could about West Africa, with particular attention to Nigeria and getting together the equipment that would be required for the type of work that had been outlined at the interview. This was much easier than I anticipated – I was referred to a dedicated company in Golden Square, Soho, whose main trading staple was outfitting officers, mainly on first appointment, for service on the West Coast.

They had answers to virtually every question, then provided everything I was likely to need, from a can opener to rifle and shotgun. These were dispensed with advice on how to conduct one's self in what was going to be a novel environment and a dramatically new way of life.

On top of that, with a very knowing look, the salesman who attended me indicated that there was no need to broach my outfit allowance to pay for my purchases as experience had shown that most first appointments were nearly always short of spending money. As a consequence, they had an arrangement with the Colonial Office whereby an agreed sum would be deducted from my salary until the debt had been discharged, plus, of course a small amount for interest.

All I had to do was sign the piece of paper he had ready, and I could take my outfit allowance home to spend as I wished before I left. Needless to say, I took up his offer and never regretted it.

It had been good to see my mother and siblings again, but Africa was calling. It seemed as though each day of the three-week voyage became a little warmer, a little more humid. The expectation built inside me like the rising mercury. We had already made landfall at a couple of ports on the West African coast, but Apapa, the main port for Lagos, seemed to take chaos, confusion, and heat to new highs.

The docks were alive with people shouting and bustling about, as passengers and cargo were offloaded, and Nigeria's exports – cocoa, palm oil, nuts and cotton - were prepared for shipment back to the UK. It seemed a minor miracle to me in all the chaos that surrounded us, that my own luggage was reunited with me after I'd been whisked off the ship to an hotel near the main railway station.

The same competent shipping agent who had looked after my bags had booked me on a train, the next day, to the agricultural station at Zaria, nearly 900 kilometres into the interior, to the northwest.

Zaria, in Kaduna Province, was one of several city states inhabited by the Hausa people. Formerly known as the Kingdom of Zazzau, a settlement had existed at Zaria since 1536. The people were followers of Islam, both men and women dressed in flowing robes, the likes of which I'd never seen before arriving in Nigeria. Zaria was just a stopover for me, however, and I struggled to take in the exotic sights and sounds and to try and retain all the tips and advice that various old timers in the Colonial service were passing on to me.

Nigeria had been one of Britain's colonial possessions since the mid nineteenth century, but much of the countryside was still wild and empty of European settlement, which was not encouraged.

Jobs such as mine were conceived by one or other of the 'think tanks' within the Colonial office as an altruistic means of trying to raise the living standards of people who had lived, and were still living, perfectly well adjusted to their environment since the middle ages.

Islam had come from the east via the attentions of the Mahdi and the flow of traders who brought salt and other goods, returning with grain and slaves. Britain had been instrumental in officially ending the slave trade, but nomadic businessmen still came from as far as the Arabian Peninsula, Egypt and the Sudan, trading horses, livestock and other goods in the Muslim dominated cities of Chad, Nigeria, Niger and other Saharan regions. Maiduguri, Zaria and Sokoto in Nigeria were amongst the main trading destinations. Some of these caravan journeys would last up to three years before the wanderers returned home with whatever money and goods they had been able to garner.

I had further to go to get to my destination and was told to start recruiting my staff from the hordes of people who showed up at the gates of the agricultural station every day, clamouring for a job.

I recruited a cook and a house servant from Zaria and we headed further northwest, another eight-hundred-or-so kilometres to get to my journey's end, Maiduguri, in Bornu Province. There being no railway, we were given the privilege of travelling in an Agricultural Department truck.

Maiduguri truly was a far-flung outpost of the British Empire. The European contingent was made up of a few hardy traders, dealing mainly in hides and skins, and running very basic supply stores on the side.

Government representatives of various callings were housed in their own private area near the administrative buildings. My destination was even more remote; I reported to the Agricultural Experimental station a few miles out of town.

Not that I was destined to see much of either the G.R.A. – the Government Reserved Area, or the Agricultural Station. In fact, not even a room had been set aside for me, as my job involved almost constant 'touring' in the bush. Instead, I was banished yet further into the wilds, to an abandoned wartime army hospital, which became my base for the next three years.

Before starting my first tour in the bush, it was necessary to assemble a small army of people to accompany me. There were very few vehicles in the province in those days and certainly not for any first appointees. Travel would be by foot and horse, so I would need a number of carriers, as well as an interpreter or two. There would be a 'Wakili' an agent provided by the Shehu or 'king' of Bornu, who was also the spiritual leader of all Muslims in West Africa. The Wakili, therefore, was a very important person and would be accompanied by his own little string of hangers-on. There would then be another Wakili supplied by the head of whichever district I would be travelling in; he, too, would have his own entourage, including a Dogari or two - messengers or tribal policemen of sorts. Each village area, as we passed through, would also provide guides and runners, who went on ahead to warn the next village we were coming so they could prepare a suitable reception.

On patrol in the wilds of Nigeria with some of my extensive entourage

By the time we were ready to move, quite a colourful little company had been assembled. When travelling in the northern section of the province, where no tsetse flies existed, all the important men in the caravan rode on horses, armed with a variety of weapons -

some of which would make a museum curator salivate. In the south, where flies were sometimes in evidence, horses were abandoned as they tended to attract the insects. There, everyone travelled on foot.

What a turn-up: here was I, a former wood-and-water joey, horse-breaker, and taxi driver, now with an entourage of no less than 30 people, befitting a minor potentate.

It took a bit of getting used to. For a start, I didn't have enough gear to warrant the 16 carriers I was expected to employ as a mark of his importance. It being a Muslim country, I decided to dispense with booze, but even with sufficient food, and other supplies to keep me going for weeks on end, the load was comfortably distributed on the heads of seven porters. As a result, and *at their suggestion*, my remaining nine porters carried boxes filled with sand on their heads.

In time, I must confess, I amassed enough personal gear to keep all 16 men gainfully employed, as my comfort demands increased. For now, though, I was travelling light, and champing at the bit to see what this incredible and already slightly-confounding continent had to offer.

MY JOB, as dreamed up by some bureaucrat in the colonial office, was to head out into the wilds of Nigeria and select cattle that might be bred up on a commercial scale to provide a core of suitable animals for distribution among the non-stock people in parts of the province where tsetse flies were not a problem.

The whole idea was fanciful, but no doubt looked good on paper in some hallowed office in London. It goes without saying that some politician, who probably didn't even know where Nigeria was, would pontificate on how he was improving living standards throughout the empire.

Be that as it may, at least it gave me a job, which was proving more and more interesting as the days rolled by. Bornu (known as Borno these days) was in the remote north-east corridor of Nigeria. Across the border to the east were the Cameroons and to the north and north east the French colonies of Niger and Chad, respectively.

The countryside we moved through was known as Sudan savannah, a mix of thorny, scrubby acacias and baobab trees, great swollen things with incongruously delicate branches reaching high, like fingers. It rained from June to September and the rest of the year was dry. It was hot, with an average daytime temperature of 37 degrees Celsius, climbing well into the forties as the rains approached.

To the north it became hotter and drier, as the vegetation became thinner and the soil sandier. This was the beginning of the Sahel, an Arab word for coast, or edge, a transition to the great Sahara Desert.

Soon after arriving in Maiduguri I heard of what appeared to be a unique breed of cattle called 'Kuri' living along the south-western shores of Lake Chad. From the stories filtering through, the breed appeared too exotic for our development purposes but, nevertheless, if time ever permitted, a trip to see them in their unique environment would be an experience not to be missed.

Among the stories was the intriguing snippet that they had so adapted to the torments of the mosquitoes and biting flies that infested their chosen habitat that they lived a good part of their lives semi submerged in the shallows of the lake. They were, it was said, able to keep their nostrils just above the water's surface through the agency of their horns, which actually resembled nothing more than an oversized onion bulb. The interior of the horn was honeycombed with air-cells, acting to all intents and purposes like a pair of water wings, keeping the head afloat while the body dangled down in the shallow water, the hind feet resting gently on the bottom.

The only area of the Kuri breed's range which was in the Nigerian jurisdiction was just south of what was then the Baga Promontory. This small spit of relatively high ground jutted into Lake Chad, roughly along the 13th parallel, not far from where the international boundaries of Nigeria, Chad, the Central African Republic (C.A.R) and the Cameroons met.

This little spot of land was so far off the beaten track that virtually no one ever visited it, apart that is from an elderly, erudite ex-major of the Black Watch. He styled himself as a 'trader', wandering around these desolate, arid areas with a string of camels, apparently content in their company, for months on end.

I found him one day, grizzled and grey haired, his skin burned and lips cracked from months under the harsh African sun, propping up the bar in the club during one of his very infrequent visits to the fleshpots of Maiduguri.

After chatting for a while, I asked him if he'd ever seen the Kuri cattle. He had, and he told me of the location of the Baga Promontory and passed on some more intriguing information, which only served to whet my appetite further.

'There's a wee village of Shua Arabs who actually live on the promontory itself,' he said, 'and they tell me that there is also a small herd of elephants who, like the Kuri, spend most of their time hiding in the lake.'

'Is that so?' I quizzed.

'Aye. They emerge only at night, to browse on the few trees growing along the edge of the lake.'

It seemed the elephants lived about 18 hours a day submerged in the water. 'And you don't need a licence to hunt these elephants,' he added.

He had me hooked. I cooked up a story for my superiors, stressing the importance of having a look at the Kuri cattle. In presenting my case I forbore mentioning the elephants' presence, as I thought it might distract attention from the true reason for visiting the area.

Quite a few months later, after completing a few trips in the bush feeling a bit more comfortable with the whole business, an opportunity came up for me to consider heading for Lake Chad to look at the Shua Red cattle living along the western shores of the lake.

Coincidentally, Keith Hallam, the senior police officer for Bornu, was taking some local leave and was also interested in seeing that part of the country. He sweetened the pot of accompanying me by offering transport by police vehicles, as well as an escort of askaris to help with the chores. This was a distinct improvement on my proposed modus operandi and much quicker too.

Needless to say, I was delighted, not only for his company, but also with the trucks, as we could do the whole trip in a couple of weeks instead of the six weeks or so it would have taken me by foot and horse. His askaris, the term for African levies to the colonial military and police forces, would also come in handy.

The trip itself was not entirely unpleasant. Initially we trundled east in the stout Bedfords towards Dikwa, then turned north and bush-bashed our way for the best part of three days until we came to the southern end of the Baga Promontory.

We consciously took this route as opposed to the more direct route straight north to Kukawa from Maiduguri. It seemed to me we might have more chance of running into some of the Kuri cattle I was so anxious to see by hitting the southern shore of the lake, then turning north along the shore to the promontory, rather than approaching from inland.

As it turned out, it was the right decision as the travelling wasn't too bad and we did come across two or three villages near the southernmost point of the lake, where we saw a few unusual looking small herds of cattle. They weren't the fittest looking specimens of the genus, but sufficiently different to other cattle for us to conclude that they must be Kuris.

To my untutored eye they looked rather like a *Bos taurus* edition of the *Bos indicus* Fulani White, but graced with oversized, bulbous horns, as had been described to me.

Interesting as they were, they hardly conformed to the specifications of the type of animal I was looking for. I took a few photographs and spoke, via my interpreter, to some of the tribesmen tending them, and we continued on our way.

Turning east, we pushed out onto the promontory, finally coming upon the village, if it could be called such, which the trader had told me about. It consisted of about 15 rather interesting grass huts of a design I hadn't seen before, each one surrounded by 'zana mats', made of woven phragmites stalks.

The unusual Kuri breed, with their large horns which helped them stay afloat

The huts themselves were made up of what looked like a continuous mat of small reed stalks, wound around a framework of bent poles, ending up with a topknot of twisted grass/reed stalks.

Although we had made no attempt to warn the village of our arrival, it was nevertheless apparent that we were expected. All the local people had turned out and were waving and calling out as we arrived. When we turned the engines off and climbed down out of the trucks, we were shown to a hut that seemed newly constructed and empty, as if awaiting our arrival.

Once settled in, we asked the villagers for any information they might have on the elephants we had been told lived in the area. To our surprise it appeared that some years earlier a white man had based himself in their village for nearly two years.

'His name was Johannes Oberjohann and he was trying to capture young elephants for a zoo, in Germany,' we were told.

It turned out Oberjohann, had caught a total of four young elephants. He had learned, quickly, that the elephants seemed to not only prefer living in water, but they actually needed it to survive.

Three of the elephants he caught died after a very short time on dry land, without the stimulus of the water to keep them functioning.

Oberjohann had the sense to take his time and slowly wean the fourth young elephant from its natural watery environment, to a point where he was actually able to get it down to Lagos and aboard a ship for Germany. Unfortunately, the sea voyage proved too much of a strain on its constitution and it died en route.

Other than Oberjohann's efforts, it seemed the only other white men to visit the area in search of elephants, in the villagers' memory, were two separate British army officers, one in 1903 and the other sometime in the 1930s.

The villagers seemed to know quite a bit about the elephants, however there was one glaring hole in their collective knowledge – other than the four youngsters that the intrepid, if eventually unsuccessful Oberjohann had captured, no one in the village had ever seen them!

The reason for this rapidly became very evident as we stood around talking. One of the first things I had noticed on arriving, as I started slapping my exposed skin, was that even in daylight there were plenty of mosquitos about. That, however, was nothing, because as soon as the sun started to set a great, black, floating, buzzing cloud emerged from the swamps on each side of the promontory.

I swiped my hand in front of my face closing my fist as I did so. Keith and I looked in amazement as I opened my hand, it was black with crushed mosquitoes showing just how dense the air was with them.

To overcome this menace, the villagers had developed a system of retiring to cotton tents set up inside their huts at dusk, reappearing only after the sun had well and truly risen the next morning.

Keith and I and our men went on a very sharp, intensive learning curve; we gave up on the idea of an evening meal and our whole crew were under their respective mosquito nets and tucked in hermetically by the time the sun had reached the western horizon.

The next morning, once it was safe to emerge from our protective cocoons, we made up for our missed dinner, planned our future activities around early retirement and late rising, then turned to the subject of elephants with our hosts.

To repay the hospitality we had been shown, Keith took one of the Bedfords out with some of the crew to see if he could shoot something for the pot, while I stayed in camp to get as much information as I could on how to find and close with the elephants.

By the time Keith returned to camp, with a Red Fronted Gazelle and a Kob, another type of mid-sized antelope, I had come to the conclusion that the only way we could hope to get in touch with the elephants was to wade into the water and try to follow their paths through the phragmites reeds as they returned from their night's feeding.

Clearly, this was not something to be undertaken lightly, but, as I told Keith, probably preferable to trying to shoot one at night, where we risked being carried away by mosquitos.

Keith agreed and we spent the next five days 'hunting' elephants. Like water buffalo, we waded, partially submerged in the stagnant swamp water as deep as we could, to try and escape the persecution of the insects. Even the slowest movement disturbed thousands of them, which swarmed our exposed heads and upper bodies mercilessly.

We floundered along through the phragmites reeds, using the passages cleared by elephants and hippos, which they used to exit and enter the lake. It was a tense, dangerous business, because although I was new to Africa, I had already learned that a hippopotamus, either in the water or out of it, was one of the most dangerous animals one could encounter.

It seemed the Gods look after fools. In all our days of slogging through water, mud and reeds we neither heard nor saw anything worse than our constant companions the mosquitoes.

Wet and filthy as we were, neither Keith nor I were prepared to brave a bath back at the village as that would simply expose even more of our skin to attack from the daylight squadrons of insects.

Needless to say, our crew were not at all impressed by what they saw as downright stupidity, proving beyond doubt that white men were from another planet, not to mention the fact that what we were doing had absolutely nothing whatsoever to do with their normal duties.

After five days of misery, we came to the conclusion that elephant hunting in Chad was a fiasco and should be left to others. Having made the decision to quit, we allowed ourselves a day to clean up as best as we could, and put in an afternoon going up onto the plains to see if we could shoot something for the village, by way of repayment for their hospitality, and maybe get a bird or two for ourselves.

With debts repaid, we left the following morning, headed back to Maiduguri, this time by the more direct route through Kukawa.

'Now I know why they don't charge licence fees for hunting those bloody elephants,' Keith said over a beer in the Maiduguri Club the night we arrived back.

'I agree,' I said, clinking glasses with him, 'anyone who wants one of those things is welcome to it.'

Nature had conspired to protect the elephants of Lake Chad in my day, but the mighty body of water I knew, covering some 25,000 square kilometres in the 1950s, has dwindled to just 1,500 square kilometres today.

Chad's elephants, which were said to number some 150,000 as recently as the 1980s, are now down to about 2,000 thanks to massive poaching and doubtless the loss of their main habitat. Desperate efforts are afoot to save them; but it seems man's greed combined with environmental changes, eventually defeated even the mosquitos' protection of them.

10

I loved my job. My qualifications in the farming side of agriculture weren't much use to me in the harsh, waterless tracts of Sahel savannah, however, I was learning that the nomadic peoples who lived in the remote areas of Bornu lived in stable, symbiotic harmony with their environment.

They moved their cattle, sheep and goats across the vast sub-Saharan landscape with little regard to local government dictates or restrictions, nor the abstract lines European colonisers had drawn on pieces of paper in faraway countries.

My rough overview of the population structure of the province was that in the main there were three distinct groups of people: the itinerant nomads, mainly Fulani, who moved with their herds and flocks all over the northern savannah areas, the more sedentary Kanuri people, and the omnipresent Hausa.

The Kanuri were a small, isolated tribe, found only in Bornu, but as a result of being particularly adept in the arts of war they provided the backbone of administration in the province. The Kanuri were the only people to defeat the mighty Mahdi, when they met on the plains of Dikwa. The Mahdi had swept undefeated, west from the Sudan, near the end of the 19th Century, spreading the faith of Islam to all whom he encountered until he met the Kanuris, who stopped his westward drive.

The Hausa provided the lingua franca of the country, and were mostly found in the administration sectors of government and commerce.

My duties required me to travel in the more remote parts of the province, to areas where the people seldom, if ever, saw a white man. Some regions, especially those around the western shores of Lake Chad and along the eastern border with the Cameroons, were pretty wild, with bands of cattle thieves and outlaws posing a constant threat to travellers.

My little caravan of carriers, a ripe target, was always accompanied by representatives from the local administration, from the district head down through village head, to hamlet chief, plus the odd policeman or two, if they could be spared. My own headman, Ali, always carried a rifle; whether he had any ammunition or not I was fortunate enough never to be in a position to find out during the three years he worked for me.

Travel was usually about 16 miles a day, the porters carrying 15 kilograms or more on their heads and me riding my horse. For the benefit of my entourage, and for my own comfort, most of our travelling was by night. It was so much cooler for both the animals and men and, in those areas where they existed, the tsetse flies were asleep.

Provided we could arrive at our destination before about eight o'clock in the morning, I could complete whatever work I had scheduled by lunch time, which was then followed by a short sleep during the heat of the day. After a cup of tea I would go out bird shooting or hunting.

Returning to camp around sundown, I would wash in a little portable canvas bath/basin combination. During my dinner the bulk of the camp would be packed up around me and the carriers sent off on their way, while I retired to bed for a short sleep until about midnight. Then it was back on the road, my bed being carried behind me by a man called Buba Gombe, specially designated by the headman for the job, and paid slightly more than the average for the privilege.

Our daily regimen worked very well for me. I saw a good deal of the country, acquired a reasonable idea of how the people lived, and best of all, from my point of view, enjoyed some pleasant and successful hunting. It was the romanticised life of the big game hunter, which I had seen in the cinema in Sydney, that had drawn me to Africa.

I WAS SHOOTING for the pot, to feed myself and my retinue, and it was Isa who noticed my change in mood one day when our supply of food suddenly dried up. It seemed the animal tap had been turned off.

'You must take the day off, sir,' said Isa, my gun bearer-cum-groom and mentor in all things pertaining to the bush, 'and visit the local Serekin-ma-Harbi.'

'What? A witch doctor?'

'Yes, sir. He controls all the hunting and hunters on behalf of the Shehu.'

Isa had noted how despondent I was becoming, following weeks of fruitless hunting.

'He can help.'

Interesting, I thought, that a practitioner of magic and traditional healing would control hunting. I was willing to give anything a try, as something very strange was going on and it was upsetting the daily routine I had quickly grown accustomed to.

Though we were constantly on the move, the habitat had not changed and there was nothing in the subsistence life we were leading which would have indicated I had 'over-hunted' or in any way upset the local game population density. While I realised that not every day could necessarily include a successful hunt, the increasing lack of even a sighting of any game was disturbing and mysterious.

It really did seem as though there were some other force was at work here. I would trudge for miles through the bush and see not a single buck. I could not even hear a bird calling. This went on for days, and then weeks. It was eerie. Unnerving. At Isa's suggestion, I rearranged my itinerary to take in the village where the Serakin-ma-Harbi lived.

A few days later we arrived at a village a day's march away from the witch doctor's place of residence. This allowed me to attach a personal messenger to the Dogari's retinue, which always went on ahead of me, to warn the next village of my arrival. My man took a little gift for the Serakin-ma-Harbi to ensure he would be there to meet me, and to sweeten him up – another of Isa's suggestions.

Our arrival at the village was greeted with the normal assembly of people, consisting of the village head and his elders. Women ululated, raising their voices to a crescendo as we moved through the assembled ranks.

The headman led us to the centre of the *dandal*, or village square, where a big shady tree offered us a respite from the fierce sun. I took my place in a chair, which had been set out for me, and waited as courteous extended greetings and gifts were exchanged.

When this ceremony was over, I got up and Isa, who seemed to know exactly where to go, led me to the hut of the Serakin-ma-Harbi.

Here, I was offered another seat, in the shade of the overhang of the thatch roof. The witch doctor was grey haired, serene and reserved. He politely insisted I sit in his chair, then sent a child, one of a group of curious onlookers, to go fetch him a seat from another hut. He had probably seated me on the only stick of furniture he owned.

When he was seated, beside me, Isa squatted down between us, like a kind of go between. More gifts were exchanged.

'He asks if you and your family are well,' Isa said, translating.

'Very well thank you.' I asked after his family and we discussed the weather and the condition of the countryside at this time of year.

'I think the hunting should be good at this time of year,' the Serakin said.

'Indeed, it should,' I said, but instead of making demands I got the feeling that we should just let the conversation flow, gently, back and forth. We discussed cattle and sheep – the merits of one over the others.

'I wish you good health and a long life,' he eventually said to me.

'And I you.'

That, apparently, was that. There were no spells, not magic potions, no money exchanged – just the mutual giving of gifts.

Isa and I left the village and once we had returned to the bush, Isa pointed to an open, grassy stretch of savanna. When we had passed through this area earlier on our way to the village it had been barren of wildlife. As I blinked, I saw, dotted amongst the dry, golden grass a small herd of antelope, the first I had seen in months.

IN THE WAKE of my meeting with the Serakin. my caravan and I did not go hungry again. If for no other reason, my diversion to meet him paid ample dividends, even if I could find no logical or reasonable explanation for it.

Nearly a year later, we were camped outside a village about sixty miles to the west of Maidugeri. I was wandering about, ostensibly still looking for suitable cattle, but not being very serious about it when out of the blue a battered old Bedford 30 cwt, one of the very few vehicles used by the government in the province, turned up, bringing a dust cloud that settled over everything as the driver came to a halt.

The messenger travelling in the truck climbed out and handed me a note from the Resident, the Governor of the Province, asking me to return to Maidugeri in the truck as soon as possible. The note also suggested I send my caravan of porters and attendants westwards across country, to the township of Damagum, the headquarters of the district head of that section of the province.

Once back in Maidugeri, I was asked if I would take on a most unusual task, something far beyond the scope of my normal duties.

'Word has just come in that an elephant has killed a man,' the Resident told me. 'somewhere near Damagum, in the south-west of the province. It would be to everyone's benefit if we were to be seen doing something about it.'

'Certainly,' I said.

I had never seen an elephant in the wild, but I was judged to be the right man for the job. More probably it was a case of: *in the land of the blind, the one-eyed man is king*, as no one else I knew of in the province was keen on hunting. To sugar the offer, I was told: 'You can take the Bedford, for as long as you need it, or until we need it for other duties.'

The next day, having supplemented my domestic supplies from the various trading stores in town, I set off on the long journey west to Damagum, where I hoped to meet up with my little caravan.

On arrival I found the others had made it that morning, having walked more than seventy miles over the four days and three nights since I had left them, an impressive effort. Ali, my major-domo, had my camp already set up at the government rest house on the outskirts of the town, which was comfortably situated under some shady trees. It was a good spot, handy, but far enough away to avoid the bustle and noise of the township.

It being too late for any of the usual ritual formalities attending the arrival of an officer in the district, I had my dinner before gratefully retiring to my bed for what I hoped would be an undisturbed night.

The next morning, shortly after breakfast, heralded by the cacophonous toots, squeaks and bangs of his band, and followed by all the ululating women he could muster, the District Head arrived to extend all the due courtesies as required when meeting a visiting representative of the government.

No doubt his main aim was to find out why an officer, whom he had never met before, had arrived out of the blue. Also, without having been given any notice he would have had no time to hide any or all of the things that went on in his town which he certainly would not want the administration to become aware of. As a result, he seemed quite restless.

Taking pity on him, and to put him more at ease, I explained the reason for my unusual arrival: 'I'm here to shoot the elephant.'

'Oh!' On hearing this prosaic reason for my arrival, the

atmosphere changed dramatically from one of obsequious, rather nervous enquiry to instant camaraderie and near-joy.

'Oh, yes, yes, yes, that is good. Among my retainers I have the most accomplished elephant hunter in the country; a man who had killed so many elephants that it is a wonder there any left,' he said.

'Wonderful,' I said, wondering, in fact, if this paragon of the chase was merely going to be a spy in my camp, to make sure there wasn't a hidden agenda to uncover some racket designed to defraud the colonial administration.

If the truth be known, I was more than happy for the offer of any help, especially from an 'experienced' elephant hunter. There were few elephants about and hunting them was strictly controlled by the colonial overlords so, assuming this person truly knew what he was doing, I had to wonder under what conditions he had gained this experience.

Sometime later that afternoon, when I was settling down to what I hoped would be a nice leisurely evening of reading, Ali came into the hut.

'The elephant hunter has arrived,' he said.

I went out in the golden light. There I met a Hausa man who, in any context, would be considered impressive.

'I am Dan Maine,' he said.

He appeared to be of early middle age, about five feet eight inches tall, well built, without out an ounce of fat on his frame. He was clad in the traditional hunters' blue riga, a robe rather like a long, sleeveless shirt or smock, gathered at the waist by a plaited belt from which hung all sorts of little pouches and bags. His upper arms carried traditional amulets and he wore a knife about six-inches long in a sheath.

Other than his outward appearance, it was his demeanour that really drew my attention. Dan Maine radiated quiet confidence, and had an open, trustworthy face. I took an instant liking to him.

'You look like a man I can rely on,' I said.

'My family have been elephant hunters for several generations,' he told me, 'in the service of our chiefs for many years.'

'Is that so?'

'Our duty was to supply ivory tusks for our masters, but now, because things have changed there is not so much need for elephant hunting. Well... sometimes.'

Under the colonial administration Nigeria's formerly loose arrangement of smaller chiefdoms had given way to a more unified system of provincial control. Local chiefs could no longer shoot protected game, such as elephants, willy-nilly, but it seemed Dan Maine had been able to keep his skills honed despite the presence of the police and those who took a dim view of such activities

As he was obviously far more conversant with the area and the conditions we were likely to encounter, I was only too happy to defer to his advice as to where we should start. Actually, were I to be completely honest, I was more than content to let him take complete control of the whole operation.

The next morning, following Dan Maine's directions, we set off south and west of Damagum, to an area several kilometres east of where the killing had taken place.

'The elephants follow a migration route,' Dan Maine explained. 'For centuries they have been travelling at this time of year from the west, near Sokoto, across the country to the western Cameroons, just north of Adamawa. They will spend the dry season there. '

'Where should the elephant be by now?' I asked.

He looked to the distance. 'They are heading for a series of pans and waterholes, which would take them about 10 days to reach. It has been that long since the killing so they may be there now. We probably won't catch them but we might pick up their trail.'

When we arrived on the edge of the plain where the pans were, we found plenty of evidence that the elephants had been there. Their dung was everywhere and there was freshly shredded vegetation – elephants consume about 180 kilograms of leaves and bark a day.

As expected, though, they had moved on. We knew the general direction in which the herd was moving, but Dan Maine could not be sure how far they would have travelled, nor what lay ahead. We were now moving, he explained, into unfamiliar country, outside of his chief's area of influence.

We decided to make a big sweep south and east, before turning north to see if we could cut the herd's tracks. For the next two days we followed this plan without any success and I was beginning to wonder if we had reached the end of our search.

On the third day, however, just after our midday rest, we were heading north and east to pick up the road back to Damagum, when we came across an old honey hunter travelling along the track we were following, but going in the opposite direction.

As was usual in these circumstances, we stopped to talk to him and offer him some water and such food as was available. He asked what we were doing out here, in the middle of nowhere.

'Ai, I have just passed a herd of elephant, no more than one hour ago,' he told Dan Maine.

Time being of little consequence to these very rural people it had to be a matter of judgement just how far away it was that he had actually seen the elephants.

This called for some discussion, especially as we would possibly be using the Bedford to follow the old man's tracks back along the way he had come.

'These elephants will not be used to the sound of vehicles,' Dan Maine said. 'They may run when they hear the noise of the engine. I think we must go on foot.'

The honey hunter agreed to accompany us and he, Dan Maine and I, set off. After about twenty minutes' walking the old man stopped us and indicated that he had last seen the herd just to the east of us, in the tree-line just across a small open donga, or dry river bed.

Moving from the edge of the track to the western side of the donga, we stopped to take a look and had only been sitting a few minutes when both the old man and Dan Maine stood up, pointing to some movement in the tops of the trees on the far side. I stared at the bush and a little while later even I, too, could make out the odd, large grey back, moving rather like an old ship in choppy water, through the trees. At this, Dan Maine told the old man to go back for the Bedford and bring it up to where we were at that moment.

As soon as the honey hunter was out of our sight, Dan Maine pulled a couple of small sheets of paper out of one of his amulets. There was script of some sort written on both sides of each sheet. He took one of the notes, tore it up into little pieces, then put the whole lot in his mouth and began chewing.

When the paper was reduced to pulp, he spat it into his cupped hands. Next, he began rubbing the masticated mix all over his exposed skin and under his robe.

As if that wasn't strange enough, he repeated the process and then rubbed the resulting pulp all over me! 'What on earth is this for?'

'This will make us invisible,' he said, his face betraying nothing other than sincerity and seriousness. 'We can now cross the donga and look at the herd. We will see the elephant we want, the one that killed the man.'

I must admit that I was not entirely convinced that his magic would work, nor wildly enthusiastic about the idea of blithely wandering across to, and in amongst a herd of elephants.

However, having come this far, and put myself in his hands, I couldn't falter now. We set off, and crossed the dry donga to the other side.

Once in the tree-line I could see elephants scattered over quite a large area, cooling themselves with their ears and quietly browsing off the tree tops. Elephants have an intricate web of blood vessels close to the surface of the skin of their ears. Flapping their ears generates a breeze which cools the blood, and, therefore, the animal.

I could even hear their stomachs rumbling as they communicated, contentedly, with each other. There was the crack of branches being snapped off and whole, smaller, trees being knocked down as the herd fed.

I had heard tales that animals, in general, could smell fear. That had to be an old wives' fable, I now realised – I was scared witless and as such should be thoroughly tainting the air for miles around, yet apparently none of them could smell me.

This was the first time I had seen elephants in the wild and, to add to the experience, I was now close enough to see just how enormous they were. The realisation was quite frightening. Dan Maine, however had no qualms or doubts in the efficacy of his pre-hunt sorcery and boldly moved into the herd.

It truly seemed as though he was invisible to them, as he moved about the bush, looking each animal over until we came to a youngish bull on the northern periphery of the herd. Without hesitation, he pointed the animal out, clearly indicating that this was the miscreant.

Holding my rifle in a white-knuckled grip, I manoeuvred into what I considered a suitable position, with Dan Maine next to me, and I lined up what I imagined would be a brain shot from the side. I squeezed the trigger, totally shattering the peace of the bush.

The elephant appeared stunned by the hit, but stayed on his feet. Quickly, I worked the bolt and put another shot into where I thought his heart would be.

Still very much on his feet, the elephant turned to his left and headed off into the bush at a great rate of knots. As he was charging off, I fired a third shot into the soft area under his tail in the pious hope that it would penetrate through all the soft body tissue in the abdomen and reach the thorax, where some real damage would be done.

Two things penetrated my subconscious when all this was going on; at the first shot, everything went deathly quiet, not even a bird twittered, but after the second shot - and they were not far apart - there wasn't an elephant in sight. The rest of the herd had silently vanished, as if they had never been there.

I heard nothing and saw nothing, and if it hadn't been for the steaming piles of droppings scattered around the area, one would have been hard pressed to convince any outsider that there had been a herd of elephants browsing just minutes ago.

Dan Maine was convinced that our elephant had been very hard hit, and would not go very far. We followed his trail for a little while but as it was getting late, decided to go back to the track and make camp for the night.

The next morning, we were all up early; the old honey hunter was sent off around the local villages within easy reach to call in anyone who wanted some free meat, such was Dan Maine's confidence that we would find the animal dead.

Dan Maine and I headed back to where we had left the tracks the previous evening. We picked up the elephant's spoor easily enough, and followed it for a couple of kilometres until Dan Maine suddenly stopped.

Imitating him, I also listened as carefully as I could – my hearing had never recovered from flying with a head cold during the war. Eventually, I also managed to hear what had stopped him in his tracks - the sound of very laboured, deep bubbly breathing, quite near at hand.

Quietly and carefully, we followed the sound. It was our elephant, in a very bad way, although still on his feet, leaning up against a big baobab tree. By the look of him he was very close to death, but I was too inexperienced to judge whether he would have enough strength to exact his revenge on us, if disturbed.

At this point I must make a confession. The situation we were in, and that included the elephant, was entirely due to my total inadequacy to undertake the task I had so blithely accepted.

In every way, I was unqualified, having absolutely no previous experience hunting dangerous game. I was armed with the only rifle I owned, a little 6.5 x 54 mm Mannlicher-Schonauer carbine, admirable for small deer or antelope, but certainly not big enough for anything larger than a bushbuck.

There is a truism that if one hits an animal in the right place they will die, however knowing that place is what really counts, not making an uneducated guess. The great ivory hunter Karamojo Bell almost invariably used a 7-millimetre rifle with great success, but then he was an excellent shot and knew exactly what he was doing. I was the total opposite, neither a good marksman, and nor did I know what I was doing.

The little Mannlicher with its 160-grain bullet was totally inadequate for anyone, let alone a novice such as myself, and it was only with the greatest piece of luck that my second and third shots both managed to penetrate the animal's lungs, damaging them sufficiently to prevent him from going too far. While we had not had to travel too far to catch him, my inexperience had, without doubt, denied him a quick, painless death.

Left on his own, in the condition we found him, he might possibly have lingered on for up to three days before dying. As inexperienced as I was, I was not prepared to allow that to happen.

I still really had no idea of how to find a guaranteed route to the brain, either from the side or from the front. The only certain killing shot I could think of that would not include a long chase through the increasingly heavy bush, would be to try and get as close as I could, and, by lying on the ground, wriggle into a position where I could, with luck, get a shot into his brain through the soft tissue of the mouth and throat.

I only had two solid cartridges left so it had to be a case of do or die.

I told Dan Maine my plan.

Pragmatically, he said: 'Just leave it to die.'

I couldn't. I had made this mess and I had to clean it up. I dropped to my hands and knees and crawled towards the elephant. The closer I got, the lower I wriggled. I can only think that the poor creature was in so much distress that it was unable to notice me. Lying half on my back, I took aim and when his mouth opened for his next laboured breath, I fired. The round went up through the roof of the mouth at sufficient angle to penetrate his brain fairly and squarely, dropping him instantly onto his knees.

The elephant did not go to waste; villagers from the surrounding area arrived en masse and quickly reduced the carcase to little more than a bloody spot on the ground. The meat was shared out. Allah, in His wisdom, according to my information at the time, dispensed with the ritual halal in the case of dangerous animals, allowing the faithful to take full advantage of a bounty such as this.

Dan Maine, my crew and I repaired back to Damagum to be duly thanked by the District Head, before loading up the Bedford once again, and returning to Maidugeri.

My arrival back in Maidugeri coincided with the annual visit of the country's Conservator of Forests, a venerable Scot, Duncan Macintosh. Mr Macintosh was a man of immense reputation, having in his day been one of the leading hunters of the colony, as well as being a prominent naturalist and authority on both the flora and the fauna of the country.

One of my main friends in the expatriate community of Maidugeri was Jock Masson, the local forest officer, and on my first evening back I was invited around to his house, for dinner and to meet his boss, Mr Macintosh.

The dinner, as usual, was an excellent groundnut chop, one of the specialities of West African cuisine, and afterwards, over coffee and brandy, I was induced to tell the tale of my elephant hunt.

At the completion of my doubtless somewhat-embellished tale, rather than the applause I expected, Mr Macintosh, sitting comfortably in his chair and smoking his pipe, subjected me to one of the most complete and devastating dressing downs I have ever experienced. His message was made infinitely more effective by it being delivered quietly in a beautiful, measured, Highland accent. In excruciating detail, he took me apart for my lack of preparation and knowledge and for the way I had subjected the elephant to unacceptable pain and distress.

I don't think I have ever been made to feel so small, nor to appear such a total fool. There was no malice in his dressing down - he was doing it for my own good, making sure I understood what he was saying and would remember it. Once I got over my embarrassment, I realised the value of what he said and would definitely benefit from his sage advice over the rest of my time in Africa.

The next day, when I got back to my quarters after doing the rounds of reporting fully to the administration, I found a gift and a note from Mr Macintosh. The gift was a lovely little double barrelled

.450/400 Jefferies rifle plus four sealed boxes of ammunition, and a note.

Mr Whitehead, I am passing this rifle and ammunition on to you for the very modest sum of fifty pounds, which you may pay to me whenever you have enough money to spare. I wish you luck, and pray that you heed the advice I offered, to never go after dangerous game unless suitably armed.

From my personal point of view, the whole episode was a very steep and dramatic learning curve from which I had emerged unscathed only by the benevolence of providence.

And what other forces had been at work? The eventual death of the elephant proved that Dan Maine had selected the right animal from the herd – traces of dried blood were found on the elephant's tusks. These were not from the gunshots I had inflicted, but from his human victim, who had been gored repeatedly and knelt on.

I can accept that, from his background as well as his local knowledge, Dan Maine was able to deduce where the elephants were likely to be up to ten days after the incident occurred. I can even, if I stretch my imagination and credulity to the utmost, accept that he could convince himself he was able to become 'invisible' as elephants are well known to have notoriously bad eyesight.

However, it beggars belief that he could eliminate both his and my scent. Elephants have an incredibly acute sense of smell. Confirmation of that is that no matter where on the continent elephants are hunted, whether by indigenous hunters with bows and poison arrows, or the more sophisticated variety armed with high powered, heavy calibre rifles, the dust bag with its contents of light wood ash is an essential part of the true elephant hunter's equipment.

A puff of ash from a hunter's dust bag will tell him accurately which way the wind is blowing, dictating his approach from downwind, whether the wind is steady, gusting or swirling, and much other information on which a successful stalk depends

In many subsequent hunts I would later see elephants disturbed by human scent from distances of a quarter of a mile or more, if the breeze was blowing from behind the human, towards the herd. Yet there we were, Dan Maine and I, walking around amongst the herd as though going through Mr Brown's dairy cows, and they didn't even stop browsing.

What were the sheets of paper he chewed? How was he able to produce a situation whereby he could reduce to invisibility, not only himself, a devout follower of the prophet, but also me, an unbeliever?

Magic.

11

The village of Marguba was well known for its witches.

'These witches,' Ali, my senior man had told me. 'they lure young men into their clutches and then take their souls for their own use. They turn them into zombies, before returning them to their normal lives, without their souls.'

After spending a good deal of time wandering about looking at the local breeds of cattle and evaluating them in terms of their potential to help raise people above the level of subsistence farmers, it had been decided that the time had come to put my recommendations to the test, and set up a working farm and cattle breeding station. Marguba, witches and all, was chosen as the location.

Someone in a pay grade far higher than mine had picked this place, but all I thought at the time was that it would have taken considerable effort to find a less suitable location for the project. For a start, Marguba was 60 kilometres west of Maiduguri and considering how short we were on motor vehicles this was quite a cumbersome distance to travel by foot or horse. There was little water at the village, so a well-digging crew was despatched while back at base we readied the buildings supplies that would need to be transported all the way to Marguba to erect the farm buildings.

Apart from the distance and lack of water, Marguba was a village with a very unsavoury reputation for many reasons, not the least being that the village head was a devious, corrupt rogue well known to both the police and the administration. Any co-operation or assistance from him, or the village would be unlikely to say the least. Along with many other shady enterprises, it was rumoured that he ran a coven of witches who used their soulless Zombie victims for all sorts of sordid, unmentionable activities.

When all the basic infrastructure was in place, it was expected that I would take up residence and start stocking it with cattle. Fortunately for me, because of some unexpected and unplanned for interruptions in my normal schedule, I didn't actually spend much time on the farm, but those times I did more than confirmed my original view that it was going to be an oppressive, unpleasant place to live in, let alone work from. Ali and the rest of my retinue would only accompany me there under protest. On the whole, the village was shunned by decent people, and anyone who valued their soul.

Having experienced the village headman's attitude in the past, on the advice of Keith Hallam, the Superintendent of Police for the Province, I took the precaution of hiring a gang of Maruwa Fulanis, from the nearby Cameroons, as a workforce and for security purposes. Purportedly fleeing French harassment, the Fulanis felt themselves vastly superior to the locals. They were warriors and traditional stockmen, so they would be a good fit for a cattle farm in witch-territory, I thought.

On one occasion, I stayed at the farm at the beginning of the wet season. Even for that time of year it had been an unusually hot and humid day. A monumental tower of dark cloud built on the horizon towards sunset and when the storm finally broke the rain fell in torrents. Ferocious flashes of lightning lit up the night sky and deafening rolls of thunder boomed like an artillery barrage.

The poor quality of the thatching on the roof of the newly-erected farm house was exposed as rainwater poured in by the bucketful. Luckily, I had anticipated just this possibility, having watched the thatchers at work, and had erected a canvas sheet over my bed. I became busy with my house staff, battening down the canvas and rescuing my vulnerable possessions, stacking them on and under the bed. Above the noise of the storm we all heard the door being assaulted vigorously, hands banging on timber and the cries of excited voices.

'Help! Help! Let us in, let us in,' someone yelled.

On opening the door, it appeared that more than half my whole work force was crowding onto the veranda, clamouring to get into the house. Once in the house the clamour slowly died down and eventually Dan Sokoto, the much-respected headman in charge of my porters, took me to the door and carefully opened it to show what had frightened them all so much.

At nearly the limit of vision, from the direction of Marguba village, were four or five little winking, flashing lights, appearing and disappearing at random, yet steadily coming towards the farm. The tension amongst the labourers crowded behind me was like an electric current through the room.

'It's the witches, they are coming to take us,' Dan Sokoto said. Old Dan had been around the clock a couple of times, but was now as pale as a ghost and shaking like a leaf. It wasn't surprising that the younger men were petrified.

The hair on the back of my neck stood up like a row of crowbars and goose pimples ran riot up and down my back. The fear of the workers was infectious and the only reason I didn't succumb to the general panic was that I had recently acquired a dog. Although of very dubious ancestry, he had an engaging nature and was brave as a lion. I had recently seen him take on a troop of baboons, which had been making themselves a nuisance in one of the villages when we were passing through.

Incredibly strong, and armed with wicked yellow fangs, a big baboon can cause a lot of damage. While omnivorous and usually sticking to plant matter, they are not above taking down a small buck or a smaller primate when opportunity presents and feasting on meat when available.

'Dog', as I had rather unimaginatively named him, showed no

signs of anxiety at all at the witches outside. Rather, he was more intent on driving all these unwanted interlopers from our house. He barked at them and, for fun, chased a few of the workers around the room, much to the distress of those near him. As Muslims, they thought dogs unclean and something to be avoided. Inspired by Dog's lack of concern over the witches, I pretended to be unimpressed and completely calm.

'Get the Tilley lamp,' I said to Ali. 'I'll go outside and take a look.' When Ali came back with the light, I took my walking stick from behind the door and went out to find out what the 'lights' were. Within meters of the house, I was drenched to the skin, but again taking my cue from Dog, I pressed on. The closer we came to the lights, which were still flickering about, disappearing and reappearing randomly with no fixed pattern other than to be approaching the farm, Dog seemed to be getting more and more aggressive.

He growled and snarled, then made a darting charge towards the nearest light, only to turn and come rushing back to my side. As we closed on the flickering lights, they seemed to become more intermittent and more widely dispersed. I focused on one, in particular, and walked steadily towards it. As I walked and watched, the light flicked on and off, then appeared to move randomly over a fairly large area.

Dog started growling again. 'What is it boy?'

He seemed to be adopting a posture of aggression, rather than fear, as though getting ready to ward off an intruder. Had Dog started showing the slightest sign of apprehension, by whining or cowering, I would have turned tail and beat him home to the farmhouse. I gripped my walking stick tighter. Dog let out a low, menacing growl. We carried on a little further and I paused. Over the howling wind I heard a weird sound. It was like a human, mumbling.

Witches, I wondered?

A figure staggered out of the bush, towards me, a light shaking in its hand.

Dog looked ready to launch at it.

Was it a Zombie?

'Master' the being approaching me said, using the term of address commonly used in colonial West Africa at the time. He hiccupped. 'We are lost.'

There were five lost souls, I reported to Ali and Dan and the other terrified men in the house when I got back. They were not the walking dead, merely some of my workers who had gone into Marguba and got drunk. They had become lost on the way back to the farm and were staggering about. Their intermittent, spooky lights came from cheap battery-powered torches they had acquired in the village – with each drunken lurch in the rain the tiny bulbs flickered on and off and the torch had to be shaken to restore connection.

On my return to the farmhouse the quivering, shaking mob that had been cowering there, quickly transformed into a vengeful, masterful force hellbent on seeking redress. Luckily Dan Sokoto, recovered his composure rather more rapidly than the others, and took control of the situation, promising to dispense discipline as required to the five miscreants. As the embarrassed party filed out, Ali drew me a hot bath in thanks for 'rescuing' them. I laughed it off.

Outside, thunder echoed through the heavens and the window was lit by lightning. I shivered, perhaps from the cold, or perhaps...

AS WELL AS super and not-so-supernatural events I witnessed other spectacles in Nigeria, involving men, horses and insects.

One of the more spectacular events held in Bornu province was the festival of Babbar Salah, which accompanies Eid al Adha, signifying the end of the fasting for Muslim people during the holy month of Ramadan.

The Salah was held in the Dandal, or 'city square' of Maiduguri. One end of the Dandal was taken up with the Shehu's palace and its ancillary buildings, while the opposite end was open. Along the two sides of the square were the houses of important members of the Shehu's retinue.

The Salah itself was also a gathering of all the Shehu's senior people and their own retinues, mounted on their best horses, dressed in their finest. Their horses, too, were decorated with armour inlaid with coloured glass and semi-precious stones and richly coloured blankets and tassels. The trappings on the horses had been handed down from generation to generation and some were said to date back to the Crusades. All the men, without exception, were armed with swords, together with a variety of firearms, from ancient intricately-decorated Jezail muzzle loaders through to modern single-barrel shotguns. Many also carried small, round shields on their arms which I was told were made of rhino hide. They, too, must have been very old indeed as even back then rhinos had not been seen in Nigeria for a very long time.

Gentlemen of rank took it in turn to lead mounted charges down the full length of the Dandal, whooping and hollering, firing their weapons or banging their shields with their swords. The man in the lead would steer straight for the Shehu, who waited at the far end, and then at the last possible moment the horseman pulled his mount back on its hocks, making the horse rear as high as it could. They would then wheel round and gallop off to be followed by the next contingent, and so it went on for most of the day.

The noise was indescribable as the crowd packed in along the edges of the Dandal ululated and cheered. Gunshots split the air, horses whinnied and a cloud of dust rose over Maiduguri. The whole thing was pretty hair raising, but everyone seemed to enjoy themselves. Homage was paid and the festivities went on throughout the night. If a horseman took a fall, the casualty was very quickly disposed of by being dragged unceremoniously out of the way before the next band of warriors charged.

OUT IN THE COUNTRYSIDE, however, there was less to celebrate or give thanks for. A plague of desert locusts had migrated south from the Sahel and black clouds of insects were laying waste to northern Nigeria's agricultural areas.

Myself and other members of the field services took to the air day after day, flying missions from Second World War-era Dakota transport aircraft. The 'enemy' this time was not the Japanese, but rather insects. Stripped to the waist because of the heat, and tied to the aircraft with safety harnesses, we laboured tirelessly, spreading bags of poisoned bait out the open door of the 'Dak', letting the slipstream scatter its hopefully-deadly cargo onto the ravaged lands below.

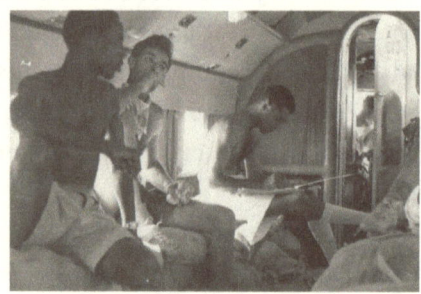

Flying again - this time the enemy were insects!

Some little time later, after the locust problem had moved on, I returned to Maiduguri from another trip into the bush. I had paid my labour off, done all my paperwork and checked my stores in preparation for another trip and was at a complete loose end. It was a Saturday morning and lunch time would bring the usual session followed by a curry lunch at someone's house, so I had gone to the club early to wash a bit of the dust out of my throat before the day's festivities started in earnest.

I was sitting at the bar alone, interested in nothing more than another beer, when a stranger came in. I glanced over at him, confirming he was no one I knew. I went back to contemplating my next drink when, from the corner of my eye, I became aware of the newcomer staring at me rather more than casually.

After a little while I became somewhat irritated. I was about to get up and do something about this situation when he called, from the end of the bar: 'Is your name, by any freak of chance, Whitehead?'

I was taken aback. 'Yes.'

'Have you got a brother called Glen?'

'Yes.'

'Well,' he said, 'I was best man at his wedding!'

'Bloody hell.'

'Yes, I was in the same squadron as him.'

I sat down next to him and had several more beers with the chap. It turned out he had been working in the Cameroons and had come from Fort Lame in French West Cameroon where he'd been working on a water development project. He and Glen had served in Italy together. Glen had met a WAAF during the war and married her. I looked enough like my brother for him to have recognised me, here, in the wilds of west Africa.

My sister Mary had ended the war as a Flying Officer, the same rank as me, in the WAAFs, having served as a fighter plotter, directing Spitfires on to the German aircraft. She later became a chiropodist.

Wendy and the Norwegian naval officer she married had two daughters. One of these, Anita, a fellow lover of horses and Africa, went on to become a Countess.

As for me, I was still single, with little chance of finding a wife in Maiduguri – not that I was looking. While Nigeria had been fun, I was itching to see more of Africa.

THE NORMAL TOUR of duty in West African postings in those days was 18 months in Nigeria, followed by a mandatory five months leave in a temperate climate.

Personally, I didn't find the climate in Bornu in any ways enervating. Certainly the living conditions, while primitive, were a vast improvement on those of rural Australia, so when my name seemed to slip past the leave roster, I was in no hurry to bring the matter to anyone's attention.

Throughout my time in Nigeria, I had continued to harbour the urge to get to East Africa and become involved somehow in the wildlife business. To that end I had sent endless letters of application to all the wildlife departments and organisations from the Sudan to South Africa, asking to be considered for any vacancy that might arise. It was just another coincidence, one of the many that have dogged my life, that when I was finally being pressed to go on leave from Maiduguri in 1953, two letters arrived for me. One, from the Kenya Game Department, said that if I could present myself at the departmental office at a given date, my application would be considered. It did have a proviso stating that there may be better qualified applicants also being considered, therefore not to take the letter as a job offer.

The other letter was from the then recently developed Northern Rhodesian Game and Tsetse Department, which actually offered me a definite job if and when I could arrive to take it up. Although every fibre in me favoured taking a chance on the Kenya offer, I elected to go to Northern Rhodesia.

Located in south-central Africa, Northern Rhodesia (which would become Zambia on gaining independence in 1964), along with Rhodesia (later Zimbabwe), had been claimed as protectorates by the businessman Cecil John Rhodes, in the late 19th century. Control of the protectorates later formally passed to the British Government.

On arrival in the capital, Lusaka, I was received by the then Provincial Game Warden of the Central Province who, with his wife, made me very welcome. Over the next three days I was 'signed on', being brought up to date on the aims and objectives of the department and introduced to all and sundry staffing the department's headquarters in Chilanga.

I was then outfitted with a vehicle, a Land Rover, a big change from Nigeria where first appointees travelled everywhere on foot or horseback, and a rifle. I had the choice of a Holland and Holland .375 magnum or a Cogswell and Harrison .404, and selected the former. As if all that wasn't good enough, I was still collecting pay from my previous posting in Nigeria, where I was officially on leave.

From Chilanga, I was packed off to Mumbwa, to relieve Gerry Taylor, the game ranger in charge of the central section of Kafue National Park. Gerry was due to go on his three-yearly furlough to the UK.

The park had been in existence for some time, but had only recently been officially proclaimed. It had been set up under the guiding hand of the well-known conservationist Norman Carr, who would later become a pioneer of tourism in the reserve. Kafue was a 22,000 square-kilometre expanse of wilderness and wild animals – I couldn't wait to get to it.

It was also only in recent times that any serious effort had been made to properly staff and develop the national park. To this end three rangers had been appointed – Len Vaughn in the southern section, Gerry Taylor in the middle, and Barry Shenton in the northern section. The whole park was under the overall control of the Game Department, based in Chilanga.

In reality, all three sections were run virtually independently, although I was told on arrival, somewhat vaguely, to do something about making contact with the other two sections as it had been decided to try and encourage a bit of tourist interest in the park as a whole.

It seemed there was never going to be any tourism allowed in the central section, because of a serious tsetse fly problem, but a link between the northern and the southern sections, west of the Kafue River, was a possibility, and a link on the eastern side of the river for park service issues would cut travel times down considerably - if they could be established.

The Kafue River ran through the park, which was located about 160 kilometres west of Lusaka. Mumbwa, where I was to be based, was about 30 kilometres east of the eastern border of the park's central section. The river had its source to the north, just below the border with what was then still known as the Belgian Congo (it would late become Zaire, then the Democratic Republic of Congo). Lying wholly within Northern Rhodesia, the river was about 1,500 kilometres long.

Most of the park, I soon learned, was covered in miombo, or brachystegia woodland, semi-deciduous forests. In the south and centre of the reserve were evergreen forests of teak and mopane trees and sections of open grassy plains. Interspersed in all of this were low lying depressions, colloquially known as 'dambos', which filled with water during the summer wet season, from November to April, and served as drinking places for game until they dried up near the end of the long, dry winter and spring. Large termite mounds were dotted throughout the landscape and these rich deposits of insect waste were home to their own rich vegetation which sprouted from them – and which I would later carve into a cave for the survivors of a certain aircraft crash!

Arriving in Mumbwa, I was met by Gerry, a larger than life, hearty ex-major from the Regular British Army who, in a whirlwind two hours, showed me the very modest little house I was to occupy, and the department's office in the government compound, or boma. The boma was the collection of buildings assigned to the various officers of the colonial administration. The grounds were tended to by prison labour, who were also responsible for filling the 44- gallon drums on stands by the houses – the source of domestic running water.

My requirements were not great; living in the bush I would be catching fish and shooting birds for most of the time, and dry goods and anything else, such as beer and kerosene, I could get from Jukes Curtis, a South African trader operating in the village. For the times I would be in the boma I had a Silent Night kerosene fridge to keep my booze and other luxuries cold.

Gerry introduced me to the key people in the camp, including his sergeant major of game scouts, his clerk, and finally to the District Commissioner, or DC, with whom his relations were not the most cordial.

'He's a bit of a stuffed shirt,' Gerry confided in me after our meeting with the DC, 'totally obstructive to the wildlife side of the department, as opposed to the tsetse control side.'

The tsetse control people existed solely to improve the lot of the indigenous population, without any regard for the damage they did to the environment or the wildlife. They were happy to slaughter wild animals and clear the bush to try and prevent infestations of tsetse flies. These mean little insects gave a bite that felt like being stabbed with the point of a red-hot knife, and carried potentially lethal sleeping sickness.

The wildlife side of the department, conversely and ironically, prosecuted the indigenous population for doing exactly the same thing – hunting or fishing - without the necessary piece of paper authorising them to do so. The movement of locals was restricted to those areas outside of the game reserve and controlled hunting areas, and there were also controls on them purchasing firearms, fencing wire and other materials that could be used for illegal purposes, such as snare lines and making leg traps

In taking over the house in Mumbwa, I also took on the staff. The first of the problems was that the staff left behind had, in the main, been accustomed to working in and around the house as my predecessor was a fairly fertile gentleman whose wife had produced quite a few offspring, all of whom were under the age for boarding school. The second problem was that the staff were used to being dealt with by the female member of the family, not by a youngish, single male who had only been in the country for six days and had no idea of the language or the customs of the people.

The staffing matter was very quickly resolved when one of the more senior of the game scouts, a Nsenga from Nyasaland, told me that his brother, another Peter, was a well-trained cook and was looking for a job. On interview, I immediately took to the applicant, employed him and sent all the previous staff members on their way. Peter the cook remained with me for the next ten years.

A COUPLE of days after taking over the station, I was sitting in the office trying to come to terms with all the paperwork involved in being a game ranger and wondering if I would ever become sufficiently conversant with it to be able to capably carry out my duties. The issue was giving me food for thought.

I was reading up on the law books of the territory, as they applied to poaching and at the same time, getting to know my staff. A couple of the scouts and the clerk spoke fractured English, but to give them their just due, they were infinitely more competent in making themselves understood in English than I was in trying to speak their language.

Lost in this world of insecurity and doubt, I was slowly aware of an unusual amount of noise coming from the clerk's office next door to mine. The adjoining door opened and my clerk, a game scout and another man came in waving and talking at a million miles an hour. My clerk began to translate.

'He is a fisherman, Bwana,' the clerk said, 'he lives and fishes at the north end of the Big Concession.' Bwana was a term meaning sir, in Swahili and bits and pieces of that language were spoken in Northern Rhodesia, which was a kind of transition zone south of Tanganyika and Kenya to the north, where Swahili was common.

This Big Concession, I had already learned, was a large parcel of land set aside for future European agricultural development, situated just outside the national park. The thinking there beggared belief.

'He and his brother were fishing on the Kafue River yesterday, Bwana,' the clerk continued, as the man spoke animatedly to him, and pointed to his leg with a chopping motion. 'He says they were attacked by a hippo, which overturned their canoe and then bit off his brother's leg.'

Blimey, I thought.

The man's story was not over. 'He says he managed to rescue his brother and get him ashore and up to the village,' the clerk said. 'Bwana, the man says his family has sent him here to get help for his brother and to ask me do something about this hippo, which has been tormenting the fishermen for some time, and is very dangerous.'

On my whirlwind tour of the boma I had met Andre Geyser our Afrikaans medical man so I sent one of the scouts to the clinic with a note explaining what was going on and to ask him to come to the office. I then told one of the senior control scouts to bring his gear and his rifle, a .404, as we had a job to attend to. Control scouts constituted a small cadre of selected men within our little group, and were trained for, and trusted with shooting – 'controlling' - dangerous game that posed a threat to humans, or wounded animals that had been left behind by irresponsible hunters.

Andre arrived in his own Land Rover, a long wheel-based version equipped to support a stretcher, together with one of his assistants. I took my control scout and the departmental driver, in case I needed him, in my own short wheelbase four-wheel-drive. We travelled the hundred odd kilometres up to the top end of the Big Concession in convoy.

When we arrived, the fisherman directed me to the house of Bwana Jeffrey, situated not very far from his village, while Andre continued on to the village, to see to the injured man – if he was still alive.

Bwana Jeffrey, I learned when I met him, had been a fairly successful trader on the Johannesburg stock exchange. His health had broken down and he had decided to leave the hectic city life for the wilds of Africa and invest his money in the romance of pioneer farming on a block in the Big Concession.

His house overlooked the river, not far from where the hippo attack had taken place.

'I know this hippo,' Jeffrey said. On cue, one of the big animals, perhaps even the same one, gave its deep, honking call from somewhere down river. 'It's well known for harassing the locals and I've warned them to be careful. As hippo are on the list of protected game, there was nothing I could do about it, so I was going to report it to you people in Mumbwa next time I had to go to Lusaka.'

A short time later I received word from Andre the medic. The fisherman was alive – just – and Andre was rushing him back to Mumbwa in his Land Rover, leaving my scout and me to deal with the troublesome hippo.

Now that I was there, as the local game ranger, I decided to go down to the river with Jeffery and make a plan on how to proceed. The Kafue is a fairly substantial river and at this point was three to four-hundred metres wide. As I got closer, I could now see the source of the noise I'd heard. There were pods of hippo surfacing, grunting and expelling air all over the place.

My immediate reaction was that the job was just about impossible. I had no idea how I was going to pick out one rogue hippo from this lot, let alone isolate it and get close enough to shoot it. After tactfully waiting a few minutes for me to come up with some sort of plan, Jeffery tentatively offered a solution.

'This hippo likes to attack canoes' he said. 'If you go out in a canoe, he's most likely to take the bait and come straight for you – and then you can take it from there.'

Put like that, his plan sounded oddly reasonable, however, neither my game scout nor the fishermen showed any enthusiasm for it – rather, the reverse. They refused point blank to have anything to do with it. Eventually, after quite a long exchange of what sounded like a heated argument between Jeffery and the fishermen in the local lingua franca, of which I understood not a word, one of the fishermen volunteered himself and his canoe.

At this, the game scout rather reluctantly agreed to join the party and the three of us got into the canoe. I was in the bow, the game scout perched precariously on a bit of wood in the middle, and the fisherman, as master and navigator, sat in the stern, using his paddle to provide the propulsion and steering

We hadn't gone more than 30 metres when it became obvious we were the centre of attention of one very large bull hippo, who detached himself from his pod and started approaching. Every few steps – hippos, I learned, walked on the bottom of the river, rather than swam – his nostrils, pink ears and evil beady eyes surfaced to make sure he was still on course to intercept us.

From the rippling wave on the surface which heralded his approach, I could see he was running true to form. I gripped my newly-issued Holland and Holland .375 tight, trying to steady my nerves. The free board of the canoe, loaded as it was with three men, was probably little more than 10 centimetres and the water quite choppy, providing a less than stable platform from which to get a steady shot.

When the hippo surfaced, about twenty yards away, I judged he was about to make his final charge so lined him up and squeezed the trigger. The hippo's whole body reared up out of the water as he somersaulted backwards and disappeared into the depth of the river. The resulting waves from this violent evanescence threatened to capsize us. As the paddler tried to stabilise the canoe, and turn it around to head back to the bank, the river churned and boiled from the hippo's thrashing about below the surface.

While we were struggling to stabilise ourselves, a hippo head suddenly appeared in the centre of the vortex. With no time to think, I took a hasty snap shot, and once again the body reared up out of the water, and fell backwards with a huge splash. Again, the water swirled and roiled with subsurface disturbance. By now, we were heading in the right direction and made for the bank, at flank speed, as they would say in the navy, the paddler's arms flashing in a blur.

'It's well and truly dead,' Jeffrey laconically said by way of greeting as we nosed into the bank. 'All we have to do now is wait and it will eventually float to the surface.'

'How long will that take?' I asked, forgetting, in the excitement that I was supposed to be the expert here.

'Maybe up to three hours,' he said. 'Let's leave the fishermen here to keep watch and we'll go have some tea. I'll organise the tractor, as well, as we'll need to pull the carcass out of the water.'

A couple of hours later, Jeffrey and I were comfortably sitting on the veranda of his house having a much-needed cup of tea when the game scout arrived and informed us the hippo carcass had surfaced. We finished our tea and went back to the river bank. On arrival, I was astonished to see not one, but two bodies floating on the surface!

One was huge and the other slightly smaller. The conclusion, supported by a subsequent examination of the bodies indicating that both had been killed instantly by a brain shot, was that the second bull had been overcome with curiosity and come over to see what all the commotion was after I had shot the first one.

Unfortunately for him, the second one had surfaced in roughly the same spot that the original one had gone down in and I, thinking it was the original bull surfacing again, had knocked him off too. After helping to drag both carcasses up onto the bank I headed back to the boma. The meat and fat from the dead hippos would not go to waste; they would provide relish for the village for some time to come, while Jeffrey said he would make sure the injured fisherman's wife got some of the profits of the animals' by-products, as compensation for her husband's disability.

I, however, was worried. From perusal of the law books, and from what Jeffrey had said, I knew that hippo were high on the protected species list in Northern Rhodesia. I felt I had been quite justified in shooting the first one, but the second, although unintentional, might be stretching my friendship with my superiors a little too far. I also knew that the DC had little time for the game department. In my imagination I saw him rubbing his hands in glee at my imminent fall from grace.

I decided the best thing to do was go into headquarters and make a clean breast of what I had done. I travelled to Chilanga and unburdened myself, with all due justifications, to the Provincial Game Warden.

'Don't worry about it,' he said, after I had finished. 'These things happen, and if there's any unpleasantness from higher up in the administration, I'll take care of it. Off you go.'

I'd had an exciting, if rather terrifying introduction to life as a game ranger and realised I had a great deal to learn about my proposed new way of life. One other thing I learned, once I had settled into life at Mumbwa, was that the DC and his staff were actually very nice, helpful people and we quickly became friends.

Perhaps, I thought, the DC and my predecessor had clashed because they were like a couple of bull elephants - headstrong, intolerant individuals, each convinced he was the dominant male. Benefits come few and far from that sort of behaviour.

12

Persistent rumours had been filtering into the game department office of suspicious activities going on in a remote area of the province, the Iwonde Forest.

Strangers had been spotted in this region, which was usually only visited by the more itinerant members of the Kaonde people, as they moved from one location to another within their tribal boundaries. I suspected it was poachers - from either the copper mining town of Broken Hill, or the capital, Lusaka, in search of elephant, for their ivory, or hippo and antelope for 'bush meat'.

Whatever the true story was, it needed looking into. I loaded the little aluminium dinghy allocated to me for the Fisheries section of my duties, and its notoriously temperamental, unreliable five-horsepower Seagull outboard, onto the trailer. I also packed my two cameras, fishing gear, rifle, and enough provisions and gear for a four or five-day trip for three people. We were travelling very light, intending primarily to live off the land.

Accompanied by Light Lucheta and Jim Musonda, the best of my African game scouts, I set out to reach the river at the edge of the Iwonde, a distance of some twenty miles east of where the Kafue National Park boundary crossed the river. This point was the demarcation between my central section and Barry Shenton's northern section.

My plan was to search for any signs of intruders from the river, using it as my patrol route. Ideally, had I had plenty of time to plan my trip, I would have liaised with Barry and arranged to meet him, so that we could carry out the patrol together. However, time was not in my favour, so I decided to do the trip alone.

The journey from the boma to the river was not far as the crow flies, but on the ground, it was going to be pretty slow travelling, as there were no roads and very few tracks to follow.

We set out, making our own track, 'bush-bashing' most of the way. Eventually we reached the river by mid-afternoon and set up a temporary camp for the night. Luckily, we had enough time to test the dinghy out, catch some fish for our evening meal, and make sure everything was ready for an early start the next morning. The outboard motor, I was pleased to note, was co-operating, running like a sewing machine.

From the very rudimentary map of the area that I had, I estimated our proposed journey along the river would be somewhere between 50 and 70 kilometres. As we would be travelling downstream, I felt that with reasonable luck we should be at our destination, the Lubungu ferry crossing on the Mumbwa/Kasempa road, by late evening on the day we left. However, having no idea what we might encounter along the way, such as rapids, and other hazards, I had allowed for up to five days.

Before we set off next morning, I told my driver, a Mongwato from Bechuanaland named Petros, a man I trusted implicitly, to clean up our little camp.

'Go back to Mumbwa,' I told Petros 'pick up the cook and his equipment, get anything else you think we might need and drive straight up to the Lubungu crossing. If all goes well, we'll see you this evening, but not to worry if we don't show up. There might be all sorts of things that could hold us up, so give us at least three days before you start worrying.'

'Yes, Bwana,' he said.

'If we're not at the crossing by then, go to the Kasonso mine and raise the alarm.'

He nodded his understanding. Kasonso was a copper claim, run by Raymond Brookes and his wife.

Light, Jim and I set off, letting the Kafue's current do most of the work. The river was so wide at this point that if the dinghy was close inshore on one side, one could barely see the bank on the other.

We stuck closer to the south bank, as this was my area of responsibility and by hugging it I hoped we might see the tell-tale signs of a poacher's camp, such as smoke, meat drying racks, a boat, or even a human scurrying off.

The combination of the little outboard's co-operation and the current enabled us to make very good time, and there was no indication whatsoever of any human activity which might have caused us to pull into the bank to investigate.

In fact, my waterborne anti-poaching patrol was rapidly becoming just plain tedious. Thick riparian bush precluded us from seeing anything beyond its first line on the riverbank and the river itself was so wide and flat that there was nothing much to break the monotony on the water. Only the odd rock breaking up through the surface provided a diversion, and they were few and far between.

About four o'clock in the afternoon, I judged we should be approaching the main bend in the river's course. Here it turned from flowing roughly east-west, through ninety degrees, to flow north-south and with the change in direction came a problem; up ahead, stretching right across the river, was a barrier of islands covered in trees and scrub, with rocks in between. I saw white water boiling ahead of us, where the river funnelled, tumbling between the boulders.

Thinking the current would not be quite so strong nearer the bank, I turned the bow of the dinghy to the left, intending to drive diagonally across the current to the slower water inshore. My plan was then to beach the dinghy while we reconnoitred the route ahead to see whether we would have to carry the boat, or if there was a calm water channel we could use.

Putt, putt, putt... At that moment, the Seagull motor, having performed in an exemplary fashion all day, decided to live up to its reputation and quit.

'Use the paddles,' I said to Light and Jim, 'keep the bow heading towards the bank, but make sure we don't turn broadside onto the current. And watch out for rocks!'

Light and Jim did their best, but clearly, they were not from fishing people. As I turned to check on the motor, the little boat broadsided into a submerged rock and capsized.

All of our gear disappeared under water, as did we. As I broke through on the surface, gasping and spitting water, I saw Light making good headway towards the bank. It appeared that Jim, however, could not swim. He was floundering about, waving his arms and splashing, so I swam over to him and grabbed him

I half swam, half waded us both to shore and with Light's help got Jim into the shallows and up onto the bank. Once on the bank, it was pretty obvious that we were in a fairly sorry state.

I had on a shirt, shorts and a pair of rubber-soled canvas ex-army boots, whilst both Light and Jim had only their shorts and soaking wet, heavy leather boots that the department issued to all scouts. Everything else had disappeared under the water. With no means of lighting a fire, or even drying the few clothes we had before nightfall, the prospect of huddling soaking wet in the dark was not appealing.

'The best thing we can do is start making for the road,' I said to the others.

None of us had any factual knowledge of either where we were, nor where, definitively, the pontoon crossing lay. Reason told me it had to be a few points west of south so, for better or for worse, that was the course we set, using the setting sun as a reference.

Once darkness fell, we continued on roughly the same course by guess alone until the stars started to appear. Once they came up, I could clearly see the Southern Cross and establish with a fair degree of certainty, true south. Using that as a guide, I felt quite confident of the line we should follow, so we plodded on for the rest of the night

The going was tough, and stumbling about in the dark was not a very pleasant experience. The moon was new, so there was not enough light from it for us to see where we were going, but at least now we had a definite course to follow. As we crossed the low-lying dambos we stumbled and tripped as our feet disappeared into mini sink holes – tracks where elephant and hippo feet had sunk deep into the mud during the wetter months and then dried in the dry season.

On the higher ground in the miombo forest we were impeded and skinned by thorns and branches as they whipped and slowed us. Mosquitoes took the heaven-sent opportunity to feast on us, while the constant, underlying fear of predators did nothing for our peace of mind.

Just after dawn, as the first rays began to light up the morning sky, we saw a clearing through the trees ahead.

'Let's hope it's the road,' I said.

It was, and we hit it and turned west. After about seven kilometres of much easier going, we saw the welcome sight of the thatched huts of the pontoon crew at the river crossing and, not far away, my camp, in the shade of some trees further along the river bank.

Petros and the cook were more than a trifle shaken to see us walking in. Breakfast was soon on the table, and after a short rest to recover from the night's efforts, we packed the camp up and headed back to Mumbwa.

About twenty minutes along the road, I noticed some very fresh tracks superimposed on our footprints from the night before, they were crisp and clear. When I stopped our little convoy to check, I saw, quite clearly, the spoor of two very large lions - they had been walking in the same direction as us.

We followed the tracks back along the road and when we came to the spot where Light, Jim and I had emerged from the miombo woodland onto the road, so, too, had the lions, proof that they had been following us, either out of curiosity, or possibly for some more sinister reason.

. . .

TIME PASSED and despite the odd hiccup now and again, the life of a game ranger in Northern Rhodesia could not be bettered.

I was living a dream and getting paid for it, albeit not very much. I spent the bulk of my time wandering about in country untrammelled by others, with the odd bit of tension to liven things up if one became too complacent. In the dry season I was able to spend up to 28 days a month camped out away from the boma whilst in the wet, despite the difficulties and the unpleasantness of possibly getting stuck, there was still enough of interest to do to keep one occupied.

I was living a dream

In the next dry season following my disastrous river patrol, I bush-bashed my way back to where the dinghy capsized, to see if there was any gear that could be retrieved. I found the dinghy and the outboard, and also managed to retrieve my Holland and Holland .375 rifle, but that was all.

The dinghy was still reasonably serviceable, but neither the outboard nor the rifle were useable. Despite taking my weapon to several gunsmiths when I returned to England on leave, no one, not even the makers, was prepared to take it on. In true government fashion, the rifle, being government property, was replaced. Although knowing I had no insurance for my personal belongings – the premiums were too high for the type of work I was doing - the department refused to compensate me for my lost personal equipment, even though the cameras and fishing equipment were used in the department's interests. It was just one of those little anomalies one had to accept, if one expected to enjoy the other benefits of the job.

Africa's cycle of mild, sunny winters and blistering hot and stormy wet seasons rolled on as my posting stretched across the years. The main rains had finished and the ground was drying out. The resultant growth in vegetation was luxuriant, with grass standing up to two metres high and the brachystegia scrub bursting into full leaf.

It was always amazing to see the transformation of the bush each year, from the dusty khakis of the dry to the rich emeralds of the wet. The new growth, however, always made hunting, or any movement in the bush, a slow, difficult exercise, to be avoided whenever possible. Not only was the thick bush hard to navigate, predators were harder to spot and the risk of stumbling into a lion or a lone, cranky old buffalo was high.

Being now a sensible game ranger with a certain amount of experience, I spent as much of the wet season as possible at my station at Mumbwa, completing the onerous chores so beloved by governments the world over, such as catching up with report writing, balancing the books, writing assessments on the staff, and checking equipment. I also used that time preparing for, and looking forward to, the rapidly approaching dry season when getting back to the bush became more and more attractive.

This quieter, wet season time was also the party season, when one was able to catch up with one's social life. Although Mumbwa was a very small boma, parties were very much the order of the day, especially at weekends. They tended to become pretty rowdy as a good many of the people involved were young, unmarried and bored with being cooped up by the rain.

So it was, one Sunday morning, that I found myself in my house, nursing a very sore head and trying, without much success, to focus on some paperwork. Peter, my cook, knocked and came it. 'There is someone who wants to see you, Bwana.'

I was in no mood for trivialities, but if Peter was bringing a local then, I reasoned, it must be about some game problem. The man I was introduced to was the school teacher from Peter's village and had travelled 50 kilometres to get to the boma.

'Bwana,' he said, as I yawned, 'a lion has been killing our cattle. We set up a trap gun and the night before last, it went off. We found some blood and a trail leading into some long grass. We threw stones into the grass and there was movement and growling.'

A trap gun is a firearm, in this case an old muzzle loader according to the teacher when I quizzed him for more detail, which had been tied to the posts of the cattle kraal. A string was tied to the trigger and the twine was then played out and attached to a bait. When pulled by the (hopefully) target animal, in this case the lion, the string would pull the trigger.

The trap had been set less than fifty metres from the nearest hut, and the grass patch into which the lion had retreated was nearby. Now, they wanted me to come and sort it out.

In my hungover state, I must admit I wasn't too enthusiastic, but duty being duty and with the village apparently so close to the problem animal, I felt I had better go and try and do something.

'Peter,' I said, 'please go to the game scouts' compound and rustle up someone competent, who can track.'

Meanwhile, as I was due to have a recovery lunch with the agricultural member of the boma team, I went over to his house and told him of the change of plans.

'Can I come along?' he asked, looking rather excited.

'If you like.'

We went back to my house, where Peter was waiting, with a trainee control scout.

'Ah, Bwana,' Peter said, 'all of the duty men are too drunk still, and the rest have gone away for the weekend. This is the only one I could find.'

I had no personal experience of the man Peter had found, but he looked quite stable, didn't smell of drink and was prepared to come along, so with nothing better in prospect I gave him a shotgun, and a couple of SSG – special small game – cartridges.

The three of us and the school teacher, together with his bicycle, set off for the village. On arrival, we were met by all the men, talking, shouting and generally confusing the situation to a point where I had to get our school teacher friend to send them all away, except for the man whose cow had been killed.

He took us to where the action had taken place. The area of long grass was in a depression, and given the time of year it probably still held some water. There were a few clear tracks through the two-metre-high grass, that were made by either village animals or the villagers themselves

From the trap gun, a clear trail of blood, now quite dry, led into the grass. Our guide pointed to the spot where they had last heard a growl and seen any movement.

'We have been watching, Bwana, while we waited for you,' the man told me. 'We are sure it is still in there.'

I took a quick walk round the whole patch, about half a hectare in area, with my control scout. We found no fresh tracks indicating the lion had left the long grass so it seemed it was, indeed, still lying up in there somewhere.

This was now about to become a very hairy situation.

'Climb up on top of the Land Rover, please,' I suggested to my agricultural friend. 'Keep a watch on the grass for me and let me know if you see it start to move.'

I looked to my trainee scout. Although he was a bit grey around the gills, he assured me he wanted to accompany me, so putting him on my left side, we started to follow the tracks into the grass.

The low, afternoon light was golden, and it was airless in the grass. I moved as quietly and as carefully as I could, but every time I put a foot down, the crackling of brittle undergrowth sounded as loud as the Armageddon to me.

The first 15 metres felt like kilometres. We showed down, then stopped. Ahead of us was a small patch of flattened grass, perhaps where the village's cattle had rested at some time. I took one, two, three slow, careful steps into the clear patch, perspiration running down my face. My hands were clamped tight on my little Jeffry's double 450/400; the safety catch was off and I was ready for instant action.

It was just as well I was so keyed up, as I had just steadied myself when the grass on the other side of the clearing parted before my eyes. A huge face, full of teeth, snarled at me and then I saw the bulk of its body as it launched itself at me like a missile.

Instinctively, I squeezed the trigger, firing the right-hand barrel. As the rifle roared, the lion, half in the air, hit me at shoulder height, a glancing blow that sent me spinning around as the cat passed me. As I spun, I fired again, close enough to clearly see a puff of smoke or dust fly off his hide, just behind his ribs.

The lion seemed to somersault, as he disappeared into the curtain of grass at the other side of the clearing, not far from where we had entered it, without a sound.

I looked around. The trainee scout hadn't moved a centimetre. I think he was rooted to the ground in either surprise or fright, but at least he hadn't tried to use his shotgun, which was something to be grateful for. If he had fired at the lion his pellets would have probably hit me – the animal had been almost on top of me.

My heartbeat had gone off the clock; my hands were shaking as I reloaded my rifle. With the light now getting pretty bad, I had a good excuse to put off following the lion up until the morning.

'Be careful,' I said to the school teacher and the other men of the village, 'I'm pretty certain I hit the lion hard, especially with my second shot, but I can't be certain he's dead. I'll come back tomorrow.'

Once home in the sanctuary of my house, before cleaning my rifle or doing anything else, I reached for the bottle of Johnny Walker whiskey. When I was done, the level of the spirits was lowered significantly.

The next morning, with a couple of experienced scouts as back-up, together with the trainee who I thought deserved to be in on the finale, we went back to the village. All was quiet, although the usual mob of rubbernecks had gathered on the outskirts to watch the entertainment. Making sure they kept out of the way, the four of us followed yesterday's tracks back into the grass to the little clearing, then on to the spot where I had last seen the lion.

'Throw a couple of rocks in there,' I said to the trainee, pointing to the spot where the lion had disappeared after bouncing off me.

He did so. There was silence. Slowly, we moved forward, into the wall of grass. I held my breath, rifle in the shoulder, ready for a snap shot.

We found the lion. He was dead, stretched out where he had somersaulted after my second shot, which we found had hit him, just as I had thought, behind the ribcage on the right side. The soft nose bullet had torn right through his thorax and killed him, virtually instantly.

On a closer look I saw that my first shot had hit him just below the eye on his right cheek and split his skull up towards the ear, turning him slightly away from me as he charged.

My agricultural friend told me that from his vantage point on top of the Land Rover he heard my two shots go off almost simultaneously. The whole action must have happened in a heartbeat or two, but in my recollection the episode took place in very slow motion, with every aspect clearly etched in my mind. This, I guessed, was the power of adrenalin.

Although I wouldn't recommend it as a regular practice, I had learned that the best way to cure a hangover was a brush with death.

13

KAFUE NATIONAL PARK, NORTHERN RHODESIA, 1957

'Lions!' I cried to Ted and Gerry, who were lying in the little cave I had hacked out of the bush for them after our Auster Aircraft had suffered a head-on collision with the ground near the Kafue River, in 1957.

At the precise moment that I had identified the intruders stooging just beyond the illumination of our camp fire not as craven hyenas, but rather that other apex predator, the largest of the lions broke from the other two and charged.

He came straight at us. I snatched a burning branch from the fire. The lion skidded to a halt in front of the boma wall I'd constructed from the bushes I'd removed to make the sleeping area.

Flimsy though it was, the thorny barrier halted the lion's rush.

'Hah!' I yelled and threw the burning branch at the big cat to try and frighten him away.

Gerry and Ted, injuries forgotten, exited their little hidey hole as if shot from a gun and took station by the fire, hands on burning pieces of wood ready to repel any further attacks.

I could now see the lions were a male and two females. The male re-joined his harem and the trio began to circle our encampment.

Throughout the night they crept around us, as the three of us took turns tending the fire, as a deterrent. Every now and then the lions made short rushes at us, running up to the barrier, but then baulking and backing away. If they had taken that extra bound or two they would have realised just how easy it was to pick up an easy meal of three unarmed men.

It was terrifying.

Just before dawn, the lions retreated back into the tree line, leaving us exhausted and not overly happy with our situation.

'I just had a thought,' I said to my two tired companions. 'A while ago, when I was pottering about the bush I came across an old track; I thought it was probably made when the national park boundaries were being surveyed.'

I tried to visualise the map of the area we were in, and the orientation of the river. The last of the evening's mosquitos buzzed around us; soon it would be the dreaded Tsetse fly shift taking over. Out by the river a fish eagle made its mournful, pining call.

'The track runs north-south,' I said, 'and if my guess is right, I reckon it's about 12 miles east of us.'

We discussed our options. There was no way of further strengthening our little bush fort, so we made the decision to try and walk to the track. It would be marginally safer than walking through the night, and if a rescue party was coming overland, they might think to use the same access track.

We laid a very clear, large arrow signal on the ground indicating which way we were heading, on the basis that an aerial search was most likely to pinpoint the wreckage of the Auster aircraft first, but would then notice our marker.

Gathering up what supplies and kit that we could carry, we set off. For some time we followed the river, which meant the going was not too hard and drinking water was always available. We took it slow, keeping an eye out for dangerous lone, male buffalos, which liked to laze about close to water, and elephants coming to drink.

Gerry and Ted were suffering from the bumps, cuts and bruises they had suffered in the crash. After a long, tedious day, focused mainly on putting one foot in front of the other, we came to what I thought was the track I had envisaged. Overgrown, it looked as if it hadn't been used in years. We reasoned that it had probably been cut from Mumbwa to Kasempa. Whatever its original purpose, it was a godsend.

Nearby, on the river bank, there were even signs of an old camp. We found some stones which, judging by their position and blackened colour, had once been part of a fire pit. We put them back in place and got a blaze of our own going, with the billy on the boil.

We had our first meal since lunch on the previous day, some bits and pieces from the emergency ration box, washed down with a hot tin of tea.

Remembering our previous night's experience with the lions, we organised ourselves into three-hour watches, so that one of us would always be awake to keep the fire stoked up, and to watch out for predators.

The next morning, after an uneventful night, we talked things over and came to the conclusion that we should consolidate our position first, then rest for the remainder of day.

'By then we'll be in a better position to decide if I should walk to Mumbwa.' I could make it, I thought, but I knew the other two needed rest and this riverside location was as good as any. It would also be easy for me to find once I located help, by following the old track back. In my absence, they could also maintain a signal fire in case an aircraft was looking for us.

With the plan decided, we spent the day gathering a stock of firewood and making ourselves as comfortable as possible.

While the emergency ration tin had not included teacups it did, thoughtfully, contain fishing lines and hooks. We rigged up some angling tackle and baited the hooks with some baked beans and bully reef from the emergency ration tins.

About three o'clock that afternoon we were sitting on the banks of the river.

'Listen,' said Ted, cocking his head.

With my poor hearing I strained, but then caught the buzz of an aero engine.

'There!' Gerry pointed to the south, over the horizon.

He was too far off to see our fire. Ted reckoned he was flying a search pattern, looking for us.

A while later, a second aircraft appeared, this time flying much closer to our position, heading due west, across our front.

'This way, this way,' I willed him.

'Damn!' one of the others said.

Much to our disappointment, he continued on his course rather than flying a square search. If he had, he might have turned our way and seen the smoke from our fire. Disappointed, we settled in to wait, hoping one of the search aircraft would return to our part of the river.

Again, we heard an engine, a short time later. Judging by the direction from which the aircraft flew, from west to east towards us, it looked like he might have seen the Auster, and our arrow marker.

In anticipation of a search, we had gathered a mountain of green leaves and branches, Quickly, we threw as many as possible onto the fire. A column of grey smoke shot up, leaving a grubby stain on the clear blue sky.

The pilot dived, aiming right at us, levelled out low and waggled his wings as he buzzed us. We waved in joy and then shielded our eyes as we watched the aircraft disappear eastwards, towards Lusaka.

By the time all the excitement was over it was about 5 o'clock.

'I'll go down to the water to check the lines,' I said to Gerry and Ted, 'you two get a meal on and boil some water for tea.'

Keeping a wary eye out for crocodiles, or hippos preparing to leave the water for their nocturnal browsing. I knelt and checked the lines.

'Yes!' We were in luck. The lines were both wriggling and jerking in the water. As I pulled them in, I found we had hooked two barbel – be-whiskered catfish.

Barbel were bottom feeders, known for their muddy taste, but beggars couldn't be choosers. I cut off the heads and gutted the fish, flaying and opening them, then threaded each of them on to a long, green stick, ready for barbequing.

I used the intestines to re-bait the two hooks. I hoped the new bait might attract something a bit more substantial, though to give them their credit, the baked beans and bully beef had worked a treat.

Knowing that the outside world now knew where we were, we could settle back and wait.

Between us we figured that it would take a road party a couple of days to reach us. We made ourselves as comfortable as we could and we ate well – it seemed the fish in that part of the Kafue were not used to the threats posed by fishermen – they were keen to snap up anything we placed on the hooks.

On the third day, just before midday, we heard the rumble of internal combustion engines pushing their way through the heavy secondary growth of the old track.

Eventually a Land Rover appeared, followed by a second and then a three-ton Bedford. They pushed out onto the plain and trundled up to our camp. The first man out was André, the medical man from Mumbwa, armed with all the things he thought necessary to treat grievously injured survivors of an aircraft crash.

'Oh, you're alright?' he said after we had greeted him. His disappointment was pretty obvious, although he tried valiantly not to show it when he realised all he had to deal with were a few superficial cuts and bruises.

'We just need to be sure, though.' Andre said. He ordered Gerry and Ted, who had been walking around just fine for the last few days, to lie on the stretchers he had brought along, for their journey back to Mumbwa in the Bedford.

I've had more comfortable journeys in my life than bouncing and rocking our way for several hours overland, but I can't remember a road trip I enjoyed so much.

Just before dark, the African sky painted a deep red, we broke out of the bush and onto the Mumbwa-Mankoya, road just west of the Nansenga River bridge. From there it was about thirty minutes into the boma.

No sooner had we arrived than a parade of visitors started rolling up. Our disappearance had caused such a stir. Everyone wanted to see us, make sure we were still alive, and ply us with something stronger than tea. Very soon, a full-blown party was underway at and around my little house.

The stories were told and retold. Gerry and Ted had risen, Lazarus-like, from their stretchers and the beer and the whiskey were flowing.

At about 2 o'clock in the morning, Peter, my cook, who had been working through the night, serving food and booze, came to me, in considerable distress.

'Bwana, there's a body in the bath!'

'A what?'

'A dead man, Bwana.'

I stumbled after him, into the small bathroom. The floor was inches deep in water that had overflowed from the tub.

In the tub there was, I saw to my horror, a wrinkled white body, arms over the sides, gently bobbing in the water.

'Ted!'

I sloshed through the water. It looked as if Ted had slipped away from the party unnoticed, stripped off and climbed into my bath. It appeared that the effects of exhaustion, relief, strong liquor and hot water had done him in. By the look of his shrivelled skin it looked as though he might have been in there, drowned, for hours.

People had heard me cry out and were rushing to squeeze into the little room. As well as being the medic, Andre was one of the die-hard party-goers. He immediately took charge and we hauled Ted out of his liquid coffin.

He was alive, just, but he was clammy and shivering.

We dried him and wrapped him in towels and blankets – anything warm we could find, and put him in my bed. Peter re-heated some chicken soup and spoon-fed him, forcing the hot broth into him.

Ted was conscious; Peter must have found him just as he'd fallen asleep. If his head had gone under, he might very well have drowned in the tub. Having regained consciousness and finished his chicken soup, Ted promptly passed out again, sound asleep.

THE NEXT MORNING, my house looked like a battlefield. There were bodies everywhere and while none of them was actually dead, some would have wished they were.

At breakfast, or, more appropriately, brunch, the tall stories and vast quantities of coffee brewed by Peter were flowing.

Ted walked out of the bedroom, bleary eyed.

'I'm hungry,' he announced.

All eyes turned on him and there was a moment's silence.

'What?'

He was none the worse for wear and, seemingly, oblivious to his midnight swim.

The finger at the end of the long arm of the game department was wagged at Gerry and me soon after – big time. We were told, in no uncertain terms, that our decision to deviate from the original flight plan was stupid, and that we should have had enough sense not to even contemplate such a thing. Although we were made to feel like very naughty school boys, given what we had endured, no further disciplinary action was taken.

About 15 months later, when I had a lull in the seasonal routine of a game ranger, I thought it would be a good idea to try and recover the bent Auster aircraft from its resting place in the bush.

I assembled a gang of labourers, borrowed a five-ton Bedford from the Tsetse Department, stocked up with enough food and fuel to last a week, and set off early in the morning along our erstwhile exit track to the river.

We arrived at the river bank in mid to late afternoon, and set up camp the first night at the spot from which we had been collected earlier.

The fish were still sufficiently uneducated to provide enough for all to enjoy a very good meal. As I'd brought along more sophisticated equipment, we were able to catch some bream, which were infinitely better quality than the barbel of the previous occasion.

The next day we slowly made our way along the river to a spot some two miles or so from where I judged the aircraft to be. The going was very slow, as during the previous wet season the hippos and elephant had made good use of the riverine floodplain, leaving tracks like potholes, some of which were 45 centimetres deep.

Driving over that terrain was like riding a bucking bronco. Most of the labourers climbed down off the slow-moving truck, preferring to walk alongside at the same pace.

I decided to make camp early, to allow the drivers time to check their tortured vehicles, and the labourers enough daylight to make a secure place to sleep, given that I knew we were deep into lion country.

The men were used to this and began cutting down a number of small trees. They then upended them and arranged them around the trunks of two much larger, mature leadwood trees at an angle. This created a couple of natural bell tents, with the big trees as the centre poles. To reinforce the structures, they cut down more branches and wove these horizontally in and around the base of the vertical limbs. This made quite a substantial barrier; certainly, we thought, sufficient to deter all but the most determined lion.

Eventually, everyone settled down for the night. All the men retired from their fires to their leaf tents, while I climbed onto the back of the Bedford where my bedroll was laid out against the back of the cab.

The night sky was clear, and I could have read by the bright light of the moon. An owl hooted nearby and a hippo honked contentedly from the Kafue River. There was the splash of a fish jumping. It was times like this that reminded me how lucky I was, to be paid to live and work in this natural paradise.

The serenity of the night was shattered by the shouts of the labourers as they scrambled in panic to exit their leafy shelters.

I looked over the side of the truck, the moon still bright enough for me to see by, and I saw men streaming, eyes and mouths wide in terror, towards me.

The source of their fear was a lioness standing on her hind legs, clawing at one of the shelters, trying to rip it apart and feast on whoever might be left inside. Meanwhile two other big cats prowled menacingly near the other shelter.

I crawled off my bedroll and snatched up my rifle, which I'd left by my side.

Men's lives were at risk. I took aim at the lioness raking the shelter and squeezed the trigger. She went down, so I turned my attention to the other two, one of which I got as she started after one of the workmen who, slower than his comrades, was only just emerging from the shelter next to her.

The third lion suddenly lost interest in the proceedings and headed off towards the tree-line, but another lucky shot bowled her over before she reached it.

Meanwhile the Bedford was rocking and squeaking on its well-worn springs as men clambered up on all sides around me, and squeezed into the front cab. There was absolutely no way that any of them were going to leave me in peace and go back to their tree shelters – and nor did I blame them.

A male lion called menacingly in the distance.

As soon as it was light enough to see properly, I went out with one of the game scouts to find the lionesses. All three were dead; at least they hadn't suffered, and none of my men were injured.

By late afternoon we had the aircraft in pieces and on the back of the truck and were back at our campsite. As it was too late to make a move, we decided to reinforce the shelters and arrange for watches to be undertaken by the game scouts and myself to ensure there were no further surprises.

Lions called all through the night, some quite near, and others further away. Dawn couldn't come too soon.

As the sun's first rays lit up the sky, we had a hasty breakfast, cleared the camp and set off. The large truck was too heavily loaded for us to risk damage on the elephant and hippo-ravaged flats alongside the river, so I decided we would bush-bash cross country to the track, which I guessed was about fifty kilometres away.

Weaving in amongst trees we made reasonable headway, only having to stop and cut our way through the foliage a couple of times. The reason I hadn't taken this route on the way in was that I knew the bush would be thick with tsetse flies – it was. The other driver and I suffered the worst; being continually engaged in steering and changing up and down the gears, we didn't have a hand free to swat away the flies.

About three in the afternoon we broke out of the trees and on to the track, from where it was an easy trip into the boma for a well-earned bath and a good night's sleep.

I've often thought about those lions at Kafue Hook.

Chief Kabulwebulwe's people had been moved out of the area due to the attentions of man-eating lions some thirty years before our aircraft crash. This was a remote, now uninhabited part of Africa and it was likely that generations of lions had been born and died in that area without ever having encountered a human.

I have been in lion country many, many times. For all their fierce reputation, a lion will, usually, not go out of its way to attack a human, unless surprised or provoked. Generally, their first response is to move off. An old or a hungry lion might go for a human, as a last resort, but the cats I had seen at the Kafue Hook were in excellent condition, and spoiled for food – the area was rich in game.

Yet there, by the river, more than a year after our crash, the lions were ready to once more attack humans in a most aggressive manner. Perhaps it was hereditary, a genetically-inspired preference for human flesh? As idyllic as Northern Rhodesia was, one thing was for sure – it was not for sissies.

14

I was at a loose end. From Kafue I was given a short stint filling in as the Provincial Game Warden for Northern Rhodesia's Central Province, but after that there was nothing immediate on the books for me.

When Eustace Poles, the game ranger responsible for Eastern Province, came due for leave I was bundled off to his part of the country, to take over the Southern Luangwa Game Park, which was about to open to the public for the first time. South Luangwa National Park, as it would later become known, would end up as one of modern Zambia's most famous tourist attractions – but that was still a long way off.

On the way to the Luangwa Valley, I was asked if I could call into Feira as the District Commissioner there had reported a lion making a nuisance of itself around the Catholic White Fathers' school and mission, located some fifteen miles north of the DC's boma.

Although Feira was some 60 miles off the main road, I saw no problem in making the detour. After talking things over with the DC, I headed back up the road to the mission. On arrival I was met by the most delightful character I had come across in many a long day.

Father Wadigora, who was Polish, was a giant of a man, sporting a long white beard. He was grizzled from years spent in the African bush, yet maintained an irrepressible sense of humour which became evident from the moment one met him.

He engulfed my hand in one of his spade-like appendages, then led me up onto the shady veranda of the mission's administrative block. He arranged for one of his staff to bring refreshments as we sat. 'What can I do for you, my son?'

Over fresh, cold orange juice from the mission orchard, I told him why I had called in, to sort out a problem lion.

Father Wadigora let out a roar of his own, of laughter. 'I am so sorry you have had to make such a long deviation,' he said, 'and I now regret I even said anything to the District Commissioner.' He chuckled away. His English was not great, which seemed to account for a misunderstanding between him and the DC. 'Lion was calling in distance. I just mention it to the DC when he call in to visit. I only hear the lion!'

'I see,' I said.

He looked at me, earnestly. 'Young man, please don't disturb the lion. I tell you why: he is doing the mission most desirable service – he keeps the young boys out of the girls' dormitories at night, something, no matter how hard we try, we have never succeeded in doing!'

With a request put in such a manner, what else could I do? After drinking some more of his very welcome orange juice, I took my leave, with some regret, to return to the boma. As it was fairly late by the time I got back, I called into the DC's house to let him know the results of my visit.

I had obviously disturbed him in some esoteric activity as my reception was somewhat less than cordial. Although tact was not one of my strong points, I made every effort to be polite and was careful not to pass on either the whole of the good Father's comments, or his irreverent view of the DC's misunderstanding. I limited myself to the essentials, which were that no complaint had been made as the lion had never been near the mission rendering my trip totally unnecessary.

The DC was not in the slightest bit apologetic for sending me on a wild goose chase, and nor did he have the courtesy or grace to offer me any hospitality for the night, as was usual when strangers visited remote stations. He left me to camp en route on my way back to the main road.

It certainly takes all kinds to make a world, I thought to myself as I lay under the stars in the African bush. With such manifestations of imperial superiority, it was no wonder the foundations of the empire were beginning to creak a little.

EUSTACE, the man I was going to fill in for, was based on the plateau at Mpika. For years, his annual routine had been to walk down the Muchinga escarpment at the end of each wet season, to do his game ranging on the inaccessible west bank of the Luangwa river.

This activity kept him fully occupied throughout the whole of the dry season, as this narrow valley contains one of the greatest concentrations of wildlife on the whole of the African continent. This period lasted roughly from June to November-December, when the short rains started and the animals were able to disperse back into the dry, relatively waterless areas away from the river.

Over the years, Eustace and many others had been advocating opening the area up to tourists, by approaching it from the Eastern Province rather than from the Northern Province under which it fell administratively. Eventually, with the bureaucratic problems resolved, a rather shaky pontoon to cross the river was installed and the road down from Fort Jameson (modern-day Chipata) was upgraded to provide a reasonable dirt road access.

Once it had been agreed that the park should be opened for tourism, Eustace had spent the last couple of years toiling away, laying out game viewing tracks and setting up a beautifully sited, though fairly basic, tourist accommodation camp, at a place he called 'Big Lagoon'. It seemed ironic, now, that he should be going on leave at the exact time 'his' park was due to open.

In retrospect there may have been some serious thought hidden away in the bureaucratic bumblings of our masters. Eustace was a man most comfortable in his own company and could be a trifle more than curmudgeonly with those not used to his way of life or devotion to 'his' park. Having to deal with an influx of strangers might have been a bridge too far for him to cope with. Whatever the reason, I was sent down to the valley to enjoy the fruits of all his labour.

I only wish I was gifted with the fluency of language, the imagination and the ability to do justice to the wonder of the valley as it was then. The Luangwa River valley lay at the southern end of the Great Rift Valley and ran between the Muchinga Escarpment to the west and the mountainous regions of Nyasaland (now Malawi) to the east. While the eastern side was fairly well populated, the wild western bank was virtually devoid of human habitation.

The microclimate of the valley, combined with the relatively high fertility of the soil, resulted in a wide variety of vegetation. Giant red mahogany, cathedral mopane and ebony trees stood majestically on or near the river banks; huge, bulbous baobabs and sausage trees dripping with their eponymous pods dotted the landscape inland, while further inland, yellow-barked acacias and thorn scrub marked the edges of the open grasslands beyond the tree line. This variety made the whole area a habitat of sufficient resource to accommodate the vast numbers and diversity of animals that concentrated there as the dry season progressed.

Other game reserves and parks may lay claim to being the best in the world for this or that, and some may be aesthetically more attractive while others contain larger concentrations of one or more species, but none combines quite so much in such a relatively small area as the South Luangwa National Park.

Every variety and species imaginable lived in the narrow confines of the valley, becoming more and more concentrated as the dry weather continued and the inland water holes dried up, leaving the river itself as the only source of water to satisfy the huge numbers of animals needing a daily drink. Herds of elephants browsed the trees on the bank and splashed through waters that were, in places, crammed with scores of hippo at a time. Lions roared at dawn and dusk. The Luangwa Valley also claims one of the highest densities of leopard in Africa.

As if the abundance of animals was not enough, the birdlife of the area is of such an order as to drive any serious bird-watcher to doubt the credibility of what they were seeing. Sightings of rarely seen species were the norm and the intermingling of the east and central African avifauna ensured a variety that could only be dreamed of. Flocks of beautiful carmine bee-eaters made their nests in holes in the earthen banks of the Luangwa River and African Fish Eagles threw back their snowy white heads daily to issue the distinctive cry of Africa.

It was in this virtually unspoiled paradise that I now found myself. All the hard work had been done, the wet season was over, the grass was drying out and the animals were beginning to make their way down to the riparian flats. The river was still running quite strongly, so the pontoon crossing lent more than a little spice to the adventure, but once over, it was no problem to follow the twin wheel tracks that constituted the road to Eustace's camp, some 16 kilometres south of the crossing.

Along the track we passed through his tourist camp at Big Lagoon, consisting for the most part of open 'chitenges', shelters made of mopane poles and thatch. It was sited in a delightful spot, snuggled under some enormous trees on the west bank of a huge oxbow lake which was home to hippos and crocodiles and was obviously a prime source of water for large numbers of buffalo and elephant, if the tracks were anything to go by.

On arriving at Eustace's camp, I found him and his senior game scout/right-hand man in the process of retraining a martial eagle which he, indulging in one of his many passions and skills, had 'manned' recently. He had used it for the best part of a year to hunt food for his personal pot, and was now in the process of preparing it for a return to its natural way of life. The proceedings had apparently reached a point where the bird was being induced to find its own perch for the night. Eustace now discouraged the eagle in its repeated attempts to fly either onto his arm, or its normal perch. As the sun began to dip over the horizon it finally gave up and flew into one of the trees surrounding the camp, to settle itself for the night.

Satisfied that his bird was comfortable, Eustace turned his attention to me. Between liberal drafts of whisky, I was given copious instructions on how to conduct myself; what was, and what was not, permitted in his Park, and what the tourists were to be allowed to do and where they could go.

Included amongst all these instructions, I was pleased to see that he had negotiated with the Powers That Be - or more likely had just told them - that the labour working with him was to be fed from resources within the Park. Under normal circumstances, and confirmed throughout the game ordinances of Africa, was the tenet that any shooting at all within the confines of parks and reserves was strictly forbidden. Eustace, however, had very sensibly argued that with the huge numbers of animals concentrated in such a limited area, together with the difficulty of getting regular supplies in, it made sense to rely on the Park Warden's probity and provide for the labour by only taking out animals that wouldn't be missed.

For example, I was told it would be OK to shoot the odd buffalo, of which there were thousands. The same went for elephants, preferably those without tusks, a hippo if it caused a nuisance, or any other animal that would, under compassionate circumstances, be better off put down rather than left to die. One thing Eustace was adamant about, though, was that the warden should not shoot antelope for his own consumption. There were thousands of guinea fowl in the area, which, together with the odd buffalo steak from the labour rations, should be enough to meet even the most exacting demands of any normal game ranger.

The next morning, well before daylight, the camp was aroused by Eustace preparing for the day from the confines of the dining chitenge. Game scouts and labour marched in, received their orders and were sent on their way. Eustace's driver then came in to report on the condition of his vehicle and any other machinery that was in use, by which time the sun had well and truly risen, so it was time to call the eagle out of the tree where it had spent the night. The bird was given some meat, which it took very delicately, much to my surprise. When, in Eustace's opinion, the eagle had eaten enough to keep it from starvation, but not enough to satisfy it, it was dispatched to fend for itself for the rest of the day.

Only then was breakfast brought in. As we ate, I was given a rough idea of the limits of the park and the extent to which Eustace had made arrangements for the advent of any possible tourists (none) - that side of the development was left to me, as he didn't want to have anything to do with visitors.

Eustace's view was that tourists were a necessary evil, and had to be tolerated if the park was to retain its privileged place in the scheme of things. That did not mean, however, that he had to get personally involved with them in any way – or like them. The rest of the day and the next two were spent with Eustace showing me the park and going over his future plans for it.

On our second day out, travelling along one of his newly laid-out tracks, we came across an old rhino bull peacefully minding its own business with its head stuck well into the thorn thicket it was browsing off. On seeing it, Eustace decided it was an ideal opportunity to show off one of his party tricks, one which I had heard of, but had taken with a pinch of salt as it seemed too 'way out' to be true.

Making sure the wind was favourable, he approached the rhino on foot until he was about fifty metres from it, then he sat down and started towards it by bumping along the ground on his bottom. Believe it or not, he was able to approach within about ten metres without disturbing the animal, after which it did stop chewing for a moment to look at him in a somewhat myopic way, then went right back to its browsing.

Encouraged, Eustace bumped himself a bit closer, but getting no further response, he decided to retire. This was just as well, as by then I was quite ready to drop the animal had it made the slightest move towards him. Eustace told me he had used that particular ruse to photograph quite a number of animals, and invariably found it quite safe - as was evidenced by the fact that he was still alive.

Having satisfied himself that I was up to speed with all his plans, on the fourth day Eustace, having sent his Land Rover with his driver back to Mpika with the bulk of his equipment, marshalled his porters with their diminished loads and set off to walk back up the escarpment, a journey that would take him about five or six days. Left on my own, I rearranged the camp to suit my own tastes and settled down to spend the next six months in one of the most delightful spots on earth.

WITH VERY LITTLE TO do other than just keep an eye on things I was able to indulge myself in the pleasure of stopping whenever the inclination was on me, simply to sit and watch the birds and animals as they went about their daily battle for existence. In doing so I saw some incredible sights, two of which remain as clear today as the day I saw them.

Both involved elephants. In the first incident, I had been driving around the country south of my camp and as it was a hot day I had decided to pull up under the shade of a large sausage tree, on the edge of a fairly small oxbow lake some six or seven miles from my camp. Lying in the shade, I was watching a flock of white storks coming in to land on the edge of the lake.

I then noticed a small herd of elephants arrive. They were mostly cows and calves, but as the wind was in my favour, I saw no reason to do any more than just keep an eye on them. That was until I noticed a big, mature bull standing about thirty yards from the herd and looking towards the lake with an unusual degree of concentration.

As I watched, the bull appeared metaphorically to lift himself up onto his toes and creep very carefully forward, as though on tip-toe, towards an impala ram that was grazing between him and the water. Abandoning my birdwatching, I watched as the elephant, in little dashes, slowly closed the distance between himself and the impala ram until he was right behind the antelope.

Then, I swear with a grin all over his face, he slowly edged his trunk nearer to the ram until it was literally underneath it. With a mighty snort, the elephant blew a cloud of dust all over the antelope.

If heart attacks were the order of the day amongst impala, that ram would have died on the spot; as it was, he levitated at least six feet straight up into the air and came down heading for somewhere else as fast as he could lay foot to the ground.

The elephant, satisfied that his little prank had paid such an enormous dividend, strolled slowly down to the water, to all intents and purposes shaking with laughter, for a drink and a leisurely bath. After watching that, I have to believe that animals do have a sense of fun.

The other incident, which proved to me beyond all shadow of a doubt that elephants can reason and solve quite complex problems, came some months later in pretty much the same part of the Park. This time I was on the river bank watching for crocodiles, of which there were plenty. At the point I was watching there was a well-established game trail, an obvious 'elephant road' down into the river and up the other side. Not having any means to judge the depth at that point, I automatically assumed it was a shallow crossing and used by all and sundry to get from one bank to the other. As I watched, a fairly large breeding herd of elephant cows and calves came noisily down the track and with no hesitation the first of them went straight in.

It was only then that I realised how deep the river actually was - all but the tallest elephants in the herd disappeared under the water, with only the tips of their trunks appearing above the surface. Then came the really surprising revelation, that the cows with small calves went in to the water, turned sideways with their heads turned upstream and literally bent down so that the calves could go up alongside and hook their trunks over the top of the adult's ear. When satisfied all was in order, the cow then turned and waded across with the calf hanging onto her ear. On the far side the cow turned her head down stream, letting the calf off into the shallows, with her body shielding it from the current and preventing it from being swept away. As I watched, at least thirty cows ferried their calves across in this manner, and when the whole herd had successfully reached the far bank, they headed off into the bush, leaving only the churned-up mud in the shallows to show they had passed.

THE LOCAL TSETSE CONTROL OFFICER, Viv Wilson, was visiting my camp for the weekend. On Sunday we had just finished lunch and were considering a gentle siesta prior to a late afternoon drive around the rapidly drying ox-bow lakes, when one of the scouts came to report.

'There is a large herd of elephants crossing the river, about a mile north of camp, Bwana,' the scout said.

Viv and I decided to take a look. Under normal conditions, especially at that time of the year, it was most unusual for elephants to be moving around during the heat of the day. Knowing that Bert Schultz, the only licensed professional hunter in the valley at that time, had clients out with him I assumed that they must have disturbed the herd earlier on. Knowing the park was safe ground, the elephants had hot-footed it across the river.

We hadn't gone very far, possibly five kilometres, when we heard the elephants. From the sound of it, the game scout was quite right, it was a big herd. Having crossed over into the safety of the park there was no need for any further movement, so the herd was spreading out and settling down in the shade of the cathedral mopane trees that lined the bank at that spot.

As we manoeuvred around the outskirts of the herd, it became obvious that it was about three to four hundred strong - quite a sight. Certainly, it was big enough to make us realise that if we wanted to go game viewing later, it would definitely not be in that direction. On turning away to head back, we came out of the trees onto the track about a mile from camp, two miles from where the herd was. As we passed a little opening in the trees, going down to the river from the road, the game scout in the back of the Land Rover tapped me on the shoulder and pointed towards the river.

There, standing in the shade of a very large fig tree were three of the biggest elephants either of us had ever seen. We had both done quite a bit of elephant hunting, and both of us had current licences.

Ivory was the only means we game department people had of paying for our three-yearly furloughs, for the wages paid by the government were niggardly in the extreme, even for bachelors. The sight of those three made our mouths water - the smallest must have been carrying at least a hundred pounds-plus of ivory on each side, while the biggest would certainly have gone over a hundred and twenty pounds a side, representing an absolute fortune. Viv and I had licences to legally hunt four elephants each.

Although seriously tempted, I felt it was just not on. Admittedly I was also entitled to shoot elephants for rations, but it was accepted that only those without tusks would be shot, and besides, the thought of violating the tenets of the Park was something I personally was not prepared to do, nor, I am sure, was Viv.

We sat and watched the three big fellows for quite a while before reluctantly moving off, possibly relieved that we hadn't seen them some time earlier, while crossing the river, when they would have been legitimate game. Had Bert and his clients seen them, almost certainly one at least would have been shot. Elephants of that size were not seen very often, and on the rare occasions that they were, it was usually only one at a time. To see three, standing quietly under a tree on a Sunday afternoon, must have been a one off and as such a very special occasion to be treasured above mercenary avarice.

ON THE EAST side of the Luangwa River, where hunting was allowed, the elephants were generally very jittery; the slightest suggestion of human presence was enough to provoke either flight or aggression, especially among bulls.

On my side of the river, in the park, my bed for the night was laid outdoors, under a mosquito net strung from a tree. Like most other game rangers and wardens, Eustace, didn't bother with tents during his dry season safaris, and his camps didn't waste resources on sleeping shelters, so I followed his lead.

A few metres from where I slept was my dining chitenge. A grass mat wall was wrapped around the shelter, to cover my movements while I was watching game in the river and on the opposite bank. The domestic facilities' enclosure, which included the cooking shelter and staff accommodation, was some metres further away from the river. Shortly after taking over from Eustace, after settling in for the night, I woke to the sound of an elephant splashing across the river, very close to the camp.

Quietly slipping out of bed I went over to the dining area, to give the elephant plenty of room to pass by. I was quite surprised to see him; he was a good-sized bull carrying about fifty pounds of ivory a side. Having crossed the river, he climbed up the bank and sauntered casually up to my sausage tree, ran his trunk over my bed and mosquito net cover, then grabbed a few mouthfuls of grass from around the bed and tree before moving on.

For the next few weeks, this same pattern was repeated five or six times. Each time on crossing the river the elephant would stroll up to my bed, run his trunk over the mosquito net, grab a mouthful or two of grass and move on. He never went near the domestic facilities, and nor did he ever venture the short distance between my bed and the chitenge where I was standing. He just moved away into the bush as quietly as he arrived. This was an elephant whose tusks would have been a more than adequate trophy and who no doubt had been hunted quite seriously. Bert's camp was no more than five miles away on the other side of the river, so the bull's tracks must have been seen when Bert and his clients were casting around for spoor to follow up. However, here he was, quite at peace with the world, showing no sign of nervousness from the very warm scent of my bed, or from the staff area only fifty metres away.

After a few weeks, when a pattern had more or less been established, I had gone to bed as usual, drifting off to sleep to the normal bush sounds of an African night. I must have been more than usually tired that night, as I didn't hear anything until I awoke to something breathing heavily into my mosquito net. In the moonlight I saw the elephant standing right above me, and as I watched he did his usual thing of sniffing the net, then grabbing a mouthful of grass, and rocking backwards and forwards while gently flapping his ears to cool himself off. He then departed, as usual, disappearing quietly into the bush. From that night onwards, I never bothered to get out of bed, and nor did he ever, from his many subsequent visits, vary from his routine.

Some months later, I was visited by the Provincial Warden of the eastern province, Roelf Attwell, who was accompanying a very distinguished visitor, Dr. Frank Fraser-Darling, on a scientific fact-finding trip for a paper the doctor was preparing for the Colonial Office. Roelf and the Doctor elected to stay with me rather than use the facilities at the tourist camp, so we put their two beds up under another sausage tree, about twenty metres away from my tree. Their two beds were set up a couple of metres apart with a woven grass mat spread out between them and a table carrying water, a couple of glasses and such other things as distinguished visitors require to get them through the night.

The first night went off without a hitch and everyone had a nice peaceful sleep. The second night, however, my friendly elephant decided to visit us. I had mentioned the possibility that he might turn up, but had told both Roelf and the doctor not to worry if they heard him moving about as he would most likely visit me as usual, then push off into the bush.

On coming up the river bank in his customary way, my elephant friend made straight for my bed and did his normal sniffing and grabbing a bunch of grass act, but then, instead of heading off to the bush, he went straight over to the other 'bedroom' sausage tree. He investigated the two new beds before carefully stepping between them to run the tip of his trunk gently over the table, mindful not to knock anything over. That was followed by a lengthy inspection of both beds, with Roelf and the Doctor still in them, before reaching up into the tree for some succulent morsel there, which he stuffed it into his mouth before very circumspectly backing out until he was well clear, whereupon he turned and picked up his path for the bush.

Possibly prompted by the fact that he had found another place of interest on his last visit, on the next the elephant decided to explore the camp a bit further. This led him to the domestic compound, which didn't go down very well with those living in it. Despite my repeated assurances that he meant no harm they remained nervous and agitated every time he visited their compound until one night his enthusiasm, or curiosity, got the better of his judgement and he tried to push his way through the grass mat enclosing it.

The staff grabbed pots and pans and beat them with whatever was at hand, creating a din sufficient to send even a deaf elephant into instant flight. That was it - the honeymoon was over, and as I didn't intend to spend the rest of my time in the valley doing my domestic chores myself, it had to be made clear to the elephant that the kitchen area was off limits. Whether he would take the hint from his last experience there or not, his next visit would determine.

It was about a fortnight later when he made his next foray, and as soon as he had done his thing around my bed, it was obvious that he had not been deterred in any way by the pot banging of his previous visit to the kitchen. He headed straight over there once again showing every intention of pushing down the fence to see what was beyond.

Having rather anticipated this, in preparation I had stationed two game guards in the compound armed with thunder flashes, hand grenade simulators which go off with a loud bang, and .404 calibre rifles, in case things got sticky. For myself, I was relying on a shotgun loaded with light birdshot – a hit from one of those cartridges would give the elephant a sting, but not penetrate his thick skin.

At the first sign that he was going to take on the fence, the game scouts let him have a barrage of thunder flashes, which blew up all around and under him, proving too much for his courage. He turned, flattened his ears to the side of his head, stuck his tail in the air and headed off to the bush at high speed. I followed up with both barrels of the shotgun, tickling his backside as a reminder that friendship had limits and that liberties had been taken that were unacceptable. He got the message.

I heard him cross the river again many times after that night, but he never once ventured into the camp again, although we frequently saw him close by in the bush when we were entering or leaving the camp.

The fact that he knew he would not be put under any pressure on our side of the river, where there was sanctuary from the harassment of hunting, was something that had been observed amongst elephants in many other parts of the continent.

Having obviously been hunted on the east bank, his apparent acceptance that being very close to humans was not necessarily cause for alarm or caution, was, to my mind, raising the whole intelligence element to another level. However, his subsequent behaviour, especially when he purposely and very carefully went between Roelf's and the Doctor's beds, when he could easily have taken what he wanted from any other part of the tree, showed that he knew exactly what he was doing, and his care in manoeuvring his bulk in such a confined space confirmed that.

Finally, when he had overstepped the mark, his recognition of the fact, and his realisation that he was no longer welcome in the camp, took the whole concept to an even higher level altogether. It seemed the more one saw of animals such as dogs, dolphins and elephants, the more one realised that humans are not the only ones gifted with a substantial intelligence.

BETWEEN MY CAMP and the one built for the tourists, a distance of about eight kilometres, there was a large grass plain cutting through the belt of mopane trees, right down to the river. This was used as a highway by a very large herd of buffalo.

Two or three times during my first week of duty, after I took over from Eustace, I ran into the buffalo as they were either going down to the river, or going back inland, depending on the time of day. On each occasion they didn't appear too disturbed by the passage of my Land Rover, so, being basically a cattle man at heart, I thought I would see if I could get them to tolerate my passing right through them, now and again.

Over the coming weeks I made a point of getting to the plain at a time when I thought they would be there, hopefully resting. Sometimes I drove straight through the herd very slowly, and at other times a bit more rapidly until they barely parted to let me through, no matter at what speed I approached. I would then stop once I was well into the herd.

Initially they moved away from the car, but gradually got so used to it in amongst them that once I stopped, those that had got to their feet to let me pass would then lie down again, taking not the slightest notice of either the car, or the people in it. I never tested their tolerance to the point of getting out of the car and trying to walk in amongst them, as that was not what I was aiming for; rather, I just wanted them to accept the car in the herd.

As a result, I could sit and watch them for an hour or so, to see if they differed in any way from a herd of domestic cattle resting during the heat of the day. As far as I could see, they didn't. I hoped that sometime in the future, should there ever be a serious effort to domesticate the species, any information such as I was gathering could possibly be of value in planning any such program.

Despite their formidable reputation, I was convinced that the buffalo I was seeing were remarkably similar to domestic cattle in that there were some wild, intractable ones at one end of the spectrum, and perfectly docile ones at the other end. Based on their temperament, as I watched them I was convinced that competent, thinking cattlemen would have every chance of success in domesticating the African buffalo just as the Asiatic species had been in various parts of Asia.

The benefits of such a scheme would be immense for the exploding rural populations of Africa. Buffalo were resistant to many tick and tsetse fly-borne diseases to which traditional, domestic ungulates commonly succumbed, and could be a much more viable prospect, given the right environment and management. All that was required, as far as I could see, was for a sound operational methodology to be established, which could be transferred and customised for any area or country where buffalo herds exist.

Of course, the other aspect that had to be considered in my argument was consideration for the rapidly-diminishing, pristine areas of the continent where ticks and tsetse flies acted as the most efficient, incorruptible means of wildlife preservation yet devised. I did wonder, however, if domestication might be the best way of saving the buffalo for the future.

ONE NIGHT I awoke to the sounds of what appeared to be a real knock-down drag-out fight between lions and some other animal, most probably a buffalo from the bellows and grunts that intermingled with the sounds of the lions.

As it was nature going about its business, there was no reason for any interference from me, so I just lay back in my bed and listened to a blow by blow account of the fight as there was no chance of any further sleep. The battle went on for the rest of the night, dying down just before dawn, when, apart from a few grunts, nothing much more seemed to be happening.

As the action had obviously taken place quite near the camp, I decided to have a look and satisfy my curiosity. Once I had finished my breakfast and seen to the work program for the day, I headed out in the Land Rover, pushing through the bush in the direction I thought the noise had come from. About three hundred metres from the track I came out of the trees into a small clearing.

The grass was trampled flat and daubed red with blood. By a small termite mound, roughly in the centre, stood a very old buffalo bull, literally torn to pieces. Despite his injuries he was still on his feet and full of fight. He turned to face the car as we broke through the trees. I wasn't sure whether he could see us or not, as his head was virtually stripped of skin from the boss of his horns to his nose. However, he sensed where we were and lowered his head threateningly in my direction as I stopped the vehicle.

However, from his condition, there was no question of him leaving the shelter of his backstop, the termite mound, unless forced to do so. I didn't need binoculars to see how desperately badly he was hurt but used them anyway. It was unbelievable, in view of what I saw, that he was still on his feet, let alone prepared to fight on again if forced to. There didn't seem to be a part of his body that wasn't injured. Blood dripped from him like a red shower. Even though the standard approach of a game ranger was to let nature take its course, I just didn't have the heart to let this old fellow suffer any more. I put him out of his misery with an easy brain shot, from no more than ten yards away.

The surprise came when we returned to the site with some labourers to cut up the buffalo's carcass for ration meat for the staff. While the carcass was being dismembered, I walked round the site and was astonished to find three large male lions, probably siblings. They had most likely not yet managed to take over a pride of females and were still going around as a group.

All three lions were dead. Though mortally wounded, that tough old buffalo had taken out all of his attackers.

The following day, returning to camp in the late afternoon, one of the scouts in the back of the Land Rover drew my attention to a mob of vultures rising out of the bush about a quarter of a mile from the site of the lion and buffalo fight of two nights earlier. When we went to the place where the vultures were feeding I was amazed to see yet another dead lion. Unlike his brothers, this male had not died immediately, but had dragged himself away, no doubt looking for water, and had died after a day and a night of what can only have been considerable suffering from his injuries.

It beggars belief that one fairly decrepit, very old, buffalo had been able to stand up to the combined attacks of four fully-grown, healthy male lions, for at least four hours, and inflict enough damage to kill all four and still be standing, prepared to fight on. This tragic, yet inspiring experience convinced me, if it were needed, to never, ever take buffalo cheaply, especially if they were alone.

THE FIRST TOURISTS to South Luangwa National Park were a group of internationally-respected ornithologists who, having wound up their conference in Livingstone, were offered a free trip to the newly-opened reserve.

I did what I could to direct them to places where I thought they might see something out of the ordinary, such as the nesting carmine bee-eaters burrowing into the river banks in large colonies, and some quite large concentrations of water-fowl still residing on the larger oxbow lakes and the marshy land surrounding them. All of this they seemed to find interesting and enjoyable.

'I've been told there's a chance we might see a Pel's fishing owl,' one of the bird spotters said one night, as we were all sitting around the campfire.

The Pel's is a bird rarely seen, due to the fact that it is nocturnal and has a habit of perching mainly in the denser foliage of the larger trees surrounding quiet waterholes, or sometimes in those on the banks of slow-moving rivers. Apparently, the prospect of seeing one of these birds had been the motivating force that had induced quite a few of the visitors to take up the 'freebie' offer, as the journey to the Park in those days was no easy undertaking.

'I can't just show you one, I can show you several,' I said. My guests were now very excited. Eustace Pols was a very keen and competent ornithologist and had pointed out a large gathering of the owls on the edge of one of the bigger waterholes not very far from the camp, while he was showing me around.

The next morning, I duly took those interested to the waterhole and showed them ten or twelve of the birds as promised. The excitement was of such an order that I left them to it after about an hour for, while quite interested in birds in general, the only reason I was prepared to spend any serious time in pursuit of them was when I had a shotgun in my hand and the prospect of a good meal to justify the time.

However, it appeared that I had, in absentia, established a reputation for myself as being 'one of them', an ornithologist no less. For the rest of the time they were in the park I really had to keep my wits about me, dodging their penetrating questions and wracking my brains to think of something to offer them in support of their view that I knew what I was talking about!

Fortunately, the pressure only lasted about forty-eight hours before they were on their way, much to my relief. Later, back at headquarters I was the butt of some serious ribbing as all there knew to the nth degree the standard and scope of my ornithological background. It would seem a reputation can be established as much by luck as by the more conventional way of industry and hard work.

15

In the bush, I came across a wounded kudu, trapped and left to die the most horrible death, with a wire snare around its neck – it was too far gone, so I put the poor thing out of its misery. We could save one in a hundred snared animals, if we were lucky.

Poaching, mostly for the illegal commercial bush meat trade, was getting worse. About a sixth of Northern Rhodesia was covered in national parks and other protected areas and illegal hunting had been well controlled, but things were changing.

Strict laws which had restricted local African people from buying fencing wire and owning four-by-four vehicles were being relaxed under the new Governor, Sir Arthur Benson. While these were well-meaning changes, we were seeing an immediate effect on the country's wildlife. I would regularly come across snare lines two-to-three miles long, with rotting, fly-blown carcasses of animals hanging there.

In the past, we'd been fair and exercised common sense when we came across poachers. If it was a little old man from a village with a bow and arrow or maybe an ancient muzzle-loader, who took an impala to feed his family, I'd give him a stern warning or even bend him over a log and give him six across the arse and then let him go.

This new breed of criminal was killing on an almost industrial scale. The poachers could not even collect all they killed – they would cut the meat off the freshest animals and leave live creatures to die a slow death. They made my blood boil and if I'd been allowed, I would have shot the bastards and left their bodies in the bush. When we did catch one, we would take him to town to be prosecuted, but the poachers would often laugh at us, knowing the courts would now most likely go easy on them.

My best friend in Northern Rhodesia, Major Ian Grimwood, who had been the second in charge at Chilanga, had left to become the Chief Game Ranger in Kenya, somewhere I still wanted to get to. Under Benson, plans were afoot to start replacing white officials in the country with mission-educated Africans, so I thought it might be time for me to move on.

A job came up in the game department in Tanganyika in 1959 and I decided to take it. The colony was north of where I was, and another step closer to Kenya. I made my way up by road in October, stopping overnight in the town of Morogoro, to the west of Dar es Salaam, on the coast, where I was supposed to report the next day. However, the next morning I received a call from an officer of the game department.

'Go straight to Same (pronounced *sah-may*),' he told me, 'Gerry has died on safari.' Gerry Swynnerton was the Chief Ranger, aged in his mid-fifties, and passed away in his sleep from a pulmonary embolism near Mikume in the Rufunsa Game Reserve.

When I arrived in Same I found the incumbent, Peter Bramwell, was something of an eccentric, who used to go into the bush dressed in a pair of yellow swim shorts and sandals made from old car tires. On my second day, I was getting the lay of the land. The boma was built in a U-shape, with the local court in the centre building, along with my office. I was sitting there with the chief game scout and the clerk, going through some handover notes. Next door, court was in session, with a District Officer presiding.

The next instant, the adjoining door from the courthouse burst open and two bloody great policemen came through, dragging a squealing 17-year-old youth between them. They headed through my office and outside, whereupon they threw the lad down, strapped him across a big log and administered 12 strokes across his arse with a cane.

After four months in Same, when Peter was due to return from his leave, I was told to go to Arusha, south-west of Mount Kilimanjaro.

Arusha was proper Africa, a town right out of a Rider Haggard book, and exactly what someone who had never been to the continent would expect Africa to look like. Tall Maasai warriors, dressed in colourful red shukas and carrying spears walked streets lined with rustic, low-rise white-washed buildings. At the end of the main street there was a German colonial-era fort, which served as the main administrative building.

When I arrived, in 1960, one still went into the bush in a Land Rover, though soon after ghastly tourist vehicles started showing up – zebra-painted Volkswagen Kombi vans, with pop-up roofs sprouting people with cameras. More tourism and hunting outfits were moving in, from across the border in Kenya, and lodges were starting to pop up.

All the same, it was still wild back then and as a game ranger I could camp down in the Ngorongoro Crater by myself, doing so-called 'scientific research' on game movements. Big herds of zebra and wildebeest roamed the floor of the caldera, along with lion, leopard, cheetah, elephant and a host of other wild animals, all squeezed into what looked like a natural amphitheatre.

This was Africa just as I'd imagined it, when I'd sat in that darkened cinema in Sydney, down on my luck at the end of the war. This was what I had dreamed of.

The game department and national parks were well-run and while they were focussed on developing the tourism industry, the huge influxes of new lease holders and tourists were still yet to arrive.

As much as I was enamoured of the country and the landscape, I was not particularly impressed with my particular job, which was to monitor and keep a beady eye on the gentlemen of the professional hunting industry, across virtually the whole country. This required me to spend a good deal of time in the office in Arusha.

One did get the odd call-out now and again, to liven things up, but unless one financed the trips out of one's own pocket they were, of necessity, short and brief. There were no departmental vehicles, and the fuel allowance was niggardly to say the least.

My secretary's sister was Gerry Swynnerton's widow, Lorna, then aged 38, and she and I got to know each other.

Lorna and her sister were Bousfields – their family was safari royalty, pioneers of making a living out of wildlife. Her brother, Jack, was a first-class PH (professional hunter) and the greatest crocodile hunter of all time. He would account for 53,000 of the reptiles by the time of his death at the age of 69, many of them in Lake Rukwa.

The Bousfields were English-speaking South Africans and the family had trekked their way up to Tanganyika, where they set up an early-model tourist hotel on the lake. Lorna was the eldest child and, as such, she was given the responsibility for supervising her two brothers and her sister on their three-day journey by three-ton truck, from the Lake to and from their school in Arusha, on every holiday for several years.

Eventually the Bousfields moved to Botswana, where they became big players in the local tourism industry. The luxurious Jack's Camp, on the Makgadikgadi Salt Pans is named after Lorna's brother.

I'd had nothing to do with women, apart from the brief wartime relationship with Marie, and had no idea what to do with them. I'd been too busy living life, much of it alone in the bush. Now, I was living in a civilised little town, for the first time in my life. There were hotels where one could have a proper meal and a drink and I suppose I got civilised.

In 1960 Lorna and I married. She'd had four children with Gerry – Brian, Massy, Colin and Geraldine, known as Deanie. In the way of these things, another one, Anne, came along in 1961.

. . .

AROUND THAT TIME some people from Hollywood came to Arusha to do some advance scouting for the filming of a movie, *Hatari!*, which was to be released in 1962.

Starring John Wayne and Elsa Martinelli, the film was to be the story of a game capture unit, catching animals for zoos and circuses abroad. Being in charge of the hunting side of things in the game department, I had a good deal to do with the production crew, whom I first met in an hotel, in Arusha.

'We want the focus of the film to be around the capture of a rhino,' the producer explained to me.

'No, no, no,' I said. 'I'll give you as many buffalo as you want but as for rhino: no, you can't touch them.'

Even back then we were busy doing everything we could to protect rhinos. These prehistoric-looking creatures had been hunted and poached for their horns, which were marketed as traditional medicine in China and other parts of Asia, and, at that time, for use as carved dagger holders in Yemen. Today, rhinos have been exterminated from much of their home range and the writing was on the wall in the 1960s.

Game capture, as would feature in the film, was not done as it is now, by darting animals and tranquilising them, but by chasing them in vehicles. A rope man sat in a seat on the front fender of a truck, ready to lasso a wild animal once it had been exhausted by a chase. It was a very risky business and the creature being targeted could die of stress and over-heating. Rhinos could be temperamental things and the other big risk was that they might injure themselves once in captivity.

'You're not going to get a licence to capture a rhino,' I told the film people, emphasising my point that there were too few of the big mammals left to risk it.

The Hollywood men were adamant and they began asking around the department, going over my head to continue their negotiations. This went on for several weeks; the game department was in a state of flux as a replacement had not yet been found for Gerry.

Another senior officer, whom I did not care for, was to take over liaising with the *Hatari!* crew.

The film was at a point where the producers had to decide whether to accept the compromise of capturing a buffalo, or to pack up and go elsewhere. I met with the Americans again in a bar in Arusha and the man above me came along as well. He introduced himself to the film people and the Yanks soon got the impression that this newcomer had the power to make a decision and overrule me, so they began sucking up to him

The next morning the senior man came to the office and questioned me about what the producer had told him, that I had refused them a permit to capture a rhino. I confirmed that I was adamant that this should not happen.

'You know, his means a lot of money - the whole picture is in the balance,' the senior man said to me. 'One rhino won't make a difference. I think we'll give them a permit to catch a rhino.'

I shook my head. What could I say? He had the right to overrule me.

THE BIG-NAME ACTORS came out to Tanganyika to film. As well as John Wayne and his leading lady there was the comedian Red Buttons, the German actor Hardy Kruger, and Michèle Giradon.

My job was ostensibly to supervise during the filming of the game capture scenes and I watched on as the cast and others did their best to flip over their vehicles, chasing down animals.

The film's director, Howard Hawks, hired Willy de Beer, a licensed animal catcher, to do the game captures. After catching two rhinos, for filming purposes, Willy gave up on a third and I ended up having to step in and catch it for them, despite my opposition to the whole process.

Central to the plot of *Hatari!* was the exploits of an orphan baby elephant. Lorna and the children can be seen in a shot of Arusha when the little elephant, whose name was Congo, goes running down the main street of town on a rampage. Congo, incidentally, saw out his later years in Australia, at the Western Plains Zoo at Dubbo, in central-western New South Wales, where he died at the age of 60.

Anyone who knew anything about game capture realised that to successfully catch one live rhino, you were going to kill one or two more trying, so catching three was always going to bring risk. To the best of my knowledge, two rhinos were killed during the making of the film – not during the actual captures, which were filmed and used in the opening scene of the movie, but when the animals were in the boma and became stressed.

When Lorna and I had married in Tanganyika we had been allocated a government hovel to live in. It soon became apparent that I could not afford to keep a family of seven on a game ranger's pay.

I had been dealing with all of the big hunting outfits as part of my day-to-day work, so when Ker and Downey offered me a job heading up their operations in Kenya, I accepted it. With the money they were offering I could keep all the children in good schools and provide Lorna with a nice house in Nairobi.

On the face of it, the position sounded like a dream come true. I was a keen hunter and I had always wanted to live in Kenya. In reality, however, it was mostly administrative work. While I could occasionally get out to the bush, I was the front man, so I had to meet and greet clients, take them to their hotel and virtually act as their servant.

One client, an Indian Prince, came to Kenya. Members of the local Indian community came to my office and the delegation extolled the virtues of the great man. I met him at the airport, where we had laid on a fleet of cars for the Prince and his small army of retainers. I put him up in the best suite in the Norfolk Hotel, along with his acolytes, who waited on him hand and foot.

The Prince went off on his safari and we were very pleased, indeed, when he returned.

'I am going to give you a present, which you will treasure for the rest of your life,' he told me, when he returned to Nairobi.

Oh goody, I thought. Perhaps it would be a diamond?

When I got home, Lorna asked me what I'd been given.

'A bloody photograph of him in his Indian royal gear,' I told her, holding it up in disgust. 'And not even in a decent frame!'

A BIG, fat German pilot was the first person to espouse the virtues of Botswana to me.

He had moved from Germany to South West Africa (now Namibia), and then to Botswana, where he had set up a one-man airline flying political dissidents out of South Africa to Tanganyika. When I met him, at the Ker and Downey offices, he told me there was potential in Botswana to set up a profitable hunting business and offered me a free trip down there to look over the prospects.

I discussed his offer with our managing director, who was interested, so I packed a bag, jumped into the German's twin-engine aeroplane and flew to and around Botswana. In those days, Riley's Hotel, a landmark establishment in Maun, the nearest town to the Okavango Delta, was just a tin shack. The place looked unused and primitive, nevertheless the pilot convinced me that there was the potential to expand hunting in the country.

I fed the idea to Ker and Downey and at the same time we were in negotiation with a Portuguese man, Jose Simoaz, to become our representative in Mozambique, where the hunting was also quite good.

I knew the chief game warden in Botswana from my time in northern Rhodesia and had tentatively arranged a deal with him in which K and D hunters would move to various parts of his country and act as honorary game wardens, as well as leading their commercial safaris. Our experienced hunters would be able to advise the Botswana game department about which animals should be taken off and which should be protected – it would be about commercialising game, but also keeping it under control.

Around the same time, I was involved in a merger with another Kenya hunting outfit, Selby and Homburg. After the merger, Harry Selby, the co-owner, was given a directorship and for a while the company became known as Ker and Downey & Selby Safaris. Harry

Selby talked Jack Block, the owner of K and D, into letting him set up the proposed Botswana operation.

Harry Selby was a charismatic hunter with a big following, especially after the publication of Robert Ruark's book covering his safari with Harry. He was obviously a good man to head up the new operation; however, his view of the venture was entirely different from mine. His was more conventional and commercial, without any cross pollination with the game department.

I must admit, I was very disappointed as I had put in a great deal of work into my idea and thought it had great potential; however, that's the way things go.

16

As the chief Game Warden of Kenya, Ian Grimwood was, by association, a respected member of a number of international conservation bodies.

In 1961, he was approached by one of these august bodies to see if he had any ideas about how to save the last known remnants of the once large herds of Arabian Oryx (*O. leucoryx*). These animals were once found from Syria to the southern shores of the Arabian Peninsula, but were now squeezed into a relatively tiny area defined by the western boundary of the Dhofar province of Muscat and Oman, and the eastern boundary of the East Aden Protectorate, where it met the southern border of Saudi Arabia's Empty Quarter, better known as the Rub-al-Khali.

To add urgency to the enquiry, it had recently been reported that a body of hunters from Qatar, using specially adapted four-wheel-drive vehicles, fitted with balloon tyres, had crossed the desert, located and shot most of the last known members of the species. Amongst reports of the carnage there was an indication that a handful of survivors might have escaped.

Based on his experience monitoring animal capture in East Africa, Ian was asked about the feasibility of mounting an expedition to go into the Empty Quarter, in order to catch any of those possible survivors – if they could be found.

Over one of our many curry lunches together, Ian raised the subject with me and over the following weeks we explored and thrashed out details about how to find and capture these animals in such a remote and inhospitable place. We came up with a plan which had enough of the basics covered for him to offer it up to the people in London who were trying to finance the rescue. Some traction began to develop and Ian was asked to head up a project, which would be mounted in April or May of 1962.

As most of the professional catchers and trappers in East Africa were fully occupied, Ian asked me if I would be interested in filling that slot on his team. It was an honour and I was very anxious to accept; however, being the manager of Ker and Downey, I had to put the proposition to my employers.

Although no real benefit to the company was likely, they agreed without hesitation to me taking two months or more leave of absence. On top of that, their generosity included an offer of any help they could possibly give to the enterprise. This was appreciated and the expedition immediately sought the help of our garage, mechanics and staff to redesign and modify a Ford F200 utility into a catching car. We based the design on the catching vehicles that had been used in the making of the film, *Hatari!*

Although we couldn't compete with the bottomless pockets of the Hollywood moguls, or the oil rich Qataris who had hunted the oryx to near extinction, the company mechanics and staff produced a vehicle in record time and at virtually no cost to the expedition.

The car they came up with would have given Heath Robinson nightmares, but it seemed functional and met all our requirements in spades. When we trialled it on the Athi plains, just outside Nairobi, it proved to have the agility and acceleration required, while remaining stable and manoeuvrable over rough country. It proved able to cope with the fastest and most evasive animals, such as hartebeest and grant's gazelle, while keeping pace with slower-moving species, such as zebra, wildebeest, and eland was a walk in the park.

Our custom-made catching car. It looked the part...

Interest was growing in the project. The Fauna Preservation Society in London, under the guiding hand of its secretary, Colonel Boyle, acted as a bell-weather for other like-minded societies, who dipped their toes into the funding pool. Eventually, one of the larger London daily newspapers took up the cause. Being a very minor player, I was not involved in any of the meetings and negotiations that went on behind the scenes, but got on with supervising the development of the catching car and getting together the few bits of equipment I thought might make the actual job a bit easier. I was very aware of the problems attached to catching the East and Central African oryx, both of which were big and strong, making up for their lack of agility by being very aggressive and dangerous. I based my preparations on them.

Christmas and New Year passed with plans progressing well. As it was the season of the short rains in Kenya, the safari business was pretty slack, so we could spend a bit more time on matters concerning the oryx expedition. The careful, methodical planning received quite a jolt in early February when a message arrived from

London reporting that the Qataris had made a second raid and had reportedly killed the last few animals that had escaped their earlier effort.

Mercifully, though, we then heard follow-up reports that one, or maybe two, oryx, had since been seen in the area between the Wadi Mitan and the sand dunes. A decision had to be made – go ahead, or cancel.

The telephone lines ran hot between Nairobi, London and New York. Making the decision even harder was the fact that the London newspaper which had been supporting the project had decided to pull the plug on its funding, based on the news of the latest hunting foray. That left us short of a major sponsor.

Much to-ing and fro-ing ensued but, eventually, based on advice from the Colonial Advisor to the Aden Protectorate, it was decided to go ahead. Some other sponsors duly came on board, and while not quite as generous as the newspaper had been, it was enough to allow us to carry on, albeit on a tighter budget. By March, all was in place; the team was selected; the contacts in England, Kenya and the Aden Protectorate were alerted. and we were ready to move as soon as the word was given.

Murphy's Law now reared its ugly head - one disaster followed another. Our specially- modified catching car was supposed to be loaded on board a ship sailing from Mombasa to Mukalla, but when it arrived at the docks in Mombasa, for some unspecified reason, the captain of the ship refused to load it. So, back the car went to Nairobi, where the RAF, our faithful, steady backstop in so many instances throughout the whole operation, stepped in and flew the vehicle direct to Aden on one of their routine cargo flights.

Then Michael Crouch, one of our two Arabic speakers and an administrative officer in the Protectorate, with jurisdiction over the area we would be operating in, was hospitalised in Aden with malaria. Consequently, he would not be able to join the expedition until he had recovered. As he had undertaken to top up the ration supplies in Mukalla before the party set off, a very hasty and disorganised replacement effort was put together to do the job, resulting in some quite unusual meals being put on the table once we were in the desert.

The next of Murphy's efforts involved the catching car, which showed its dislike of the country and conditions over which it was required to travel very early on during the overland drive from Aden to Mukalla. It only just made it into the Hadhrami Bedouin Levy (HBL) workshops in Mukalla by the skin of its teeth. There, it took all the energy and imagination of their engineers and mechanics to get it going again.

The gearbox and differential were totally unsuited to the loose, uneven surfaces encountered even on the road from Aden, let alone what was expected once we started into the wilds. We went through all the spares we had brought from Kenya, and all those we could find in the local souks, but in the end, we had to accept the inevitable and abandon our custom-built vehicle. It was simply not up to the task.

To fill the gap, we modified Michael Crouch's personal vehicle, an old 30cwt Bedford. It was clumsy and slow, but would have to do.

The ill-luck dogging the exercise did not stop there. Myself and two other members of the party, Michael Woodford, our veterinarian from the UK, and Don Stewart, our biologist from the Kenya Game Department, were supposed to meet our second Arabic speaker, Captain Tony Shepherd of the Federal Regular Army (formerly the Aden Protectorate Levies) in Aden and fly to Riyan, the airstrip near Mukalla. There, we would link up with the others. Unfortunately, however, the meshing of the flight schedules went awry. Tony had caught an RAF flight to Riyan and arrived in time, but a rainstorm that night put the airstrip out of commission for 24 hours, delaying the three of us in Aden.

However, on the 24th we finally caught up with everyone at Ghuraf in the Wadi Hadramout. Eventually we got underway for the HBL fort at Al Abr, where we were scheduled to meet up with our HBL protection unit, consisting of four five-ton Bedford Model R, four-wheel- drive trucks. These would carry all our camp gear and heavy stores, and a wide range of people. There were instant-reaction soldiers, a couple of mechanics, our domestic staff, a carpenter, and one or two others whose duties must have been pertinent but what they were I never did find out. There was also a Land Rover wireless unit and operator, and a Land Rover scout car to carry our Bedouin trackers on the hunt.

Ian Grimwood, with me behind the wheel of the trusty old Bedford.

The final member of our party, Mick Gracie, was a pilot, who had undertaken the hazardous responsibility of flying a little Piper Cruiser short take-off and landing (STOL) aircraft, lent to the expedition by the Kenya Wildlife Society, for use as a spotter and communications plane. Mick's would be a hairy job, to say the least, but one for which he had volunteered with complete confidence, no doubt the result of his considerable experience as a bomber pilot during the war.

With the party finally together, we sorted out stores and loading arrangements, selected travelling partners and prepared for as early a take-off as possible. The novelty of our situation was not lost on anyone and it seemed that photographs were the order of the day, led by Michael Woodford, who had been designated official photographer, by dint of having a 15mm Bell and Howell movie camera.

The day passed quickly and we were all in bed early, ready for a before-dawn start in the morning. We travelled east for the next seven days, passing a string of 'Beau Geste' type forts en-route, guarding wells manned by detachments of the HBL, whose main job was keeping the peace in the area.

Quaid Grey, the Commanding Officer of the HBL, was leading our convoy, which conveniently coincided with one of his regular inspection tours. He left us every now and again to carry out his duties at the forts, but returned to his place at the head of the convoy as soon as he could. Along the way, we picked up the first of our guides/trackers, Tomatum bin Harbi, at Thamud. Finally, we found our way to the fort and wells at Sanau. From there, Quaid carried on to the final well at Habarut, on the border with Dhofar, while we started our hunt in earnest.

The plan was to make our base camp near the fort at Sanau, using one of the storerooms there as a reception area for any oryx we might be lucky enough to catch. To that end, we left the carpenter and mason there to prepare stalls and, optimistically, assemble a couple of extra carrying crates. Michael Woodford, the vet, was left to supervise this work, while the rest of us took off into the wide yellow yonder, to look for recent tracks and hopefully catch oryx.

Tomatum bin Harbi

With the aid of our tracker Tomatum, who was conversant with the area, Ian worked out a plan of square searches to cover the estimated 8,000 or more square miles of country we had to investigate. The overall plan was to undertake a number of searches, each lasting three or four days and covering about 400 square miles. In this way we would try to check the anticipated routes that the oryx might take as they moved south to leave the heat of the sands for the more hospitable 'johl' country to the south, where, hopefully, they would find shade and a little more sustenance.

At the end of each square search, it was proposed we return to our temporary base camp to replenish stores, and fill up with petrol and water. I might add here that one of the least attractive parts of the whole exercise was our water. It was carried in old petrol drums and more often than not, it was quite difficult to distinguish between the two – so much so that, after a drink of water, it might not have been advisable to light a cigarette. Ian, who was a chain smoker, insouciantly took the risk daily; nor did he seem to even notice the taste.

Mabkhaut bin Hassanan

Having completed a first square search, we returned to Sanau after a few days to find that Quaid Grey had returned from Habarut, bringing with him our second tracker, an elderly, but very experienced man called Mabkhaut bin Hassanan. He would join Tomatum in assisting Ian in his planning. Mabkhaut brought news that one of his sons, travelling recently in one of the areas we were proposing to search, had actually seen two oryx, so it was all systems go to get to that area and begin an all-out search.

In all, we spent about a week in fruitless searching, checking every area that Tomatum and Mabkhaut thought likely prospects. However, we had no success, apart from finding ample evidence of the activities of the Qatari hunters who had preceded us.

Eventually, on about our eighth day, we came across some fresh spoor and the chase was on. It was slow going, but Tomatum and Mabkhaut were like bloodhounds on the trail; all day they followed it, sometimes from the car, but mostly on foot. We camped on it overnight and picked it up again next morning, following the trail slowly and carefully until just after 9 o'clock, when the sun was really beginning to make itself felt. Our pick-up was in its usual place, on the higher ground away from the trackers and their car, with the other vehicles a reasonable distance away behind all the possible action.

Out of the blue, about 200 yards in front of us, an oryx jumped up out of a shallow depression.

'Tally Ho!' someone shouted. As the driver of the catching vehicle, I put my foot down, without regard for those in the back. My passengers had to cling on for dear life and at the same time untangle the catching pole and set it up for Ian, who was now standing up on his seat, with his head and shoulders out of the hole in the roof.

A man in the back handed Ian the pole, so that he would be ready as soon as we came up on the animal. With pole in hand, Ian had nothing left to steady himself as we crashed across the desert plain in hot pursuit. He was being shaken like one of 007's cocktails, ribs bouncing from one side of the cupola to the other, but Ian was one of the toughest men I have ever known, so the rough treatment had no effect on his concentration.

I came up alongside the running Oryx. Just as Ian was about to slip the rope over its head we hit a bump and he became airborne for an instant, missing the moment. The oryx got away and I resumed the chase. Once more I got close, but Ian was bouncing so much, he missed again. I'm sure that if he had been sitting or standing on a fixed platform, rather than the bouncy seat, he would have landed it.

Just before he could slip the noose over the animal's head on his third attempt, the oryx ducked out of my sight line. One of the worst features of the Bedford was that once the animal was close to the catcher's side, the driver lost sight of it completely, so if it ducked to the right, as it did in this case, a physical bump was the first the driver would know of where his target animal was.

As soon as I felt the bump, gentle though it was, I yanked the wheel to the right and braked, the oryx rolled over from the impact, but immediately got up and was off again. Turning the car back onto the line the oryx was taking, I floored the pedal, crashed through the gears, and caught up with him in a couple of minutes. Ian had reset his noose and this time, as I closed on the oryx, he reached over and snared the animal neatly round the neck.

I gently slowed to a stop as Ian reeled the oryx in alongside us. As soon as we came to a halt I jumped out, ran around the front of the truck, and grabbed the animal by the horns and nose. I turned its head towards my body, to avoid being stabbed by its long, sharp horns. I tipped it over on its right side, helped by Mick, who had hopped off the back as soon as we came to a halt. Mick grabbed it by the tail, helping me put it down. Once the oryx was down, I was able to get my knee on its neck, up behind the ears, holding it firmly in place while I put a blindfold over its eyes. Experience has shown that covering an animal's eyes has a tranquilising effect in stressful situations. We then put soft wraps around its legs, to assist in preventing further struggles.

The rest of the vehicles rolled up and the crews got the catching crate down off the R5 Bedford, manhandling it into place. While that was happening, I gave the animal a quick mouthful of water and poured a little on its head to cool it down after all the excitement; Ian gave it a shot of a tranquiliser drug to relieve some of the stress it was undoubtedly going through.

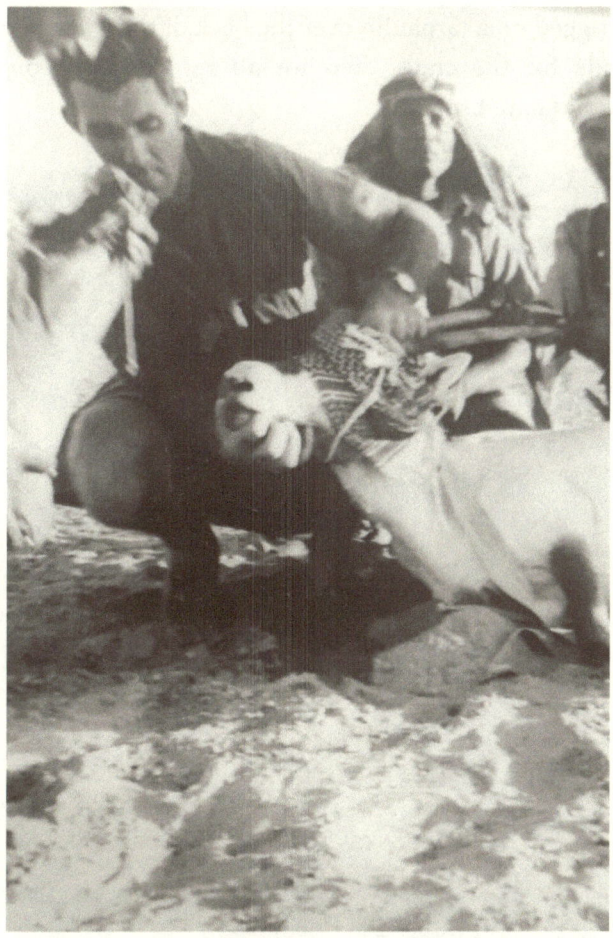

One of the captured oryx, with it's eyes covered to calm it

When all was ready, we got him – our catch was a bull - up on his feet and very gently induced him to shuffle into the crate. As it happened, the oryx was actually quite co-operative and hardly struggled at all. Once in the crate and the door closed, all hands and the cook helped to lift it onto the bed of the R5 and secure it for its triumphal return to our temporary camp. At the camp, we decided to leave the crate on the truck on the basis that too much moving about would be unlikely to benefit the animal in any way. Besides, it was unnecessary, for as soon as the heat abated, it would be on its way to

Sanau. I rigged up a tarpaulin over the back of the truck to provide a little shade for the crate, then we all sat down to congratulate ourselves and have brunch.

Safe from marauding hunters, an endangered Arabian Oryx

Ian decided Michael Woodford, Don Steward and Michael Crouch should accompany the truck back to Sanau. There were a few objections from those chosen, as everyone wanted to stay with the hunting party, as uncomfortable and taxing as it was. Ian remained firm - the men being sent back all had specific jobs to do, attached to the wellbeing of any animals caught. They had to go back with the first one, to ensure it had the best possible chance of survival, and prepare for any additional arrivals.

Back in our forward camp, the aftermath of all the excitement was that we, the catching party, would relax with a day off, while the mechanic and his minion went over all the vehicles, to check they were serviceable for the next hunt. In fact, our 'relaxing' was anything but - there was so much to do that we were all quite happy to get back on the road the next day.

As always in the desert, water was the biggest problem; our forward camp had limited resources, and supplies of both water and petrol were running low. We sent some of the vehicles off to top up and decided to send some of the HBL soldiers back to their base. We had come to the conclusion that the military men were not necessary for our protection, nor the heavy lifting - the catching team had enough muscle to lift an oryx onto the truck. Added to this, some of the soldiers, away from their officers and superiors, were not really the asset we imagined they would be. In fairness to them, they hadn't signed up to be dogsbodies or labourers on what to them was a completely unnecessary, uncomfortable trip into the desert. A little group of malcontents were continually complaining of being overworked and had been reluctant to take any instructions from anyone other than their superiors, so it was a relief to have the opportunity to send them back to the fort and get them out of our hair.

Mick, Tomatum and Tony used their day off doing an aerial search of our next hunting square, a thoroughly dangerous enterprise that I would not have countenanced at any price. Luckily, Ian came to the same conclusion and restricted the use of the aircraft for communications only.

The safety factor of flying over endless, empty desert aside, the recce did produce some positive information. Although no oryx were seen the airborne scouts did see evidence of recent rain, which had resulted in quite a substantial amount of greenery on which rhim gazelle (*G. marica*) were seen to be extensively grazing, an encouraging sight.

Later in the day, Michael Crouch and Mabkhaut returned from their visit to Sanau, which they had combined with an attempt to buy some goats for ration meat from the local Bedu. Their report was depressing; the HBL officer in charge of the fort was being obstructive, with the work there at a virtual standstill. Ian reluctantly sent a signal to Quaid Grey to see if he could turn the situation around.

We searched the area that had been flown over by the aircraft, seeing quite a few rhim and one or two other animals that were too far away to be identified properly. We spent two days looking, but there was no sign of oryx, not even tracks. On our third day, just after our midday break, we were packing up and getting ready to move, when there was an outcry from the Model R Bedford, indicating something of interest had been seen.

It was three oryx. They appeared from nowhere and were seen galloping away from us, about 400 yards to our south. A fourth animal we couldn't identify seemed to be accompanying them.

It was all hands and the cook to the helm, again! Somehow, I got the catching car and all its crew underway in jig time and the pursuit was on. The going was terrible. Normally I would have avoided the rough route we took at all costs, but this was no time to be fastidious; we ploughed on, the Bedford bouncing and shuddering.

Eventually, the animals topped a small rise and scattered. I took the one on the left and set out at full tilt after it. If anything, the going became worse. I hated to think what the crew in the back was going through - it was bad enough in the front where I at least had the steering wheel to hang on to. Ian, in the catcher's position, was even more precariously positioned, as he had to keep control of his catching pole and the attendant, but critical, noose, while at the same time wriggle himself upright through the hole in the roof, drag his pole after himself and then use both hands to prepare it for catching.

We hit an unmerciful bump; Ian gasped and there was a weak, but audible cracking sound as his ribs gave way. Immediately I started to slow up – all the oryx in the world couldn't compensate for wrecking a good man.

'Keep your foot down!' Ian yelled through tortured gasps of air.

Our quarry was doubling about and criss-crossing his flight path until it disappeared into a ravine that I wasn't prepared to take on, pulling up in a cloud of dust just before we teetered over the edge. With Ian in considerable pain, the sensible thing was to head back to camp and do what we could to make him a bit more comfortable. It was time to move,

'He's lying down!' one of the men in the Model R shouted.

I looked to where the man was pointing, along the ravine. He was right, one of the oryx had gone to ground. We set off again, but so, too, did the oryx. The going was still unacceptably bad, but if we were going to achieve anything, we just had to carry on to the best of our ability and hope that the truck would stand up to the abuse.

It soon appeared that the oryx was also finding the going pretty tough; it was limping noticeably, tongue out and giving every sign of distress. If it had been any other animal then this, too, would have made me call off the pursuit, for fear of stressing the creature too much. However, there was so much at stake I didn't even consider it.

We chased the oryx until it moved out onto a relatively flat spot and turned to face us. I pulled up alongside the antelope so that Ian, still in his catcher's position, could slip a noose over its head and pull it up to the side of the car. I ducked round the front and grabbed it by the horns. Tony and Mick, our supernumeraries in the back, jumped out and helped wrestle it to the ground, by pulling on its tail. Once blindfolded and lying quietly, I gave the oryx a little trickle of water, whilst Ian administered the usual anti-shock jab, which seemed to ease its stress considerably. The animal's breathing began to slow down to near normal; it seemed so compliant that I didn't think it necessary to disturb it further by tying its legs.

The Model R pulled up next to us. The carrying crate was offloaded, and without any trouble at all, number two was loaded into the crate, which was then lifted onto the truck ready for transport to Sanau.

When the four animals had split up, I had selected the left hand one to follow, as it had looked the smallest, fooling me into thinking it was a female. It wasn't; however, having caught it, there was no chance whatsoever that we would let it go.

It had been a disastrous chase from all angles - far too long, over totally unsuitable terrain, in conditions much too hot, and finally, but not least, it had bent Ian more than somewhat. A lesser man would have called a halt there and then, but not Ian. Once the crate was on the back of the Model R, he took his Arabic head scarf off and tied it around his broken ribs in an effort to get some relief. Having experienced broken ribs myself a number of times, I knew that his efforts at first aid would do little, if anything, for the pain, but if it made him feel better it was all to the good.

'Let's get going after one of the others,' Ian said.

About an hour later, we cut across the spoor again, and shortly after taking it up there was a shout from the back of the cars as a plume of dust was seen way out in front. It was another oryx, running away from us into the sunset.

Off we went, full throttle again, but for a long time we didn't seem to be making up any ground at all. To make matters worse the Bedford sank in loose sand. Swearing at the top of my voice and jerking the truck back and forth, through first and reverse gears, I finally got us moving again, surging forward on a tide of invective.

Initially the going was as bad as anything we had experienced up to date; we bounced from rock to rock and lurched in and out of gullies and depressions without regard for comfort or car. The engine was heating up under the strain causing me to fear that it might be giving up the ghost. Eventually, we struggled out onto a bit of ground where the terrain was better, allowing us to pick up the pace and cool the engine a little, making it a trifle more co-operative.

Murphy, our constant companion, took this opportunity to make his presence felt again. All the leaping and bouncing across the seemingly endless bad lands had reduced the back of the catching car to total chaos. Tony and Mick had the virtually impossible task of trying to sort things out and get the catching pole and its substitute ready for Ian, while at the same time trying to keep upright without using their hands, which were fully occupied. How they coped I have no idea, but cope they did and luckily so, for at his first pass at the animal when we finally caught up with it, Ian misjudged his cast and bent the pole. He jettisoned it and reached for the substitute, which luckily our two worthies in the back had ready.

This time, Ian was able to neatly slip the noose into place and draw the animal up alongside the vehicle, allowing the now quite slick capture procedure to follow its normal course. Three were in the bag

Much to everybody's delight, this oryx was a female, making us all feel so much better, as now there was a clear purpose to whole exercise – survival of a species. Up until now, the predominance of males had been disheartening; suddenly the whole atmosphere had changed.

The arrival of the support Land Rover carrying Michael, and the Model R with a second crate and its load of willing helpers was a moment of pure jubilation. There were lots of photographs, back slapping and laughter; everyone seemed infected by the occasion.

But time was wasting, and there was more business to be done. We crated our precious female, loaded her onto the Model R, and were about to send it on its way when someone called me over to the crate containing our first catch, the male.

'I don't think all is well,' the man said.

It definitely was not – the bull had died. The mood among us descended from elation to gloom. The smiles and laughter were replaced by a quiet grimness as we pulled the carcass from the crate. Our scientific fundis would have to do a post mortem to establish the true cause of death, if they could.

To facilitate this, and to avoid as much putrefaction occurring on the journey to Sanau as possible, I cut the oryx open and took the contents of the abdominal cavity out and put them in a secure box, which we covered up and loaded alongside the carcass before sending it on its way.

There were all sorts of speculation among those of us left

behind as to the true cause of the casualty, not the least, in hindsight, was the fact that the animal itself was in not nearly as good a condition as the other two we had. This was evident in death, though we hadn't noticed it during the capture; its coat was dry, brittle and 'starry'(with the hairs standing up individually and curling at the ends, rather than lying flat). Unlike the others, it had shown little of the traditional stamina expected from the species, when it was being chased. These, however, were just theories – the true cause would hopefully become clear at the post mortem.

Ian was in a pretty bad way, despite liberal doses of codeine and whisky. It was decided by all that he should go to Sanau to see if Michael Woodford, the nearest thing we had to a doctor, could come up with any way to make him more comfortable.

Ian and I lunching in the desert. Note the strapping around his broken ribs

He refused to take the easy way and fly, but had his bedroll laid out in the back of the truck, and after a quick, late meal, climbed in, lay down and declared himself ready for anything. The truck set off and disappeared into the night.

For the rest of us in camp, it had been an exhausting day, not only physically, but mentally, with the elation of finally catching a female, only to be cast down by the unfortunate death of the young bull, and Ian's unfortunate injury had taken its toll. Initially, we felt a trifle rudderless, but the show had to go on.

Before going to bed that night we decided, on the basis that nearly everybody had declared they had seen four animals, we had to go looking for the remaining oryx. Opinion was divided as to whether it could have been an immature or even a calf, therefore it was essential someone return to the site of our first contact and check the tracks. Tony and I, together with Mabkhaut as guide cum tracker, elected go in one of the Land Rovers, accompanied by the second Land Rover, carrying the wireless set and an operator.

As we set out Mabkhaut pointed to the direction we should take. Every little diversion from the line he wanted us to follow was corrected by a bang on the driver's shoulder and a finger pointing back to the right direction. This procedure went on for nearly five hours through what was a virtually featureless, monotonous, yellow-grey landscape, with the only appreciable movement anywhere being the sun slowly moving from east to west.

Finally, Mabkhaut signalled for the driver to stop. He got out of the car, walked about 30 yards ahead, veering slightly to the right and stopped. He pointed down to a slight depression in the otherwise featureless ground and, sure enough, there were the tracks. It was quite uncanny, almost beyond belief. I was most certainly impressed – with a capital 'I'. This was one of the most astonishing feats of bushmanship I have ever had the privilege to be associated with.

We carefully searched the ground around the depression in all directions, before coming to the conclusion that whatever it was that people thought they had seen, it was neither four oryx, nor was there an immature or calf. There had been only the three, of which we had caught two, and one was still at large.

We returned, following the direct line Mabkhaut had laid out on the outward trip, arriving back to an empty camp. Michael, Tomatum and Mick had flown off to Thamud to get spares for the catching car, which was now showing serious signs of abuse. Tired but satisfied, with nothing better to do, Tony and I had a quick meal and retired to our respective beds.

It was about this time that either the high levels of magnesium sulphate in the water/petrol we were drinking, or some unspecified bug, made life distinctly unpleasant for me. The severity of the problem was certainly not conducive to taking much of a part in our further activities. Nothing could be less appropriate than having to stop the car in the middle of a chase so I could rush off into the desert in full view of all and sundry to do what was necessary- not to mention the possible embarrassment resulting from hitting a big bump at an inopportune time. The hunt went on without me.

17

Over the wireless, Tony and I heard the results of the post mortem on the dead bull. There appeared little doubt that it had died from the stress of being chased for so long in the blinding heat, but the real reason for its poor condition and apparent lack of energy was a recent bullet wound, probably courtesy of the Qatari hunters. The bullet had entered just above the stifle, and the wound was putrefying inside the animal – it would have proved fatal even if we had not intervened.

It was now well into May and our window of opportunity was closing. The inactivity of hanging around the deserted camp was beginning to pall on both Tony and myself. However, inactivity was hardly an appropriate description of my state, as my problem had shown little sign of easing up.

It was quite a relief when the others started trickling back into the camp. First came the aircraft, with the spares for the catching car, followed some hours later by Ian and Don in the Model R, accompanied by a load of water among other goodies. Ian was strapped up in a nice white bodice, which probably did no good at all, but at least it drew attention to his condition.

The appropriate men of action got stuck into getting the catching car ready, working through the night, doing whatever they could to get it serviceable for some more abuse. The rest made preparations to go out and see if contact could be made with the third animal of the trio put up on our last outing.

The consensus was that I would be more of a liability than an asset, and Don was told to take Ian's place as catcher. He'd had an introduction to the art at John Seago's camp in Isiolo, when we were practicing with the original catching car. Ian took over as the driver.

The plan for this hunt followed the same as previous ones, except for an earlier departure from camp. This was most likely because no one could really sleep, with all the banging and clattering that was going on as the fixing of the catching car reached its climax.

Driving over what was now fairly familiar territory, the team was making good time when shortly after dawn someone spotted two hedgehogs (*Paraechinus aethiopicus dorsalis*) going fussily about their business across the desert. Where they came from, or where they were going, only they knew, as there was nothing around them remotely different to where they actually were – just miles and miles of blank desert. Tony and Michael jumped out and picked both of them up, discovering in doing so that one was a male and the other a female. The female, being the more sensible of the two, did what hedgehogs do and curled herself up into a ball, thereby automatically sentencing herself to be quietly collected. A specimen of the Arabian sub-species of the Ethiopian Hedgehog had been one of the items specifically requested by some boffin, when it was announced that our expedition was officially on.

The male on the other hand, being an animal of considerable character, kept everyone on their toes, scuffling about all over the car, investigating everything he came across, and causing consternation among most of the Arabs, who apparently don't like hedgehogs. Christened HH, he stayed with us for quite a time, becoming quite a pet, providing us with endless amusement.

The rising temperature did nothing for the comfort of anyone, so after the midday break, it was with considerable relief that everyone confirmed Tomatum's opinion that there was no point in continuing the search that day. Rather than make camp where they were, the team turned around and came back to the relative comfort of the main camp.

With our window rapidly closing and the fact that we had pretty well scoured all the most promising areas of the johl available to us, the decision was now to grasp the nettle and try the edges of the sand sea itself, even if it meant tackling some of the least daunting dunes

The next hunt was directed to this end and so the team headed as far north as they dared, limited by the heavy shifting sands of the dunes as well as the proximity of the Saudi Arabian border. For the next four or five days they scouted along the edge of the sands, looking fruitlessly for tracks, or any other indication that oryx might be about.

What they did see was plenty of evidence of the Qatari raiding parties, even coming across a site where they had indulged in one of their killing orgies, if the tracks were read correctly. Another very interesting feature that they came across was a deeply indented, compacted track, some two metres wide, running north-south. Tomatum and Mabkhaut both insisted this was the fabled road to the prehistoric golden city of Oubar, where, amongst others, the Queen of Sheba once held sway. They insisted that the compaction, although thousands of years old, was the result of the many thousands of camels which carried goods and supplies from the coast to the population of that fabulous city and its surrounding areas. I'm not qualified to judge the veracity of their claims, but a track was definitely seen there, and it does make a good story.

Ian, in his role as leader, now had more on his shoulders than just driving around looking for tracks. With the end very definitely in sight, he was already making plans for the onward movement of the oryx and our gear from the desert to Aden and then on to Kenya. To this end it was decided that Tony would leave as soon as everybody got back to our main camp - Mick would fly him to Sanau then onto Ghuraf, from where he would fly to Aden by commercial flight. Once in Aden, Tony would pull what strings he could to facilitate the movement of the animals and our gear from Sanau to Aden. I was scheduled to go to Sanau by truck with Michael and take over from Michael Woodford, while Ian and the rest of the crew would try another run or two at the inhospitable country at the foot of the dunes.

Some six hours after leaving camp, Michael and I arrived at the fort in Sanau in time to have a quick look at the oryx before tucking into a much-needed lunch, lubricated for Mick by fresh camel's milk, but for the rest of us, washed down by a few beers.

After lunch Mick departed in the Piper Cruiser with Tony, and Michael as navigator, for Sanau and Ghuraf, dropping Tony off there to catch his commercial aircraft. They returned to camp in time to fly a short recce, up to the border of the sands, penetrating some ten lines of dunes deeper into the desert, but to no avail. They saw no evidence whatsoever of any animal movement.

The next morning, the team set off, Ian driving the catching car, Don acting as catcher and Mick, as usual, hanging on for dear life in the back, moustache streaming in the wind. Michael Crouch travelled in the Land Rover. Their morning search having produced nothing of interest, they stopped for the normal midday break, setting off again about 2.30pm.

'Tracks!' Tomatum called out 20 minutes later. He had found some fresh spoor at the bottom of a dune. 'They are only about 24 hours old. It looks like a female.'

This was going to be a last-minute fling, and both Tomatum and Mabkhaut were determined that this one was not going to get away. For more than two hours they trotted and walked in the blazing heat, sticking to the spoor like jam on a blanket. The tracks clearly indicated the sole animal was in no way disturbed.

'It is probably looking for a suitable place to lie up,' Tomatum said.

Disaster struck. The catching car's drive wheels were spinning in soft sand – it was well and truly stuck. The members of the catching team used hands and shovels, but by the time they had freed the Bedford it was too late to carry on.

They had no alternative but to camp on the spoor. Every precaution was taken to avoid the possibility of disturbing the animal; no lanterns or fires were lit, so as to avoid spooking the oryx with the smell of smoke. Dry rations were issued and silently eaten and the bedding laid out as quietly as was practical. There was little point in making a pre-dawn start as they were already on the spoor and only needed daylight to pick it up again, so this allowed the whole party to enjoy an unexpected lie-in.

At the first glimmer of the dawn breaking, the camp was quietly broken and loaded, by which time Tomatum and Mabkhaut were able to see the spoor clearly enough to follow it. The spoor led over a gravelly plain, heading roughly south until something must have disturbed the animal. The spoor then indicated the animal had broken into a gallop and turned north, back towards the sands.

After about eight miles the tracks indicated the oryx had settled down to a walk, but further along it had once more started galloping. Fortunately, although the antelope was moving roughly north, it was actually travelling along the edge of the dunes. Had it turned into the dunes that would have been the end of the hunt. The trackers thought it might be looking for some shade. The spoor turned south and, encouraged by the freshness of the tracks, the party pressed on, harder.

Confidence was building as the two trackers trotted along crisp, clearly-defined tracks. The two men were looking ahead, instead of at the ground; the Land Rover was at their heels, while the catching car swung away to climb to whatever high ground was near at hand. Some elevation would allow for a faster take off if the animal broke cover.

From a small cave-like depression in the limestone edge of the wadi ahead, the oryx suddenly popped up like a jack-in-the-box, took a quick look at the Land Rover and bounded up on to the edge of the wadi.

It stood for a moment, assessing the situation, then galloped off across the plain. The catching car was facing the wrong direction, nullifying its 'faster take-off' strategy, however Ian was able to wrench it round and set off at high speed. He drove down the one bank of the wadi and up the other, just in time to see the animal disappear over the horizon.

Knowing the animal's line, though, Ian piled on the speed and rapidly caught up to his quarry. The oryx continued to run in a straight line, allowing Ian to draw alongside and Don to slip the noose over its head. Once the oryx was snubbed up to the side of the car, Ian slowed to a stop. Mick took over the job of getting hold of the horns, and, not being used to it, so I was told later, very nearly got spiked. However, all was well in the end; the animal was quickly loaded into the travelling crate and onto the Model R for the trip back to Sanau.

What a finale! Throughout the chase, Tomatum had been convinced the animal they were following was a female, so everyone was now congratulating themselves on a double whammy. However, on inspection it turned out to be another male; maybe it was a tad disappointing, but it was better than nothing. In fact the final oryx was an excellent specimen, young and in great condition. It was just the sort of animal we had been looking for and, in any case, beggars can't be choosers.

On arrival at Sanau, the new acquisition was freed from the travelling crate into a newly prepared stall alongside the other two animals. The Model R returned to the camp, where preparations were underway for a final tilt. Michael Crouch's doughty old Bedford pick-up had finally indicated enough was enough and given up the ghost (an indication of just how tough the last six weeks had been). For one last throw of the dice, one of the Land Rovers was jerry-rigged to act as a catching car. Not surprisingly, however, no trace was found of any more oryx, so by 10.30, the time normally set aside to lie up, it was decided to call it quits and start packing up.

We had all had more than enough. The rigours of the chase, the spartan conditions and the rising heat were all beginning to take their toll. Our Arab workers, who, after being winnowed down from the earlier, rather feckless mob we had started with, had turned out to be a sterling asset. They attended to all the unglamourous behind-the-scenes work, accepting and doing all that was asked of them without question, but now they were also beginning to unravel. It was definitely time to pull out.

Sanau was certainly not luxury living, but it was decidedly more comfortable than the camps in the desert; there was relief from the burning glare of the sun and the ever present wind, and facilities for a wash. However, the 'wash space,' involved dipping cups of the hardest water on the planet over one's head, then scrubbing curds of dirty soap off, which gathered in a foul mess at one's feet. It hardly constituted a shower, but it was better than nothing – only just. Also, it was a relief not to be waking every morning at some ungodly hour, freezing while waiting for the dawn, before moving out of camp.

The three oryx seemed to take to captivity like ducks to water. They had finally decided to try what was on offer as a substitute for their desert fare, and were showing signs of finding it quite palatable. In doing so, they were advancing their chances of survival immeasurably. Michael Woodford had done an excellent job looking after them while we had been ducking and diving about in the desert, and certainly deserved a great deal of credit for their well-being. It was going to be a hard act to follow.

Tony, meanwhile, had arrived back in Aden and set about his task of organising the efficient movement of the animals and equipment from Sanau to Aden and eventually to Kenya. We stood by the radio in Sanau, following his progress while we sorted out what would go and what would be left behind. Virtually anything was useful in a land where so little was available so our 'left behind' pile was quite substantial.

Tony was more than successful; he received co-operation and help from all corners, not least the RAF, which, whilst keeping within their remit did everything humanly possible to help us. They even arranged a supply flight for the HBL, to Thamud and Sanau, to coincide with our move, so that we had the use of an empty Blackburn Beverley four-engine transport aircraft, and its crew for our return trip. When the aircraft arrived at the strip, it seemed to have far more helpers/workers on board than I would imagine was the normal complement for a routine supply trip, but I guess the unusual cargo being loaded for the return flight might have had something to do with that.

While Ian and Tony, who had travelled up in the Beverley, escorted the RAF personnel on their 10-mile trip from the airstrip to the fort and dispensed beers all round, Michael Woodford and I organised the oryx into their travelling crates ready for their long journey to Nairobi. Tony had convinced the Veterinary Officer in Aden to issue a clearance permit certifying the animals came from a foot-and-mouth-free area, thereby eliminating at least one of the problems we might be met with on arrival at Nairobi airport.

While we were crating the animals, all the RAF people, tired of the esoteric delights of the Sanau fort, had gone back to their aircraft and the goodies it contained, such as hot coffee, fresh buns and other assorted delights. Having loaded the three animal crates onto one of the Model Rs and secured them firmly, we set off for the tedious journey from the fort to the airstrip, making slow progress to avoid any discomfort for the oryx. At the airstrip the truck was backed up to the loading doors and the crates efficiently transferred into the body of the aircraft and securely lashed down.

As soon as I was satisfied all was secure and safe, we were back in the truck and off to the fort for a last supper, and a good one it was too. A goat had been killed and Tony, with great forethought, had provided a bottle or two of champagne which had remained cool from its high-altitude flight in, making it doubly acceptable.

We all sat, or lay around, mellow and replete, going over the highlights of the trip, drowsily telling each other improbable stories until it was time to say our goodbyes to the people who had helped us so willingly – the Arab contingent. Although there was a language barrier, I think the message got through that we really appreciated all they had done for us, and some of them, strangely enough, seemed to be sorry we were going. I can't imagine why they would be sad, as our time with them must have been fairly arduous and unpleasant, even though they were used to the country.

Our support crew and 'bodyguards' from the HBL

By the time we returned to the Beverley, most of the airmen were asleep. As quietly as possible, we set out our camp beds. I went into the aircraft to have a final look at the oryx, then Tony and I had a last beer, before trying to unwind and get some sleep. HH the hedgehog, who had travelled quite peaceably up to date, must suddenly have realised that he had gotten himself into a situation that might not be entirely to his liking and was making a determined effort to get out of his specially made little box. He was making such a noise that Tony, in exasperation, took his box out of the aircraft and left it on the ground somewhere near the truck, so he says, then went back to bed.

In the morning there was no sign of HH, just an empty box with an open door. In keeping with our original assessment of him, HH was no fool; he had worked things out for himself, decided he didn't like what was happening and escaped. Hopefully he had a better future than that which we had 'saved' him from. I couldn't help but wonder if Tony didn't have a soft heart beating under that otherwise stern martial front.

It was another early start; my impression was that our friendly

RAF personnel had experienced quite enough of oryx, the desert and the lonely outposts of what had once been part of an empire, and wanted to get back to the fleshpots of Aden as soon as they could. I knew how they felt.

The doors of the aircraft closed, the engines fired up and we were rolling down the runway, lifting off into the early morning sunshine. As we climbed it got colder and colder. I noticed a few of the more experienced men were warmly wrapped up in sweaters and other warm clothing but for most of us being cool again was a novelty that very soon wore off. After about three hours of relative misery, I looked out of one of the windows and saw the sea. A few minutes later I heard the engine notes change as the power came off, and we started our descent to the runway at Khormaksar.

Landing safely, we taxied onto the apron; the engines droned down and the doors opened to a veritable deluge of people, many of whom had been incredibly helpful to our cause, and who now wanted to have a first-hand look at our prizes.

The sudden change in temperature combined with the high humidity took a few minutes to adjust to, but I hardly noticed it as I was fully occupied trying to keep the inquisitive crowd at bay. Among the crowd were some reporters and photographers clamouring for quotes and photographs of the oryx, which were said to be among the rarest animals in the world. The more acquiescent members of our group obliged and were taken off to do their thing; for my part, I made sure to be far too involved in crowd control and keeping the animals undisturbed, to take any part in such an indignity.

After things had settled down and we had managed to get a draught of air moving through the body of the aircraft, with the help of a couple of fans that some fitters rigged up, it became increasingly obvious that we would not be moving for some time to come. Mick very generously agreed to stay and guard the oryx, and Tony invited me to his home in Aden, for breakfast and a little shopping afterwards. As Aden was a duty-free community, there were lots of goodies available at prices unheard of in Nairobi.

On our return to Khormaksar, we found a whole new scenario in place. The Beverley, which had been scheduled to fly to Nairobi on RAF business, and incidentally carry the oryx there free of charge, had broken down. The oryx in their crates had been unloaded and were standing on the hardstand beside the broken aircraft.

Once again, the R.A.F. came to our rescue; somehow, they had arranged for a commercial Bristol Britannia to delay its departure. We hastily loaded the crates, all our kit and those of us who were travelling with the animals, into the aircraft and settled ourselves down for the new ETD of eleven o'clock.

On arrival at Nairobi airport, we once again discovered Murphy was at work. The worst had happened - foot and mouth disease had been reported in the Isiolo area where our quarantine pens had been built, and there was no way the authorities, nor ourselves, were going to countenance moving the oryx up there. With nowhere else to go, we decided to take them to my home in Langata and hold them there temporarily, until we could work something out.

Ker & Downey had come to the fore, providing trucks and labour to pick up the animals from the airport. Instead of the long haul to Isiolo, the oryx now had a nice, short run to my place. We settled them in the stables, unloaded the rest of our gear, then began a search for a new home for them.

John Seago, a friend of both Ian's and mine who made his living as a professional game trapper, had his holding pens on the outskirts of Nairobi - this was just the place we were looking for. He had pens that could be very easily adapted; he had expert, experienced staff; and above all John was a man of integrity who would put all of his skills into ensuring our precious animals would want for nothing.

John readily agreed to make three secluded pens available and set his staff to padding them with vegetation, to prevent any possible injury once the oryx were released from the confines of the travelling crates. He even arranged for the Electricity Board to supply, on loan and at no cost, some infra-red heaters, which were fitted into each of the pens. While the temperature in the desert could drop to below zero at night, here in Kenya the oryx would be in the damp mist-belt, 6,000 feet above sea level, a different situation altogether to the crisp, dry cold of the desert, so they would need some additional warmth.

Between Ian, John and the odd surreptitious bottle of whisky, it took less than a day for the pens to be made ready, entirely to everybody's satisfaction. Ker & Downey stepped into the breach once again, picking up the crates from my place and shifting them over to John's. We unloaded the oryx and watched them tentatively explore their new homes, before lying down in the shelters, under the infrared lamps for a much-needed sleep.

At last, my responsibilities for the oryx had come to an end. I could leave their future to others more qualified and equipped to undertake all the grandiose plans for their growth and development, towards the ultimate objective of releasing them back into the wilds of Arabia at some future date.

Contented, happy and back at home, I lay back in a nice, deep, hot bath for the first time in nearly nine weeks. As I lackadaisically scrubbed away at the accumulated dirt, wondering whether to change the water, I took a moment to smugly congratulate myself on what we had achieved. I felt I had contributed to something quite out of the ordinary. We had successfully conducted what was, to date, the first ever rescue of a species from extinction, from its own environment.

The oryx were eventually able to move into their specially built quarantine station near Isiolo, where they would serve their time prior to qualifying for entry into the United States. America had been chosen as the best place to accommodate and breed the rare antelope back from the brink, there being a suitable location, funding and expertise all available and on call.

A lot of the money for the relocation was being provided by the Shikar Safari Club, an enthusiastic collection of wealthy hunters and environmentalists, whose president and chairman, Maurie Machris, was an old client of Ker & Downey's, as were many of the club's members. All of them, when they became aware of what we were doing, were only too ready to throw their weight behind the project.

The Arizona Zoological Park, just outside Phoenix, was eventually agreed upon as the most logical place to keep the oryx; the environment there was similar to that of the Arabian Peninsula, where the animals originated. Added to that, one of the members of the Shikar Safari Club was a major share-holder in the zoo. Taking into account the conditions of entry into the club, money was easily raised to build the necessary accommodation and help finance the transport, and the maintenance of the animals, once they were installed.

When the time came to move the animals from Kenya to the States it turned out to be quite a complicated procedure, but with many friends in high places, bureaucracy was eventually defeated, allowing common sense to break cover and the way was smoothed.

Conveniently and coincidentally, I was pushed forward for a sales trip to the States at the same time as the move, not only on behalf of Ker & Downey, but also the East African Tourist Development Board, which got on the bandwagon, along with British Airways and a couple of other local Kenyan companies. Before I knew what was happening, a comprehensive, all-inclusive itinerary was set up for me to tour around the States selling the delights of East Africa to the general American public.

I very quickly learned that not many Americans knew anything about Africa.

'Do you safari operators supply porters to carry your clients' gear from Mombasa to Nairobi?' was one question I was asked by a journalist in an interview!

'I suppose we could, if it was really necessary' I replied, 'but there is a perfectly good railway service between the two cities, and Nairobi itself is served by a first-class international airport, so actually porters are not very high on our clients' requirement lists.'

My sponsors had the necessary clout to arrange TV talk-show and radio appearances in many cities, while a number of old clients of Ker & Downey arranged for me to meet quite a few prospective clients at various venues. As a means of introducing me to what I could expect during my tour, the Shikar Safari Club had arranged for me to be in Phoenix when the three oryx arrived from their brief stopover at the quarantine station for animals arriving from overseas.

On paper and publicity-wise, I was ostensibly advising on care and well-being of the animals, but as all those details had already been well and truly addressed long before I arrived, all I had to do was be photographed in the vicinity of the oryx, looking as though I knew what I was doing when the prized specimens were released into their pens.

From then on, I don't think my feet touched the ground. To say I was out of my depth would be putting it mildly, but the response was good and I was able to arrange quite a number of safaris for the company during the tour.

For two-and-a half-months I was royally entertained by existing and prospective clients, interspersed with nights in luxury hotels, where I was able to carry out media interviews and meet with interesting people at working breakfasts, lunches and pre-dinner drinks.

I crossed the country from east to west and north to south, courtesy of British Airways. At one stage, flying out of Dallas, Texas I even had a Viscount-sized aeroplane owned by one of our clients put at my disposal, complete with full flight crew and steward. The aircraft was fitted with one seat only, an imitation Peacock Throne. I sat there like the prince of nowhere, as I flew all over Texas and into Mexico for five days, before being returned to Houston and my less exalted mainstream itinerary.

I wound up my American trip with five days in Los Angeles and three in San Francisco, where I was shown the sights by Dr Lee Talbot and his wife, whose research and subsequent book had initially brought the plight of the oryx to the public's attention. I had previously worked with Lee and his wife in the Ngorongoro Crater, so our reunion in the bohemia of San Francisco was a change of venue and a novel experience.

My British Airways sponsors had told me that were I to continue my homeward journey east to west, it would save them money and I was only too happy to oblige. I had no real interest in returning to Africa via Europe, so touching down in various Pacific islands, including New Zealand and Australia was too good a chance to be missed.

New Zealand, in particular, was of tremendous interest as I had read extensively of the problem they had with the explosion of introduced species of deer. This led me to wonder if there might be a way to exploit the situation commercially, along the lines of our East African business.

To chum the water, I enlisted the aid of a stringer on one of New Zealand's larger newspapers and gave him a broad outline of what I had in mind. I made sure he had my time of arrival down pat and the gambit paid off. I was met in Auckland by not only one of the newspaper's reporters, but also by a few interested hunters. On clearing customs and immigration, I was whisked off to my hotel, dumped my bags in my room, and joined my new friends in the bar. Between us we gave the reporter enough copy to keep his editor happy for days.

For the next two days I was ferried around the country, meeting hunters of all persuasions, drinking copious quantities of beer and eating an inordinate number of pies, something I had never come across before as a regular meal. While I had a great time and met some very interesting people, it soon became clear that there was virtually no way my fanciful ideas would fit into the country.

Everything was so different to Africa that I couldn't see even the most ardent of our clients contemplating hunting under the conditions offered in New Zealand. In any case, the government had a quasi-scientific program running, whereby they paid young men to go out into the hills and mountains culling deer on a bounty system, so they certainly wouldn't want a bunch of dilettantes traipsing all over the place demanding the best heads be left for them to hunt as trophies.

It was a nice thought that hadn't cost very much, and while it had produced a definite 'no', the trip enabled me to meet many great people. It was then on to Australia, Mauritius and home.

On finally arriving back in Nairobi, having enjoyed myself beyond my wildest imagination and lived at a level way beyond my dreams, I was really glad to get back home and come down to earth.

At the office I was gratified to find that all the late-night telephone calls, urgent telegrams and other communications I had fired off had added up to nearly a full booking for our hunters, all twenty-two of them, covering just on two years. On top of this we had serious enquiries for undertaking the logistical support for five full-scale movie productions. Financially for the company, and the other sponsors of my trip, it had been well worth all the effort.

This had been a one-off experience, facilitated largely by the generosity of the contributors who bore most of the expense. Nevertheless, I would have very serious thoughts about doing it all again.

18

After three years in the management side of the safari business I was getting itchy feet. Temperamentally and intellectually, I was not really suited to life in an office, nor to living in a town or city.

As a result, I don't think it was much of a surprise to the company when I told them I thought it was time for me to move on. Not having thought things through, I suddenly found myself at a loose end. I had no real objective in sight and with the rapidly changing and uncertain political situation in East Africa, I thought the time might be right for a move back to Australia.

Lorna and I talked our situation over, coming to the sensible conclusion that I should go over and try to get some form of employment, while she and Anne, our youngest, would go back to Arusha where the bulk of her family still lived, until I could arrange for the pair of them to follow me. The timing was fortuitous, as shortly after our arrival in Arusha, the local school advertised for a matron to take over the boarding accommodation for their younger pupils – a job for which Lorna was eminently suited. Within days she was engaged, provided with accommodation, and, best of all, Anne was included in the package as a student.

With that taken care of, I flew to Perth and started looking for employment. Western Australia was terra incognito as far as I was concerned and after a few days I quickly came to realise that no one was interested in African experience. What little Australian work experience I had had been eroded away in the years I'd been away from the country.

Had I been single, I could doubtless have found all sorts of interesting jobs in the back country, but with a wife and child I had to try and think of the future, where their life could be more conventional, and there was a good school.

As Perth didn't look too promising, I bought a second-hand Land Rover, fitted it out and decided I would set off for the Northern Territory and its capital, Darwin. I knew the Land Rover was not a good choice for Australia, or virtually anywhere, but consoled myself with the fact that I knew the model better than I knew any of the other makes on offer.

I thought that what qualifications I had might be more appreciated in the frontier environments of Australia, than in built-up areas. I decided to take the long way to Darwin in case something popped up en route, first heading in the opposite direction, down to the most south-westerly spot on the continent, Albany, thence to Esperance, Kalgoorlie and from there across the Nullarbor Plain until I came to Port Augusta. From Port Augusta I planned to drive north alongside the railway track to Alice Springs and, finally, Darwin.

All seemed to be going well, until I left Kalgoorlie. I had put my Land Rover into a garage for a service and check-over in this gold-mining town, before tackling the desert. Having settled my bill and making sure I had all I imagined I would need for the maximum two days and one-night crossing, I set off. Before I had made even a hundred miles, I was in trouble – the clutch started slipping. From then on it was a case of: drive a little, stop, let everything cool down, then repeat the sequence. Using this method, it took me three-and-a-half days to reach Port Augusta!

I'd been reluctant to turn back, even though I probably should have, and did not have the tools to fix the problem myself out in the desert. In Port Augusta, I was lucky enough to find a very sympathetic small garage owner who put in the hard yards to help me.

He very quickly diagnosed the problem. The mechanic in Kalgoorlie had looked into the gear box and seeing it was apparently low - normal for Land Rovers - and not being aware that Land Rover gear boxes were fitted with dip-sticks, filled it up to the top. It was only when under heavy loading in the 'bull-dust' and loose surface of the track that the heat and the pressure blew the oil-seal. In his view I had been lucky to make it this far. To try and save me a little money, he thought he could resuscitate the clutch plate, the main cause of the trouble.

The trip north was long and wearisome; the car wasn't going well. It was very hot, and there was no real road, as such. The only way forward was to follow the empty beer cans. The trick, I soon learned, was to go where the cans were fewest, as this was the new, faster track. Wherever I came across lots of cans, that indicated the previous travellers had become bogged in sand holes, and had taken their time to extricate themselves.

I camped overnight at a stock watering point and after a trip of about 30 hours all up I finally made it to Alice Springs and booked into an hotel. I was tired, dirty and thoroughly disenchanted with my idea of coming back to Australia. However, after a good shower, a couple of beers and a decent feed I found my attitude changing. 'The Alice', I told myself, looked interesting, albeit dusty, and more than a little flyblown.

I spent the next three days camped at the hotel and looked around to see if there were any prospects of employment. If there were, I didn't find them.

From there I headed north up the Stuart Highway to Tennant Creek, where I had the address of a friend of Lorna's, who was doing bookkeeping and house management on a cattle run. I sounded out the owners, to see if they might know of anything for me, but, again, there was nothing for a man with a wife and small child. I hit the road again.

In Darwin, I found myself some affordable accommodation and

set about looking for something in earnest. I was interviewed on Radio Darwin about some of the things I had experienced in Africa and as a result became friendly with one of the listeners, a man who ran a diving and boat-selling business out of Doctor's Gully. Through him, I learned that the federal government in Canberra, who at that time ran the Territory directly, were looking for someone to open up the Coburg Peninsula, with a view to turning it into a national park.

For the first time since arriving in Perth, I thought I had actually made the right decision in returning to Australia. The job was right up my street. That, too, was the view of Canberra's representative in the territory, whom I met after applying for the job. The man told me I had the job a few days later, after he had been in touch with his headquarters.

I held off passing the news on to Lorna, at least until I had found out the terms and conditions of the appointment and been offered a formal contract. That was just as well, as two weeks later, the government representative called.

'Sorry,' he said, 'my recommendation was overturned by someone higher up and the job's been given to someone else.'

Needless to say, I wasn't very happy but had to accept the situation.

'Thanks for your efforts on my behalf,' I said to him.

In the meantime, Eddie Connellan of Connellan Airways in the Territory had been talking to me about a scheme he had been cooking up with the government and the Native Affairs people, to harvest the buffalo running wild in Arnhem Land. The idea was to provide a meat ration for the Aboriginal people who attended missions in the area.

At that time, there was not a lot of factual information about the area, so he wondered if I would be interested in having a look, to see if it was doable or not. Firstly, while the stories had it that the buffalo were there in their thousands, these numbers needed verifying. Secondly, we needed to check the access, and ascertain what movement within the area would be like. If those problems were solvable, we then needed to assess what equipment would be needed to make it a viable enterprise.

I took Eddie up on his offer, made the necessary preparations, and set off. I made it to what I estimated was somewhere between the Mary and the Wildman Rivers and spent about five days poking about. There were many buffalo wherever I went; the going varied from passable to wet, but with the right equipment and season, harvesting wouldn't be too big a problem, I thought. From my very quick trip I was reasonably sure his idea was a good one, and feasible, always providing the back-up was in place.

My whole trip took me about two weeks. On returning to Darwin I got in touch with Eddie to give him a run down on what I had seen and my opinion on the feasibility of his idea. At the same time, I stressed that I hadn't actually had the time nor resources to do much more than prove it was possible to get in there and to establish that there appeared to be plenty of buffalo. I further suggested that before getting too excited, it might be a good idea to fly over the whole area a couple of times to confirm that I had not just 'lucked' onto an area that was densely populated. He agreed, saying he would get in touch with me as soon as he had time to organise the flights.

While I was waiting for Eddie to let me know what the next move was, the government representative who had interviewed me for the Coburg job called me again. It appeared the man Canberra had put forward to develop the new national park had, after flying over the area and realising how remote it was, decided it was not for him!

'Would you be interested in re-applying?' the Government man asked.

Considering the attitude Canberra had taken over my first application, coupled with the reservations expressed by the other applicant, I re-thought the whole project over. I came to the conclusion that maybe it would be a trifle rash to subject Lorna and Anne to living in such a remote area as their first introduction to Australia. I declined.

About a week after having given my decision, I got a call from Eddie; one of his larger aircraft had a major problem, which was going to take all his spare capital to get back into the air. As a result, he was going to have to put his buffalo harvesting scheme on the back burner until things settled down.

With both my likely prospects down the drain, and having been in Darwin nearly five months, living mainly on capital, I had to make a decision. I could either get out while I still had some money in my pocket, or stay on and hope. I decided to go.

I packed up my Land Rover and headed for Perth. Seeing no reason to retrace my journey up through the centre, I turned west at Katherine and headed for Wyndham, where I was able to meet up with one of Lorna's relatives, who was working for the Department of Native Affairs there. It was quite a change from farming in Kenya, but he and his family seemed to have settled down quite happily.

I spent a very pleasant night with them before setting out again for the two-day trip to Broome. Discretion being the better part of valour, I remember camping well off the track that night, having been warned in Wyndham to be vigilant as there were some very unsavoury characters roaming about the area. Luckily, I didn't meet any of them and was in Broome well before midday the next day.

Having had a puncture in one of my rear tyres the day before, rather than fix it myself I left the car at the garage, asking the mechanic to mend the puncture and put the good wheel back on the car, returning the spare to its normal place. I also asked him to top up the fuel, oil and water, including the spare water tank on the back of the truck, having used quite a bit camping the night before, while I went across the road to the pub for a drink and some lunch.

After lunch I went back across the road, paid my bill at the garage and jumped into the car, carelessly, without checking any of the work that had been done other than noting the good wheel was back in its proper place.

After going about thirty plus miles into the Eighty Mile Beach track I noted the temperature gauge was climbing up into the red, so stopped and checked under the bonnet to find the radiator core had shaken loose from the top reservoir. I plugged up what I could and with sixty spare gallons on the back decided I would probably get to

Port Hedland before I ran out of water. I pressed on, stopping every now and again to cool down and top up the reservoir.

After about 40 miles of this stop-start going and realising I was using water faster than I had anticipated, I noticed on the horizon to the south what looked like a windmill with a tank underneath it. The windmill was turning, so it was worth diverting to on the off chance that I may be able to top up my tank. This would ensure I certainly had enough water to get to Port Hedland.

On arrival at the windmill, I came across one of the most desolate sites in the world. There was a derelict, rusty old Quonset hut, a wind-blown, tired old pepper tree and vast amounts of tangled up rusty, barbed wire. Standing amongst the wire up, against the hut, was a filthy, dirty old man hammering what appeared to be a beaten-out prune tin across what had once been one of the windows in the hut.

I got out of the car. 'G'day,' I called, and started to walk over to the man. 'I've got a problem with my radiator. Can I top up my water tank?'

The man took absolutely no notice; he just went on hammering. Thinking he might be deaf I started to repeat my story in a louder tone of voice.

He stopped hammering and looked at me. 'You'll get no f-ing help here mate.' He then went back to his work.

All thoughts of courtesy went out of the window. My response was immediate, spontaneous, and equally pithy. I then went back to the Land Rover, started it and drove to the windmill. I filled up my water tank and drove off, with not another word exchanged between us.

ONCE IN PORT HEDLAND I headed for the only garage in town.

'We're backed up with work, mate,' the mechanic told me. He nodded to my Land Rover: 'Can't possibly get around to that for at least a week, if not longer.'

The mechanic did, however, allow me to use the garage and his tools to work on the car myself, adding a little help here and there when he could. During a 'smoko' break, I told the people at the garage of my experience with the old man out at the water tank.

Apparently, he was well known in the district, had been there for years and was considered one of the 'characters' around the place. From my point of view, they were welcome to him.

Having installed a new radiator in my car and said goodbye to my new friends at the garage, I once again made a stupid, illogical decision to take the nearly-disused, old road through Marble Bar, and Meekatharra. On paper, this appeared considerably shorter than the new coastal road through Onslow, Carnarvon and Geraldton, and then on to Perth.

After about 200 miles along the track, I noticed the vehicle swaying a good deal, much more than was indicated by the poor going. When I got out, I found that the wheel which had been changed in Broome had obviously not been tightened up properly; another few miles and the wheel would have come off the hub completely. Three of the five wheel nuts were gone and the threads of all the bolts were rubbed nearly smooth. Even if I could find more nuts, the possibility of getting them to hold were pretty slim

I was now about half way between Marble Bar and Meekatharra, and with only one or two vehicles per month travelling this way, now that the new coastal road was open, I didn't think there was much chance of getting any help from any passing traveller.

I sat on the side of the road and tried to think of a solution. I had enough food and water to last me quite a few days, if I was careful, but that seemed to be only putting off the inevitable. Unless a vehicle came along, which was not very likely, or I could do something myself, I reckoned I had just about had it.

I had a large wheel spanner, a piece of piping as an extension to it, a hammer and some other tools, and a nearly full can of oil. When I rooted about in the tool boxes in the back of the car, I came across five nearly new wheel nuts. With all that at hand, surely, I thought, I must be able to get some nuts onto the wheel. I reckoned that if I could get three nuts in place, and drove carefully, I could at least make it to Meekatharra.

After two days of jumping on the shaft of the wheel spanner and the liberal application of oil, I managed to force four wheel nuts tight onto the hub. They were so firmly fastened that I doubted anyone would ever get them off without a cutting torch.

As soon as the fourth nut was locked on, I threw everything into the back of the car and set off for Meekatharra at high speed – well, at least as fast as I was prepared to go on the shocking surface.

I arrived just before dark. I had no idea how many hotels there were in Meekatharra, but stopped at the first one I saw and got a bed – in a communal room. Fortunately, the dorm was empty, not surprisingly as the whole place was basic in the extreme, but at least it was a bed. I was able to have a shower of sorts and a surprisingly good meal. All in all, I was ready for the next round the following morning.

I looked over the car carefully this time. Everything seemed to be in order, so I started it up and set off on the last leg of my trip. I made it into Perth and then onto Margaret River, where I was able to stay with another ex-Kenya resident. He had emigrated to Australia to try his hand at farming in the newly-opened-up area.

Having come to the conclusion that I was unlikely to find suitable employment easily, and anxious to see Lorna and Anne after so long away, I sold my Land Rover to the first person who came to see it, sorted out my gear and went back up to Perth to book the first passage I could back to Nairobi.

With some dismay and distress, I received the news that all available seats to Africa out of Perth were booked solid for the next three weeks, and the best that could be done for me was to have my name put on a standby list in case of a cancellation. It was a Thursday afternoon, so rather than heading back to Margaret River, I decided to spend the weekend getting all my paperwork done for an immediate take off, in the unlikely event of a cancellation.

The next day, I took my time making sure I was cleared to leave by those government departments involved, such as taxation and health, before leisurely wandering along the street to a travel-agent's office to pay in advance for a seat. I wanted to ensure there would be no hold-ups if a seat became vacant. The agent I spoke to was a very pleasant young lady who seemed to have very little to do and appeared to be only too happy for me to regale her with the stories of my trip around the western part of the country, plus a few stories from Africa.

As I was leaving the agency, she mentioned that she would be on duty the next day, Saturday, and if I wanted to call in, she would bring me up to date on any cancellations. As a further inducement, she added there would be a cup of coffee available.

The next morning, at what I imagined was a suitable time, about 11, I called in at the agency to find my new friend on the telephone. She waved me to a seat and continued on the phone; a few minutes later she put her hand over the mouthpiece.

'I'm on a call to our Melbourne office,' she said to me. 'They want to know if we can fill a seat, which has just become available for tomorrow's flight to Mauritius, and on to Nairobi. Can you be ready?'

Somebody up there was definitely looking after me – not only then, but immediately after my arrival in Nairobi.

The day after my arrival in Kenya, I went into town to touch base with 'useful' people who might be able to put me onto some activity to top up the exchequer, which was getting pretty slim by now. I called into my old office at K & D. While having a chat with my successor, two Americans walked into the office off the street.

'Do you have someone who'd be available for a week to two, to show us around the countryside,' one of the Americans asked the staff. 'We're scouting for locations for a television series. If you could find someone, maybe he could even give us some ideas for stories.'

My successor suggested to his receptionist that she seat the two men in the waiting room, while he finished with me, then bring them into see him, so he could discuss their request in more detail.

As I walked through the reception area one of the two Americans looked up and called over to me. 'Hey! Just the man we're looking for!'

It turned out he had been one of the assistant directors on the movie *Hatari!* with John Wayne, and remembered me from my time with the Tanganyika Game Department.

As it happened, K & D were fully booked, with not a hunter to spare and certainly not for two weeks, so my calling in, as far as everybody was concerned, was timely. I was hired on the spot as a K & D hunter, fitted out with a suitable vehicle, a driver/assistant and all the other bits and pieces thought necessary for a two-week run around Kenya and Tanganyika.

We set off and I learned that the TV people were looking for sites for a series about a veterinarian working in Africa. Having 'done' Kenya, we were passing through Nairobi on our way to Tanganyika. Driving down Government Road, I suddenly blacked out. I was behind the wheel, but luckily we were going very slowly. No damage resulted to the car or anyone in the vicinity, but I fell seriously ill – my appendix had burst and I was in need of urgent surgery. That ended my part in the location-finding safari and, actually, the whole idea of filming in Africa. The two producers were very kind and visited me a couple of times in hospital, but it was clear there would be no follow-up or work for me to do on their behalf.

The producers had begun to realise just how complicated and expensive shooting the series in Africa would be, compared to doing it in the 'Land of Make Believe', where everything, including trained animals, were readily available and on call. The series, which came to be known as *Daktari*, was subsequently filmed in America.

It was disappointing, but not really unexpected.

On my discharge from hospital I couldn't go down to Arusha to join Lorna, as she was living in accommodation provided by the school and was committed to stay there until the expiry of her temporary contract. Instead, I took up my brother-in-law Don's offer to go up and recuperate on his farm in Timau, just north of Nanyuki. It was all very convenient, as he had just come back into Nairobi, having completed a safari. He had two weeks off before going out again with his next client, which meant that he could take me up to the farm and be there while I settled in and got a bit stronger.

After I'd had a couple of days sitting around the house feeling sorry for myself, I needed to get out and do something. Don suggested we drive down to Naro Moru to see George Adamson, whom we both knew. George was living on Sherbrooke-Walker's farm, and had been appointed as the technical director for the shooting of a film.

The movie was the big screen adaptation of a book, *Born Free*.

19

In 1960, Joy Adamson's book, *Born Free*, was published. The story of the exploits of Joy and George raising a lion cub, Elsa, to maturity became an instant international bestseller.

After the publication of the book a number of aspiring producers had acquired the screen rights, some having even gone as far as sending people to Africa to look for locations to film the story. All had given up - the problems of filming the story in Kenya appeared to be just too great.

Some years went by until the screen rights became the property of two enterprising producers, Paul Radin and Sam Jaffe, who were convinced that a film was possible, if approached in the right manner. They managed to convince Columbia Pictures to put up the money and in-spanned Carl Foreman to act as executive producer and write the script.

A pilot company was sent out to Kenya, along with four lions, two females and two cubs, which had been acquired from a circus in Italy. Accompanying the lions were two young German handlers, Monika and Ruth, together with a skeleton crew consisting of a director, production manager, camera operator, and a few actors, including the two stars, Virginia McKenna and her husband, Bill Travers.

The idea was that Virginia and Bill, playing Joy and George, would get acquainted with the lions under the tutelage of the two German women, while the rest of the crew, including George Adamson as technical director, went around selecting locations, working out scenes and doing whatever else was thought necessary to get things up and running.

I knew George and when my brother-in-law, Don, and I sat down for a cup of tea with him, during my post-appendectomy convalescence, it soon became obvious that George had some serious reservations about the plan to introduce the star actors to the captive lions. While the rest of the crew was living in the big farmhouse, George was camping in a tent, next to a chicken wire enclosure holding the Italian lions.

Don and I looked at the lionesses and were not at all surprised at George's concerns. The cats looked decidedly surly and uncooperative. When we were told by George how the two German women went about their training, it was even more obvious that something very unpleasant was going to happen in the very near future. The lions were treated as though they were still in the circus, being subjected to the crack of a whip, or a piece of meat dangling on the end of a stick. When the trainers went into the cage with them, they did so wearing leather gauntlets and boots up over their knees. It was my view that the lions, like all cats in captivity, would be totally unreliable.

On hearing that I was out of work, George had the bright idea of offering me a job there and then.

'You can sit outside the cage with a loaded double-barrelled rifle and shoot the two adult lions when they start to eat the actors,' George said.

As the offer included accommodation and keep, it was too good to refuse, so I accepted. The next morning, I moved onto the site, where I stayed and worked for the next 22 months until the location shooting was finally wound up.

After a few weeks, it became obvious that the whole project was going nowhere fast. Tensions were high, tempers short, and progress slow to nil; doom and gloom was the order of the day. It was into this somewhat dire situation that Carl Foreman arrived to discuss progress with the other two producers and make a decision on the future of the enterprise.

Initially, it looked as though the decision would be to close the whole thing down and follow all the other companies in deciding it was just too difficult a film to produce. One evening, after a very gloomy dinner, Carl joined George and myself at the bar. I think he'd had enough of film people, and had sought out the two of us, the only 'locals' on set, as an escape.

Both George and I had been very sceptical of the way things were being handled and we were convinced that the director was out of his depth. The lions, we thought, were totally unsuitable and dangerous for Virginia, Bill and all the others involved with them - there was a serious chance of someone being hurt if things continued along the current lines.

Being well lubricated, and with absolutely nothing to lose, we gave Carl our unexpurgated view of the whole set up. We tore it apart and told him we felt the whole approach wrong. Based on nothing more than inner conviction, we told him, in our drunken state, that we could get the whole thing together and up and running if he would give us free rein.

Our arguments must have been more eloquent than we imagined, for the next morning Carl asked us to come into the office and tell him in more coherent detail how we would go about changing things. Neither of us had any idea of how films were made, but we both knew quite a bit about animals. Our proposals were based more on using ways to manipulate the animals to get responses, rather than try to 'train' them in the more traditional fashion.

We also suggested that the current director and the two German ladies be side-lined, together with the overseas lions. We would rattle the trees locally for 'pet' lions, as they were more likely to respond to the methods we had in mind.

Carl and the two other producers were reluctant to throw in the towel, so Carl gave us approval to try our approach.

'OK,' Carl said, 'I'll come back in 90 days and if you can show me what I want, we'll go ahead.'

Now, we had to find some lions to put our theory into practice. Joy weighed in – she knew that an army unit, the Kenya Regiment, had two lions as mascots, and we were able to borrow them. A defrocked Italian cardinal, who now lived with a very glamorous wife on a farm on Lake Naivasha, had a veritable pride of tame lions, so we were able to draw on those, as well.

The Nairobi National Park's wildlife orphanage had a big lion, Ugas, whom I had known since he was a cub. Ian Grimwood had asked me to go up to the border between Kenya and Ethiopia a few years earlier to collect four cheetah cubs from a police post. The cheetahs had been seized from some Somalis and when I flew up in a Cessna, I found the police had also confiscated a lion cub.

All the cats were in the possession of the District Commissioner, who was having trouble coping with them. I took the cheetah, as that was what I had flown up for, but the lion cub was surplus to requirements.

'What should I do with him?' the DC asked me.

'Not sure,' I said. 'Probably the best thing to do would be to hit him on the head. Pet lions are a pain and expensive to keep. Besides, not too many people are competent to raise them.' With that I left him with the cub.

The DC, apparently, had not taken my advice seriously and had looked for someone to take on the cub. Not surprisingly, there were no offers, or rather none acceptable. In the end he offered the cub to the National Parks; they had accepted and Ugas, as the lion was now known, was growing into a fine young male.

Some two years later, George and I were able to incorporate Ugas into our growing stable of lions taking part in the film. In fact, despite my earlier advice on what to do with him, Ugas and I became great friends, to the extent that I was able to do some really tricky scenes with him without any serious risk to either of us.

By this time, we had 10 lions. They were mostly young and George and I started getting them used to us. We took them for long walks in the bush and played with them, letting them roll and fall about us. George would sometimes sleep in one of the lion pens with his favourite lioness, Mara. He would also let Mara sleep on his bed, where she generally took up most of the space in the tent, to his exclusion.

I, on the other hand, slept in a long wooden shed split down the centre by wire netting; my bed was on one side, while four or five of the young lions had access to the other side of my room from their pens. The idea was that the lions would become so accustomed to my presence, virtually 24 hours a day, that they would become, in effect, my pride and be quite capable of doing nearly anything required of them, provided I was somewhere nearby to give them confidence. Eventually the lions became so relaxed that they would go out with nearly anyone who wasn't too nervous around them; this made things much easier from a filming point of view.

The original director's concept was that the four circus lions could be trained, or cajoled into doing exactly what he wanted them to do. By contrast, we were not trying to train the lions; we were, instead, building up trust with them, and working out what they were capable of doing. Our plan was that we would then work with the director to work out how the lions' behaviours could be incorporated into the script, and which lion would be best for whatever piece of action was required.

At the end of the three-month period, when Carl made his next visit, the actors were walking confidently in the bush with the lions running freely with them.

We had got the lions so used to us that we could pretty much do what we liked around them. George and I even had a couple of the lionesses sufficiently amenable that we could take them into the bush in the back of the car, let them out where they might kill a warthog or a Thompson's gazelle, and then allow us to take the carcass off them. We would then put the kill in the car, go back to the compound, pull the carcass out - often with the help of the lionesses - and dump it in their cage for them to eat.

Walking with lions and the film's co-star, Bill Travers

Our efforts convinced Carl and others that the film was now a possibility. This was enhanced when a new and very enlightened director, Jimmy Hill, came on board, replacing the first one. Right from the jump off, we could tell Jimmy was different.

'I'm not going to tell you what we should be doing with the lions,' Jimmy said. 'I am going to tell you what we *think* the lions should be doing, and you see if you can get them to do that.'

That was easy, and a better way to work with the animals. We could control the lions' responses by what we fed them – if a lion was full, it would be easy going and lazy; if it was looking forward to food it might be more animated and responsive. With 48 hours or more notice, and weather permitting, we could adjust the lions' diets and activities and also pick which lion we thought would be best for the action required.

After the go-ahead was confirmed, we ended up with about 22 lions, all capable of doing one thing or another. As a bonus, we already had quite a bit of footage in the can, from scenes the previous director had shot during the first three months of us and the cast getting to know the lions.

Rather than 'training' the lions, we built up trust with them

I have to admit that after more than fifty-five years since the release of the film, in 1966, some of my chronology and details of all that happened during the filming of *Born Free* might be amiss, but a number of episodes stay in my memory.

Having progressed from my job of sitting outside the enclosure, in order to shoot the lions once they started eating the actors, I became more involved in the maintenance and wellbeing of the animals on-site. Other handlers had been brought in and were undertaking some of the more straightforward scenes, under the ever-watchful eye of George. I did, however, get involved in some of the more difficult scenes.

There is a big fight scene in the film, so important that it warranted another 'expert' on lions to be brought in from Holland, to advise on how it could be staged. The objectives for this scene were non-negotiable. These were: firstly, that the correct lion, Elsa, had to win the fight; secondly, the fight had to take place in a very limited space as the camera to be used was a special one that could not be moved or panned; and finally, no lion would be hurt or injured in any way as a result of the fight, otherwise the animal rights campaigners would descend on us like a ton of bricks. It was feared that any adverse publicity could wreck the film before it even hit the screens.

When briefed, the worthy visiting expert threw his hands up in horror and exclaimed in broken English that it was impossible and he wanted nothing to do with the idea. He promptly returned to Nairobi and from there home to Holland. With no help from the outside world forthcoming, Paul Radin, Sam Jaffe, and Jimmy called me into the office and told me what had happened.

'Do you think you can work something out?' I was asked.

'Why not fake it?' I said. 'The action has to take place in filtering moonlight – we could easily dress a couple of our people up in lion skins, have them tumble about with lots of dust and bushes to hide what's really happening. With suitable sound effects, no one will be the wiser.'

'No,' I was told by the production team. 'It has to be authentic, 100 per cent real.'

I thought about the problem, and the demands.

'I have an idea,' I said, 'It's going to take a wee bit of time, but I think we can do it.'

It occurred to me that by making use of the animals' natural instincts, and taking a little time to condition them to the situation, it might just be possible to produce what was wanted. This came with the warning that it would take time to set up, and most likely be limited to one opportunity only, with little chance for any repeat takes or nonsense like that. With no other options on the horizon, the decision was made to take the chance.

The general plan we came up with was simple - once we had found a suitable site. The best location we found was the top of a small hill, on a farm in the Ndoldol area, not far from our base at Naro Moru. The hilltop itself was fairly clear of scrub and just big enough for the anticipated action to take place, while the sides and bottom had sufficient cover to hide a netting enclosure, which we strung around the whole of the lower part of the hill.

The location also provided a nice scenic approach for the 'wild' lioness, whom Elsa would fight, to arrive on the scene. This made it quite easy to put the plan into action. 'Elsa' was situated in a small enclosure on one side of the hill, where, about half way up, a tent was erected against the wire at the trap-gate, which allowed her access to the top of the hill. This was necessary, as in the story Elsa was sleeping in a tent between George and Joy, when she hears the wild lions approaching. She goes out to investigate, and gets tangled up in a fight.

On the bottom of the opposite slope of the hill, we housed the 'wild' lioness; her enclosure was attached to the main operational perimeter by a tunnel and two trap-gates, one at each end. Both lion enclosures were far enough apart to ensure no visual communication between the cats, although they were able to hear each other calling. Monika and Ruth (they were still on the set at this point), acted as handlers for each of the two lionesses. In this case they were suited to the job, as strong personalities and loud, authoritative voices were the order of the day.

The two-week conditioning procedure prior to filming was that each morning the lioness playing Elsa was allowed up onto the top of the hill and fed there, to accustom her to getting used to leaving the tent and moving confidently up to where the fight was to take place.

As soon as she had finished her food, her handler would then shout in her loudest voice, 'Raus!' and chase her back to her safe area, where she would then be petted and made a fuss of to let her know she had done the right thing.

Once Elsa had left the fight area, the 'wild' lioness would be fed in the same spot, but in her case she was allowed to spend much of the day up there; the idea was that she would develop a sort of territorial attachment to the top of the hill and be reluctant to have any other lioness usurp her.

When her time was up she, too, was encouraged back to her quarters by her handler. In this manner, we hoped to establish a pattern of behaviour that would enable both lionesses to approach the fight area confidently, and yet scoot back to their respective quarters no matter what, when shouted at by their handlers. The key to success lay in the timing. We had to keep the cats on edge, each knowing there was another, strange lioness in the vicinity, and timing the action to take place before they got too complacent, hearing each other calling from opposite sides of the hill.

On the day selected for shooting the scene tensions were of such an order that I felt constrained to ask Jimmy to clear everyone not necessary for the action away from the site, to ensure there were no untoward distractions, which might disrupt the animals' routine.

Those of us left on-site held our breath. When the two lionesses met at the top of the hill for the first time, they started snarling and spitting at each other, with the 'wild' lioness standing her ground for her territory. Next, a real knock-down drag-out fight occurred, much to the delight of the director and camera operator.

'Cut!' Jimmy yelled, when he reckoned he'd got enough of the actual fight.

'Raus! Raus!' yelled the two German handlers at the top of their voices. The two lionesses stopped their bickering, turned and scooted back to their quarters post haste. Luckily, 'Elsa' was the last off the site, and with the camera still rolling, this gave the impression she had been victorious, as she returned to the tent.

Pleasingly, for the film's reputation, neither of the lionesses received as much as a scratch from the fight; this was just typical lion behaviour. In fact, three weeks after they got back to Naro Moru, the 'wild' lioness produced three cubs - nobody had known beforehand that she was pregnant.

ANOTHER SCENE FRAUGHT with tension was that of a lion killing a woman washing her clothes in the river. It had to be dramatic and realistic, yet obviously it was vital that no one should get hurt – this was not an easy thing with a big male lion looking as though he was bent on killing a human.

To get the shot, we built a cleared track through the thorn bush on the riverbank, stacking either side with cut branches to ensure the lion followed the designated route. We had to sweep the surface of the track clean, as lions, like any other soft-footed animals, prefer not to tread on thorns or other obstructions if they can avoid it.

For this scene we selected Ugas, the male rescued from the Ethiopian Border. His 'home' cage was set out of sight of the camera at the far end of the constructed path. At the action end, a camera cage was built for the camera and crew. Immediately alongside the camera cage, but out of shot, we built an enclosure of railway sleepers, behind which stood a man with a rifle, a goat and her handler, and myself.

When everything was ready and with the cameras rolling, we tethered the goat outside the sleeper enclosure and I called Ugas. He knew me well and generally would come to the side of his compound if I called him.

As everyone watched, eagerly hoping all would go according to plan, Ugas performed magnificently. He strode along the path through the bush as though it was the most natural of settings. As soon as he got to the edge of the river bank and looked over towards us, he saw the goat. Immediately, he dropped onto his belly, twitched his tail from side to side and gathered his hind legs underneath him, ready to attack, exactly as a hunting wild lion would have done.

At the moment Ugas launched himself the man holding the goat jerked it into the enclosure. At the same time, I jumped out, in order to catch the lion and distract him from trying to follow the goat. Personally, I thought the first take was great, so I was more than a little surprised to hear the director – the one before Jimmy - call for another take.

I sighed. This was what we were in the business for, so I got Ugas back into his cage and we tried again. Four times, we went through the routine with no appreciable improvement as far as I could see, although it was evident that the lion was getting more and more disenchanted with the whole procedure. He was becoming less ready to be distracted and fussed over, so when a fifth take was called for, I baulked.

'That's it, we're not going to do anymore,' I said.

A full-blown argument ensued at which I was accused of being 'yellow' and not knowing how to do my job, amongst other things. In the end, I agreed to a fifth take, on the proviso that the director took my place to retrieve Ugas at the appropriate moment.

The idea was promptly dropped, and it is worth noting, for the record, that the first take was the one used in the final cut. I was not unhappy when this director was binned, in favour of Jimmy Hill.

THE FINAL SCENE that exercised the ingenuity of all involved, was one that called for Elsa to be seen sitting in the middle of the road, waiting and watching wistfully for Joy to return from a trip to Nairobi.

Lions in their natural state do not sit much. It is generally an intermediate position between standing and lying, and certainly not a position they sustain for any length of time, unless there is something that really catches their attention. Therefore, to try and get a lioness to sit for any length of time, looking up the road, wistfully or not, was asking for something close to the impossible. But the script called for it, and the few seconds it was scheduled to appear on the screen were apparently essential in making a point in the story.

Initially, I tried to teach one of the young lionesses we had on hand to play Elsa to 'sit', as I would a dog. I put a collar around her neck and lifted her head up while pressing her back down with no positive results whatsoever. In fact, rather the reverse. I tried for days, until I became convinced we were never going to get a result. In any case, that route was totally inconsistent with our stated approach, which was not to train the animals but rather manipulate their natural instincts to get what we wanted.

Some other strategy was required, but what? George came up with an idea – we would try and attract the lioness's attention by offering something exciting in the distance to get her sufficiently interested to sit up, long enough for the shot to be taken. That made sense, but how were we to anchor her in the middle of the roadway, until we could attract her attention with whatever the distant object was?

The solution turned out to be simplicity itself. We dug a big hole in the middle of the road and covered it with a strong piece of plywood, which in turn was covered with soil off the road to camouflage it. We then cut a small hole in the middle of the board and George got into the hole, with a chicken. The plywood cover was put in place and the lioness brought on to the set. George, sitting in his hole, kept her interested by teasing her with the chicken, whilst up the road, out of sight of the camera, we got one of the younger members of the company to cover himself totally with a bed sheet.

At the appropriate moment, the man in the sheet jumped out into the line of sight of the lioness, and hopped up and down waving the sheet to attract her attention. As soon as she saw him, she sat up beautifully, exactly as we had hoped, and held her position sufficiently long enough to satisfy even the most demanding of cameramen. After that, she was taken back to her compound and given a suitable reward for doing her job so well. I have no idea what happened to the chicken, but I suspect that it finished up in a cooking pot somewhere, as I never saw it again.

When recounting these anecdotes, it may appear that it wasn't too difficult to achieve the results required, but in fact a great deal of effort, tension and, most of all, luck were the main ingredients to their success. I feel a great deal of satisfaction from having been involved in the setting up and planning of these scenes.

The final product, *Born Free* turned out to be a great success, and remains one of the cinema world's timeless films, to be enjoyed by generations to come. It was a privilege to be involved, even in a small way.

20

During the filming of *Born Free* I had rented a farm next to the Sherbrooke-Walker place, where the movie was being made, and moved Lorna and Anne up from Arusha.

Among my responsibilities had been the feeding of all of the animals on set. To ensure there was always meat on hand for the 22 lions involved in the production I had collected all sorts of surplus horses from around Naro Moru, Nanyuki, Thompson's Falls, Nakuru and anywhere else I could find them.

Due to the politics surrounding the advent of independence, which happened in 1963, quite a number of farmers and ranchers were walking off their properties, selling what they could and abandoning everything else. Horses featured high amongst the unsaleable commodities, especially those that had no pretensions to any sort of quality or breeding.

I collected these little mobs of horses and ran them through the bush to my farm, or moved them by truck if they were further afield. There was quite a large diversity in make, shape and quality, from rough pony-like animals to some very nice ones. Some were broken in, but many were virtually wild. Anything that looked useful or caught my eye, I set aside for future use, with the result that I collected some very nice horses which later performed as polo ponies, show-jumpers, and one or two even finished up on the race course.

A few of these horses still loom large in my memory.

AMONGST THOSE DESTINED for the lions was one of the ugliest horses I had ever come across. The description in the old cowboy ballad 'The Strawberry Roan' fitted him to a tee except for the fact that he was a red chestnut. Frankly, when the lot he was in was being collected, I didn't think any more about him until an old Kikuyu syce, or groom, by the name of Ngatia asked me if I would let him take the ugly chestnut out of the mob as he was sure there was a good horse in him, somewhere.

I'd just taken on Ngatia, more out of sympathy than the expectation of any useful work as he seemed too old to be of much use around the sort of horses we were dealing with. As it didn't matter much either way to me, I agreed, and Ngatia took the horse, who was duly named Tabasco.

Certainly, Tabasco didn't belie his looks. He was a dyed-in-the-wool, no-nonsense outlaw and a thoroughly dirty one at that. Kicking, biting and striking out with his front feet were all in his repertoire, as well as throwing himself on the ground if all else failed. It was obvious that his previous owners had come to the conclusion that he wasn't worth wasting any time on as there had, without doubt, never been any attempt to handle him or try to break him in. When we finally got some sense into him and were able to check him out, his teeth showed him to be somewhat more than a spring chicken.

Despite Tabasco's dirty tricks, Ngatia remained convinced there was some good in him, and using all his wiles and skills, he eventually was able to use the old villain as his mustering hack. During the process it turned out that Ngatia's abilities were of such an order that he ended up one of the best syces I ever employed.

One of the things that tickled the old man most was to have his photograph taken with the repulsive old horse, whether just holding him or saddled up in full western rig. Why, I can't imagine, as neither were objects that pleased the eye. Actually, I think the old man tended to think he and the horse were two of a kind and wanted to record the fact - both were old, unsavoury, extremely difficult to deal with at times, and neither would ever get to the start line of even the most basic of beauty contests.

As I didn't think any benefit would result from looking too closely into the histories of either of them, I took them both at their face value, leaving the past to remain just that. Times had changed, and we were working in a new era. It was a fortuitous decision, for both he and Tabasco did me very well while they were with me.

After the best part of a year had slipped past, Ngatia established himself as an essential part of my little equine empire. He took responsibility mainly for looking after the horses in the paddocks and helping muster them up when required, always using the repulsive old Tabasco as his preferred saddle hack.

In my never-ending search for horses, I had bought a small mob from a rancher whose property was about 20 miles from my place. To get them home we would have to run them through quite a lot of unfenced bush. This was not an unusual situation, so I sent Ngatia, together with three or four other experienced syces, to the ranch the day before we were due to collect them. The syces would make sure the horses were in the yard and ready for the road when I arrived the following day, to check them out through the gate.

Usually, getting a mob started on such a journey required a good deal of galloping about, especially at the beginning, to get the horses under control. Once they had run off their initial energy, it was then just a simple droving job, particularly when one had sufficient horsemen to control them, as was the case this day, and well within Ngatia's scope to handle.

Ngatia, apart from being the oldest man, was also the most experienced and quite capable, so he took charge once the mob were on their way. As soon as all was in order and the mob had settled down, I went home in my Land Cruiser, to arrange fresh horsemen to ride out and meet the newcomers, and help shepherd them across the main road and through the neighbouring farms to my yards.

Meeting up later in the day, I was astonished to see Ngatia doing his boss drover's act from the back of another horse. Tabasco was nowhere to be seen. It transpired that not long after I left, with everything going along nicely, Ngatia felt Tabasco suddenly start shivering and shaking before collapsing on to the ground.

From the description I was given, I imagine the old horse was dead before he hit the deck. Although he was fit and quite used to the work, the only rational explanation I could come up with was that he must have suffered a massive heart attack. Fortunately, Ngatia escaped unhurt; later in the day I took him and a small crew back to where it all happened, to recover the saddle and bridle and dispose of the corpse by cutting it up for the lions.

I regret to admit it, but I think Ngatia was the only person who mourned Tabasco's passing - everyone else was more than happy to see the old villain on his way to pastures new. The story of Tabasco reminded me that from the most unlikely beginnings, something good can emerge.

HAVING WOUND up my association with the 'Born Free' production, I was, as they say in the entertainment world, resting - i.e., out of work.

The nearly-two-years I'd spent working on the film had left me with some money in my pocket, but little time to spend on maintenance of my farm. One of the most pressing jobs was to clear out some of the horses I had gathered there to provide meals for the lions.

More by luck than good planning, most of the horses that had only been fit for rations had fulfilled their duty. This left those that I thought I could do something with, amongst which were a couple of good looking mares with plenty of life ahead of them. I thought that if I could find a suitable stallion, I might produce some useful looking foals.

I shook a few trees locally and heard of a very well-bred racehorse going by the name of Kara Tepe. This horse was up for grabs at a big ranching operation just north of Lake Naivasha, which included one of the better thoroughbred studs in the country. Admittedly Kara Tepe was pretty long in the tooth - about eighteen years old – and, in the best of all worlds, not really what I was looking for. However, with little else in the offing, I thought it worth the effort to drive over and have a look.

As far as I could gather from my contacts, he had been imported shortly after his racing career had ended in the UK, but, being bred for classic distance races, he didn't really suit the Kenya scene. Initially he had been patronised fairly reasonably, mainly by his owners' own mares; his progeny, however, were not very successful on the track as the bulk of Kenya races were, in those days, framed for shorter distances.

This, coupled with the fact that he didn't prove a winner in the fertility stakes either, meant that he had become very much an also-ran on the breeding scene. With no patronage, even from his owner, he had been left very much to his own devices for years, and with virtually no contact with either horses or humans, he had become neurotic. In fact, in some circles, he was considered quite dangerous.

Neither the stud manager, nor his staff showed any inclination to much more than just show me the horse over the top of the stable door. I could understand their reluctance; when I looked into the stable, all I saw was a rather large bay horse showing lots of teeth, shaking his head, stamping and snorting at the door, clearly displaying his resentment at being disturbed. However, I did note that he was in very fair condition, if showing few signs of his age, and apart from his attitude, he would meet my requirements admirably. A further attraction for me was that they wanted rid of him at virtually any cost, as soon as possible.

With the stud manager quietly indicating he would be interested in any reasonable proposition, we came to a mutually satisfactory agreement which gave me time to prepare a suitable stable and exercise area for him before taking delivery. From the set-up I designed, the old horse would be able to see and hear the other horses, but would be far enough away from any of the action going on in the breaking yards and stables to ensure he didn't get unnecessarily upset.

I also had to work out how I was going to get him home, as it was obvious that an open truck, my normal way of moving horses, wouldn't do, and I didn't have access to any more sophisticated horse transport equipment. The solution, after a lot of thought, was to walk him to the nearest railway station, put him on the train to Nairobi, where he, still in his horse transport truck, would change trains onto the Nanyuki line, de-training at the Naro Moru siding about five miles from the farm. I would walk him home from there.

About a month after concluding the deal, I drove back to the stud with all the necessary gear and men to take over my new possession. All went remarkably well and despite the fact that the men on the stud didn't want to have anything to do with handling him, between my syces and myself, we managed to snare him in his stable, and get a bridle on him. After attaching a lunge line to each bit ring, we took him out of the stable with a man on either side, and set off for the railway siding.

It took a very short time for the old boy to settle down and by the time we got to the siding he was quite docile. He walked easily onto the truck, and after we had put up the ramp and closed the doors we loaded his food and water. The syce who was going to accompany him on the trip took his place in the service compartment, and as the train pulled out the rest of us waved them farewell.

The train duly arrived at Naro Moru station around midnight two days later. It was a filthy night, with heavy rain and wind, with the moonlight obscured by low scudding cloud. It was definitely not an ideal night to be unloading an uncertain horse and walking him five miles across country, but that is what had to be done.

I can't say I was too surprised on opening the service department door of the truck to find no syce. The combination of money in his pocket, the bright lights of Nairobi and no supervision was probably too much to ask of him. I never saw him again! Fortunately, before going to sample the attractions of the town, the syce had seen that food and water were available to the horse and everything else had been packed up nicely. From this, I concluded that he hadn't meant to abandon his charge, but had possibly had too much to drink and missed the train's departure.

The old horse, perhaps dredging up in his memory of many earlier trips during the halcyon days of his racing career, was quite happy to let us bridle him and attach the long reins to the bit. With a man on either side, he left the truck and started the walk to his new home. On arrival, with the aid of a couple of Tilley lamps, we led him into the stable we had just built for him, rubbed him down and dried him off as best we could, made sure he had hay and water, and left him to it. We all then repaired to the kitchen for something hot to drink before getting rid of our wet clothes and trying for some sleep prior to starting on the day's chores – it was by then about 5 am.

Straight after breakfast, accompanied by old Ngatia and Kipkemoi, a member of the Kipsigis tribe and another good man I had for dealing with tricky horses, I went down to the stable to see how Kara Tepe had settled in. He had taken over. It was all teeth, grunts and antisocial behaviour again, making it quite evident that last night's good manners had been nothing more than a temporary lapse, and things were now back to normal.

Having no time to indulge his fantasies, I got a rope round his neck and pulled him up to the stable door and got a good strong head collar on him. With a rein each side, he was let out of the stable and paraded around the house, stable yards, and work paddocks. Once he started showing an interest in nibbling some grass, I told the two syces to take him back to his own paddock which we had especially fenced in around his stable.

I had earmarked two of Lorna's pets, a Spanish donkey named Rominella (after the dam of the mighty Ribot, a famous thoroughbred of the era who won all his races), and a zebra yearling, to be the old boy's companions. However, for their safety I had raised the bottom rail of the paddock fence sufficiently to allow them to escape, should he take exception to them.

My dear wife, Lorna, with her pet donkey, Rominella

I left the two men with the horse, with instructions to allow him to graze as much as he wanted; at the same time, they were to try and make friends with him as they would be his attendants until more permanent arrangements could be made. Old Ngatia was especially adept at this sort of work, so by the time I went to see how they were getting on, after lunch, the matter had been settled. Ngatia was on his own with the horse, apparently on the best of terms, and Kipkemoi was resting, supine in the shade of a tree.

The old horse himself seemed to have shed half a dozen years. Even my approach didn't elicit any reaction, other than to lift his head and look at me before going back to his grazing. All being well, I sent the hard-working Kipkemoi off for his lunch.

'Come back in half an hour to relieve Ngatia, so he can have a break,' I told them. 'Then stay with the horse until we put him up for the night.'

The next morning things were much more civilized. Ngatia was able to go into the stable and put the head collar on the old fellow without any trouble, but to ensure nothing untoward happened, I had Kipkemoi put another rein on the offside before sending them off to walk the horse again. This time they went into the stable yard, around the stables, then down to the working yards where there were horses being handled, or standing around waiting for their turn to be worked on.

The old horse took a reasonable amount of interest, making those funny little wobbly noises stallions make when in the proximity of strange horses, but he was very sensible. He didn't get too excited and continued his walk quite happily when asked. On his return to his own paddock, I suggested the two men work out between themselves how they were going to handle him.

'Put a bit of distance between yourself and the horse, but keep a line on him,' I suggested. I was afraid we might be progressing too fast, and if he got loose, who knew what would happen?

Oh ye of little faith! I hadn't even gone through the gate before the two gentlemen decided the horse was quite safe to let go altogether while they went over to the nearest shady tree to spend the rest of the morning supervising (that is, smoking, talking and sleeping).

The grooms' take on the situation was, in fact, spot on; we never had any more trouble from the old fellow. Once lunch was over, I thought it a good time try out my idea of giving him the donkey and the zebra as companions. Enlisting Lorna's help, much against her better judgment, we decided to bring them to the stallion's paddock and hold them outside the rails, while he inspected them from the other side.

'If there's no signs of any animosity,' I suggested to Lorna, 'just let them go outside the rails. On the other hand, if they want to join the old boy they can slip under the rails and make his acquaintance in their own time.'

Unusually for me, my plan went off without a hitch. After a bit of walking up and down the rails looking at the two strange animals, the old horse went back to his grazing. Lorna and I joined Ngatia and Kipkemoi under their tree, to be on hand, just in case.

We needn't have worried. Within half an hour the donkey had slipped under the rails and was grazing next to Kara Tepe. The zebra might have thought that her fickle friend was deserting her for someone bigger and better, so with a little nicker, she slipped under the rails and joined the party. From then on the three of them were virtually inseparable. We tacked on a lean-to addition to the stable for the zebra and donkey, while the old fellow spent his nights in regal luxury indoors on a deep bed of straw.

With the sun on his back, and two friends to keep him company, Kara Tepe took to his new life like a duck to water. He had plenty of activity going on around him to keep his interest alive, a daily grooming before going out for about an hour's exercise, a wash and a rub down afterwards. He had a little hard feed to remind him of the old days, plenty of good grass during the day, and hay at night. What more could a retired old horse ask for?

Along with his physical improvement came a total change in his mental outlook. This was no doubt the result of his enforced exercise, having his teeth properly rasped down, being wormed, and having his feet properly trimmed thanks to Kipkemoi, who was also a good farrier.

Previously, he had barely tolerated the one syce who was supposedly looking after him, but who was actually so scared of him that the nearest he got to the old boy was to prod him with a pitch fork if he even moved when he was being fed. Any white person was a total anathema - the only time he ever saw one was when it was to stick needles into him or do something equally unpleasant, so it was not unreasonable that he was on the defensive whenever anyone, black or white, appeared at his stable door.

Now, being handled by people who appeared not to be afraid of him together with the freedom of being outside and having two companions, his outlook had gone through a 180 degree turn. He appeared quite happy to have people around him even to the extent of coming over to me – a white person - for a peppermint or any other goodies I brought him when I went to see how he was getting on.

Kara Tepe

One morning, Lorna noticed that Anne, now four-years-old, was nowhere to be found. None of the house staff knew where she was, and all the dogs, who would normally be with her if she was outside, were lolling around in the shade, meaning that she was nowhere in the garden either.

The dense bush surrounding the farm buildings was occupied by at least one big male leopard, whose tracks I frequently came across when wandering about myself. My heart beat faster and the worst of thoughts came to mind. However, with all the dogs lolling idly around, I reassured myself that no leopard could possibly have gotten near her. That settled, she had to be somewhere else. Everyone on the farm was called out to look for her.

I went into the vegetable garden, where an old man named Dumbi held sway, diligently removing about three weeds in a good week.

'Dumbi, have you seen Anne?' I asked.

Dumbi nodded and pointed to Kara Tepe's paddock. 'In there.'

I hastened to the gate and was confronted with a completely empty paddock - no Anne, no horse, no donkey, no zebra.

I heard some strange noises coming from inside the stable. I went over, not knowing what to expect but fearing the worst. Inside, there was Anne, with her arms round the old horse's nearside foreleg, stroking him and confiding all her problems to him while he had his muzzle resting on her shoulder. The donkey and the zebra, obviously feeling neglected, were pushing and nudging her for some share of her attention.

I breathed a sigh of relief, then retrieved Anne and took her back to a now very-relieved Lorna. Later, I spoke to Dumbi, about Anne, and Kara Tepe:

'She goes to the paddock often, on her own,' he said of Anne. 'She goes to talk to the horse, the donkey and the zebra; they are her friends.'

A GOOD FRIEND OF MINE, an enthusiastic novice polo player, called into the farm one Sunday evening after a weekend's polo in Timau.

Over drinks, he asked me if I would be interested in a horse, Snow Cat, which he had been offered as a gift. This was obviously a man looking a gift horse in the mouth!

One of the other players, an Afrikaans farmer from somewhere near Nakuru, had bought Snow Cat sometime earlier and apparently couldn't get on with the horse. He was a big, heavy man who rode even heavier. To make matters worse, he had hands like concrete blocks, no feeling in them whatsoever.

As would be expected from a very large, hardworking, self-employed man, he was also very strong-minded. When he found he couldn't control the horse with normal gear, he resorted to increasingly severe bits and tie downs which, coupled with his considerable strength, caused the horse sufficient distress and pain to bolt, uncontrollably.

I think the man in question thought my friend was a soft touch, new to the country, and unused to Kenyan ways. Little did he know, my friend had jackarooed in some of the tougher parts of north western Queensland and the Territory, on cattle runs bigger than the whole of Wales and Scotland put together, and knew his way around horses, quiet or rough, as well as anyone.

The only reason my friend had taken the trouble to call in on me that Sunday evening was because he was confident that the horse was a good one and, given the chance, could be rehabilitated. He wasn't interested in doing the work himself, as he had neither the time, nor the space, but he thought that if I was prepared to take the horse on, I would be in a win/win situation. If I failed, the horse had cost me nothing but time, whereas, as he fully anticipated, if I succeeded the horse could be worth quite a bit of money, and justify the effort. As always, I couldn't turn down the challenge of a problem horse, so with nothing except time to lose, I agreed.

Snow Cat's owner delivered him to the farm, and what a sorry looking specimen the horse was. I would have been embarrassed, not to mention ashamed, to be associated with such a poverty-stricken looking creature. Besides being reduced to a quivering wreck whenever saddled up, the horse had lost all its condition. On looking him over I noticed what looked like an incipient fistulous outbreak weeping from the top of his wither, which, among his other problems, without doubt had some bearing on his terrible head carriage. It was hard to believe that such a misused horse could have been allowed on the field, let alone played, yet it had!

The gentleman in question, however, seemed to see nothing wrong with Snow Cat, other than the fact he couldn't stop him, and said as much when he handed him over. Such was his bland self-satisfaction that he even had the temerity to look around some of my horses with a view to seeing if he could buy one. On this, I firmly disillusioned him.

'Anything I have that's up to your weight is under offer,' I said. 'And I've got nothing likely coming up in the near future.'

The plain fact was that I would not have sold him a horse under any circumstances. I am not, and never have been, a 'soft' man, but his lack of even the most basic consideration for his horses' wellbeing, if Snow Cat was any indication, put him totally beyond the pale. As far as I was concerned. The sooner he was off my place the happier I would be.

It was quite obvious that before any sort of work could be started, Snow Cat had to have a complete check over to ensure there was nothing more substantially wrong with him, than neglect and abuse. I rasped his teeth and wormed him, put him on a tonic and started on a feed regimen designed to build him up. At the same time, we treated his withers and one or two other minor injuries together with the odd old saddle sore and girth gall. Altogether he had a real going over.

In a surprisingly short time, he started putting on flesh. His eyes brightened and his coat began to take on a shine, all indications that he was on the mend. Before long, I thought, we should start to see if his mental approach to life was recovering in tune with his physical one.

My first concern before anything else was to try to work out a means to build up his back and his neck in front of his withers. His muscles had been eroded away by the ill-fitting saddlery used on him which was not helped at all by the excessively severe bitting that he had been subjected to. Amongst my books on horses and horse care was one entitled 'The Allen Book of Training Aids' which carried a description and picture of a simple piece of equipment called a Side Pull hackamore. This, it was stated, was designed to assist in helping a young horse get used to the bit, as well as to 'improve his outline by building up his neck and back'. Just what the doctor ordered, I thought.

To begin with, being a fairly competent, if self-taught saddler, I made up a bridle to fit the picture I had seen in the book. This resulted in a modified De Gogue martingale, with light elastic inserts.

This would work off his nose, rather than his mouth, and was possible to use with a light roller to lunge him in.

The idea was that as he walked around on the lunge line, he would be forced to bob his head up and down, thereby stretching and relaxing all the muscles along his neck and back from his ears to his tail. I knew it was going to be a very long, slow process but I couldn't see any other way of working up the muscles in question. As I had the labour and the time, it seemed worth trying.

After a couple of months of two sessions a day, each of about twenty minutes to half an hour, there was a very definite improvement. His neck in front of the wither had started to build up and his back was becoming more rounded – whether this was the result of the improved feeding he was enjoying, or my home-made physiotherapy, I am not sure. Whatever it was, the results were very gratifying. After another couple of months, with his work stepped up to include some slow trotting, Snow Cat was gradually beginning to take on the look of the horse he had once been. He was responding so well to all our efforts that I felt it was about time to start ridden work.

The abuse his mouth had suffered meant that I had to be particularly careful not to frighten him, by putting anything too strong in it. Initially, I rode him first in the Side Pull hackamore that he had been lunged in, and which he was well used to. Once he got confident in being ridden in that, I put him in an old polo training bit-less bridle, that I had bought from the Bosca Saddlery years earlier, in Sydney shortly after the war. I had used this to good effect on a number of horses who had problems with their mouths and found it worked like a Swiss watch, and so it did with Snow Cat.

He gave up his star-gazing head carriage once he realised he wasn't going to get hurt, and he also appeared to have given up any idea of bolting. Just to be on the safe side though, at no time was he given any opportunity to indulge that particular vice, he was always ridden in an enclosed area, the basic premise being that his head carriage and schooling work could be better monitored in the school, rather than the paddock.

After about seven months Snow Cat had transformed himself

from a twitchy, battered scarecrow of a horse with wide, frightened eyes, to a quiet, comfortable animal, bordering on fat, who did everything asked of him without resistance. He now seemed quite happy to have people working on and around him.

All that could possibly be achieved with the hackamore and the bitless bridle had been completed. He was going forward confidently, could stop and turn on his hocks, turn on his forehand, do sliding stops keeping his head low, and was happy doing slow stick and ball work; however, as he couldn't go back onto the polo field without a bit in his mouth, it was necessary to see what could be done to rectify that. The first bit I decided on was a soft rubber snaffle, and to make sure he was comfortable with it I spent some time on the ground, with my right arm over his neck, turning his head to the near and to the off.

'Back up,' I would ask him, while giving little gentle 'feels' of his mouth.

It all went very well, Snow Cat seemed to realise that he wasn't going to get hurt. He now had enough confidence to work quite nicely when ridden in the school, accepting all the aids and guidance cues he was given without any resistance.

The time had now come to see if all the hard work would pay off. One morning, after a little bit of warm-up work in the yard, I took him out into the large exercise paddock to see if he would revert to bolting, once allowed to gallop.

It was as though the thought had never entered his head. He responded beautifully, slowing up when asked, stopping and turning, jumping off from a stand into a gallop, bending either way to shifts of my weight in the saddle, and at no time did he try to take any sort of a hold on the bit. All this was incredibly gratifying and proved to me that we had been on the right track throughout his rehabilitation.

Now all that remained was to get him fit and work off some of that fat. While it looked nice on him, it wasn't going to do him any good if he went back onto the polo field. The bulk of his fitness work was done by the syces, who daily took him out for long walks interspersed with a bit of trotting and the odd canter. All this was done in the bitless bridle, as I still wasn't entirely sure of his mouth, not to mention that some of the syces didn't have the softest of hands.

Gradually, as his work progressed, Snow Cat became fitter, stronger and much more confident, to such an extent that the syces began to complain that he was beginning to lean into the bridle at the canter. It was time to move up to something a little more formal.

Once Snow Cat went out onto the polo field, with the best will in the world his rider would not be worrying about his horse's mouth as he chased the ball around the field. I thought, therefore, that we should start toughening his mouth up. He needed the confidence to go forward with a bit of steel in his mouth, rather than the rubber or plastic compound bits we had been using since taking him off the bitless bridle.

For this, we started him off with an egg-butted Tom Thumb, which he accepted without any fuss. From there he graduated to what he eventually settled on for the rest of his career, a Dee ring jointed snaffle, with three copper rollers each side of the joint – I just happened to have one in my tack room, and luckily it fitted him perfectly.

All in all it took me just over a year to rehabilitate Snow Cat and I thoroughly enjoyed the whole process - all the more so since it was successful. The horse had been completely reformed, both physically and mentally. Apart from the odd little scar, there was no sign of what he had been through. He had filled up in the neck and over the back, seemed to have lost all his fear of people, and had given up on his bolting. He was now quite happy to gallop about the polo field, stopping and starting when asked, without showing any signs of anxiety. His mouth, subjected as it was to some fairly rough usage in the heat of a game, didn't seem to cause him any distress.

I had developed a sneaking liking for Snow Cat during his long stay on the farm, and was determined that whomsoever I sold him to would have to be someone who, knowing his history, would take good care of him. I also wanted to know that if the time came for the buyer to sell him on, that he or she would only do so to someone equally sympathetic. On this basis I turned down quite a few good offers for him.

Eventually, I found a buyer who met my conditions, and I kept an eye on him for as long as I could. He showed every sign at his new stables of being a round peg in a comfortably round hole, which made me very happy indeed.

I was also tickled pink, one day, to see Snow Cat on the polo field, some seven months after he'd left me, playing on the same team as the farmer who had dropped the horse off to me, as a failure. It made my day that he didn't recognise the horse.

SWINDLE WAS BORN on the Athi Plains just to east of Nairobi. Of indeterminate parentage, but with an obvious heavy infusion of thoroughbred, he grew up to be a good-looking, useful type of horse, albeit a bit straight behind.

Swindle was the sort who would always put in an honest day's work without asking too much in return and, as such, much prized by Kenyan ranchers, whose margins didn't allow much latitude for those who couldn't pull their weight.

After being broken in he went to work, being ridden in the main by the local stockmen carrying out the daily tasks involved in running a working cattle ranch. After a couple of years, he started developing some very nasty habits, eventually reaching a point where it was becoming dangerous to get near him, let alone saddle him up for work.

Along with this unpleasant behaviour, Swindle also started losing weight, until, when I first saw him, he was nothing more than a gaunt bag of bones; he was hardly worth the price of a bullet to shoot him for dog food.

I heard about Swindle and his history through friends of his owners. Being in the horse trading and handling business, with a particular interest in difficult and unmanageable horses (as they were generally free, or at least very cheap) I sent word through my friend that if the owners were interested, I would like to come and have a look at him.

They were, so the next time I was in Nairobi I made time to go out to the ranch and have a look at him. Despite being in such dreadful condition, I rather liked what I saw, so made a paltry offer of 100 shillings, never dreaming for a moment they would accept. They did.

At that price, the cost of sending him by train from Athi siding to Naro Moru was considerably more than he was worth – even if he survived the journey. Knowing that within a week or so I would have to be back in Nairobi to collect my stepdaughter, Deanie, from school for the holidays, I arranged for the owners to have him available in the yard. I would load him onto my Land Cruiser for the trip home.

On the appointed day, accompanied by my Kipsigis factotum and man of all affairs, Kipkemoi, we set off from home very early in the morning, picked Deanie up at Limuru School, dropped her off with some friends in Nairobi, and went out to the plains to pick up my new acquisition.

Being well-used to handling difficult horses it wasn't too much of a problem to catch Swindle, give him a good healthy shot of the sedative Acepromazine (ACP), get a bag over his head and load him into the back of the Land Cruiser. The trip back into Nairobi to pick Deanie up was uneventful, as was the journey to Naro Moru, Kipkemoi standing in the back keeping an eye on the somnolent horse and making sure nothing untoward happened.

Shortly after leaving the road at Naro Moru, to follow the track through the bush to the farm, the situation started to change. The ACP was wearing off and it was obvious that Kipkemoi was having considerable trouble trying to keep the horse steady.

Being so close to home, there was no point in trying to give him some more of the sedative, so we pressed on, hoping for the best. About two miles from home, just as we were crossing the railway line, there was a yell from the back of the truck accompanied by the sounds of serious kicking and crashing about.

'Get out, Deanie!' I yelled.

The truck was heaving about like a ship in a gale. Just as I slowed to a stop, and Deanie escaped, there was an almighty crash on the roof of the truck. The canopy caved in, bending alarmingly, but luckily held. Swindle was demonstrating quite clearly that he had no intention of completing the journey quietly.

With Deanie safely out of the cab, I helped Kipkemoi get the horse off the roof and back into the body of the vehicle. It was obvious that there was now little chance of us completing the journey with the horse on board, so, letting down the tailboard, we jumped him off the back of the truck.

'We'll just have to walk him home,' I said.

Kipkemoi was confident that he could handle the horse, given that he had a good stout colt halter on him, with a twelve-foot lead line giving him plenty of room to manoeuvre if things got untidy. I left the two of them on the side of the track, while I shot off home taking a much shaken Deanie to Lorna.

Having delivered Deanie safely, I went back up the track to find Kipkemoi and the horse just turning into the farm, having settled their differences and come to a working agreement.

The next day, following my normal custom with new horses, I set out to check him over, look at his teeth and worm him. Trying to look into his mouth the normal way proved utterly impossible, as he reared and struck out with his front feet, grunting and bellowing all the while and letting fly with his hind feet at anything that looked in range. On the face of it, it looked as though my paltry hundred shillings had been an overestimate of his value, and I could readily see why his previous owners had been happy to accept it.

However, having heard that initially he had been such a good stock horse, I was reluctant to give up and decided that more robust means had to be the order of the day if we were ever going to do anything with him, let alone get a look in his mouth. With a bit of a struggle, we got the double side lines on him, cast him and turned him onto his back with all his legs trussed up like a Christmas turkey to prevent any chance of injury either to himself, or more especially, to those of us working around him. Once that was done, I put a block of wood between his incisor teeth to keep his mouth open while I looked inside and ran my fingers over his teeth to see what state they were in.

The cause of his bad behaviour and his loss of condition was immediately obvious. The outside shell of one of his middle molars was shaved to a razor-edged sliver nearly two inches long and digging into his upper gum, where there was a huge, suppurating abscess covering about three inches of the gum. The pain must have been indescribable, even for the horse to drink, let alone when try to eat anything. How he survived so long beggars belief, as that sliver must have been a real source of increasing pain over quite an extended period.

Not having any more sophisticated equine dental equipment available other than a rasp and a pair of electrician's side cutters I used the cutters to carefully break off the offending piece of the tooth, and then rasped all his teeth level. I cleaned out the abscess and dressed it with salt and water, then gave him a huge shot of penicillin and let him up.

The transformation was immediate and more than dramatic. Daily shots of penicillin for a week, and a light diet of sloppy food for about a fortnight made such a difference that it was hard to credit that the quiet, docile horse we were now dealing with was the potential killer of a week or so earlier.

In no time at all, Swindle had wormed his way into everyone's good books; there was little he was asked to do that he couldn't, and my little daughter Anne, then still about four, rode around on him quite happily whenever given the chance. Being a good, sturdy type of horse, unflappable and steady, it was not long before I was using him as my main handling horse, pulling and pushing unbroken horses about, while teaching them to respect the halter and to lead.

Swindle also learned very quickly to act as an anchor for me to snub up those same horses when they were first mounted, then leading and shepherding them round the yard until they were confident to move about on their own with a man on their back. He led strings of green horses out onto the plains when they first left the yards, seeming to know instinctively where game was hidden in the grass and steering away from the areas where they would possibly take fright and get into trouble. If it wasn't too fanciful, I would say he actually seemed to take a pride in seeing that they got back safely to the yards. Swindle was, in fact, a horse breaker's dream; I've had one or two other horses in my life equal to him, but seldom one better.

The Kenya Police were my main clients at that time, taking dozens of these semi-feral horses that were running in the bush and on ranches, as a result of the exodus of farmers abandoning their properties prior to, and immediately after, independence.

The reason the police were becoming interested in horses was the result of their total lack of success with other means, such as aircraft and vehicles, in controlling the increase in cattle rustling, or stock theft, as it was locally known. Raids were being carried out by Turkana tribesmen on all the areas surrounding their tribal land. Politically, as well as economically, these raids were becoming a serious problem and the powers that be were desperate to find some effective way of combating them.

With their other options seemingly exhausted, some bright spark suggested horses. The concept was that a mounted unit was a more flexible tool, capable of a much quicker follow-up, as well as being able to cross country that was virtually impassable to vehicles. Finally, making the idea more attractive to the bean counters was the fact that horses would be considerably cheaper to acquire and operate.

The men appointed to the task of setting up the unit needed a lot of cheap horses in a hurry. The difficulty was that although there were plenty of horses running wild in the bush, there was no organisation to catch them, nor facilities in which to break and train them once they were caught.

Initially, the UK government offered help by sending out a corporal-major (the cavalry's equivalent of a sergeant-major) from the remount section of the Household Cavalry. However, after a futile month or more of expensive, government-controlled effort during which he and his team had only managed to catch one debilitated two-year-old filly, he admitted defeat and I was asked if I could help.

Having done quite a lot of that sort of work in Australia before and during World War II, and having the land, facilities, and competent staff, I was more than happy to have a go. At the peak of the job, we were catching and turning out between forty or fifty horses every six weeks or so. Out of the mobs we mustered I selected only males between the ages of four and ten, which we castrated, broke in to ride, taught to carry a pack, and to be loaded on trucks – basically, all the things a good troop horse would be required to do.

Breaking a horse for the Kenya Police at Nanyuki

The officers in charge of the stock theft unit spent quite a lot of time at the ranch, watching the selection of the horses, checking the work in progress, taking delivery of shipments, and generally trying to see that they were getting value for the money. In doing so, they saw a lot of Swindle at work.

Towards the end of the program, when their various units were fully stocked with horses and remounts, someone had the bright idea that a mounted unit for ceremonial purposes and state occasions should be set up. The officer in charge of this new unit, having seen Swindle at work and no doubt fancying himself in full ceremonial rig riding such a good horse, was insistent that Swindle be the first horse acquired.

The police were such good customers, I felt unable to refuse. Reluctantly, I agreed to sell him, although for considerably more than the hundred shillings I originally paid for him. Swindle duly went to Nairobi, to not only lead ceremonial parades, but also to serve as a crowd control horse in the police crowd control armoury.

Sadly, it was in this capacity that Swindle met his untimely end. He was shot by some nameless 'hero' during one of the many civil disturbances that seemed to form such an integral part of freedom from colonial oppression. It was an ignominious and futile end of a really good horse and made me really sorry that I had let money take over from my better judgement.

IN MY SEARCH for horses in sufficient numbers to meet my commitment to supply the Kenya police, I learned of the plight of a rancher with quite a sizeable property north-west of Nakuru.

With no younger members of his family to take over the management of the place, the farmer, due to his age, had more or less lost control of his ranch. Those of his cattle that hadn't been stolen, had become as wild as hawks and were rarely seen. The horses that in the past had been bred and used for stock work were now running in large feral mobs, wrecking what little was left of the infrastructure of the once well-organised ranch.

On the off chance that he might consider letting me have some of his horses, I went over to see him. Not only was he prepared to let me have what I could catch, he was quite happy to just give them to me.

I took him at his word in terms of taking what I could catch, as far as numbers were concerned, but refused to accept them as a gift. This was a business arrangement and I would pay him the going rate for every horse I took off the ranch. Somewhat reluctantly, he agreed; I went home, collected a catching crew of syces and horses together with the necessary gear, and moved over to the ranch to set up a temporary catching operation.

Over the following weeks, my syces and I had mustered up a few of these herds with the help of the ranch labour, and had sorted out quite a number of suitable animals ranging in age from about four to nine or ten-years-old. In one of the last mobs brought in, I noticed one of the horses that had initially caught my attention had a weeping sore on his off-side hip.

The wound had obviously been there for some time as the trail of mucus exuding from it had scorched a broad channel along his hide, right down to the hock. The ranch labour told me that a couple of years earlier, a veterinarian, working on some wildlife project, had been allowed to come on the ranch to try out some new animal darting techniques and prescriptions. He had used the horses as practice targets, as they were easier to approach than wild animals.

The colt I had just caught had been part of the experiment. The story I was told was that whatever concoction was in the dart had had no immediate effect and the colt had galloped off, never to be seen again. Apart from the wound in his hip, the horse fit all of my specs, so I decided to include him in the shipment back to Nanyuki, for processing into a police horse.

Under normal circumstances, I did all the horse castrations, branding and dental work myself, as the only vets available were government employees who had other, more important, things to do than spend time cutting horses for me. In this instance, however, I arranged with a friend, Gene, a veterinarian on an exchange program from the university of Colorado's veterinary department, to bring some of his students out to the farm. Gene was currently lecturing in veterinary surgery at the local university in Nairobi, so this was an ideal opportunity for the students to get some real-life experience - it also meant that this particular bunch of about 45 horses would get the best possible treatment available, something not to be sneezed at.

I naturally drew Gene's attention to the stallion and asked him if he and his students could do anything about him, as I was sure the dart must still be in the horse's hip. Some years earlier, when serving in the Tanganyika Game Department, I had been part of a research team investigating the seasonal movement of animals in and out of the Ngorongoro Crater, and one of our tools in that work had been an early model of Palmer's CO_2 dart gun. As a result, I had a fair bit of experience in the use of such guns, and the problems involved in darting animals.

Gene and his students were keen, so we decided I would catch the horse, and handle him a bit, in order to get him sufficiently civilised to ship him down to the veterinary hospital in Nairobi. There, he could be anaesthetised under proper conditions and the necessary surgical procedures carried out in a sterile environment.

All went according to plan. The horse went down to Nairobi and was delivered to the hospital, where Gene and his team did their thing. From the report I got, they excised in excess of two kilograms of granulated tissue from the horse's rump; they had to go right down to the bone to get everything out. Needless to say, cutting so much tissue away was quite an undertaking, leaving a very large dent in the horse's hip, which required a high standard of nursing and treatment before he could be sent back to the farm.

On dissecting the large lump, once they had it out, they found the dart, and the mystery of why the anaesthetic had not worked was solved. The conclusion was that at the moment of impact, the horse was probably galloping and the skin and muscle had been slack, allowing the dart to penetrate right through to the bone. The point of the needle, on striking the femur, had turned back on itself, blocking the passage of the liquid. In fact, it was sealed so tightly that the liquid was still in the barrel of the syringe when they opened it up.

As the horse was the subject of an ongoing study, Gene was able to keep it at the hospital until its wound was completely healed; this was a blessing as I had neither the time, nor the facilities to give it the specialised attention it required.

By the time the horse was ready to be sent back to the farm, most of the hair had grown back over the scorched area of his leg, and the muscle was starting to regenerate. When I checked him over on his return, it was hard to tell just what he had gone through, apart from a large dimple in the muscle of his hip.

All the horses from that particular mob had long gone to their new home in the police stables and were actually getting ready for active duty, so it was necessary to find someone else who would take this little brown fellow over. As he stood about fifteen hands, was reasonably sturdily put together and quite active, I thought a little polo training might do him some good. Besides making him obedient and flexible, it might build up his hip a bit. It turned out to do more than that - his hip filled up to a point where, apart from a very small dimple and a slight scar, his old injury was barely noticeable.

The horse also took to polo like a natural, and in due course I was able to sell him to one of the local players for a bigger profit than I had made for the whole consignment that he had come with, put together.

All in all, the fates had finally conspired to do the little horse a good turn after his initial unpleasantness. Had it not been for the fact that I had arranged for Gene and his band of students to use that particular mob for a demonstration of castration and horse handling, and had they not been interested in investigating his weeping sore, I would have had to put him down.

21

Having worked on *Hatari!* and *Born Free*, I had been able to learn a good deal about the behind the scenes action in filmmaking and to get an idea of how a movie was structured.

During my tenure with Ker and Downey, we as a company were engaged by a number of film companies that were shooting their location scenes in Africa, to supply a full back-up service for them as a package deal, rather than their people running themselves ragged trying to get things organised piecemeal in a totally foreign environment.

The film companies' requirements were varied, sometimes even bizarre, but somewhere in our little bag of tricks we always seemed to find an equitable solution to the satisfaction of all concerned.

Of the films I handled for the company, one which sticks out was *The Lion*, with Bill Holden as the principle. It stands out not for any close association I had with the shooting, but rather a nasty situation that occurred on location in Uganda, when a hippo got hold of the back end of a Land Rover and did a considerable amount of damage to the vehicle. Luckily, none of the people travelling on board were hurt.

The incident caused quite a stir and took a lot of smoothing out. The hunter involved, although in no way at fault - these things can happen when dealing with wild animals in their own environment - was made a scapegoat and had to be replaced before the incident was declared over. My negotiating skills were never at a very high level, especially when dealing with temperamental people who didn't know what they were talking about, and they were stretched to the limit, even though I still had to replace the hunter.

The next enterprise was an English company making a delightful little story called *Sammy Going South*, about a young boy who journeys from Egypt to South Africa just after the 1956 Suez crisis.

This was a great film to be associated with and the people were a delight to work with including the star, Edward G. Robinson who was always pleasant and friendly when one ran into him. A little icing appeared on the cake when one of my brothers-in-law and I were able to help the film company out of a very big hole they had inadvertently fallen into, by not having planned their schedule adequately in advance.

Well into the shooting schedule, the script called for a very large leopard to make its appearance as a vital part of one of the sequences. The producers, thinking it was just a matter of a telephone call or two to produce a leopard in a land where leopards were presumed to abound, were horrified to find that was not the case.

Under normal circumstances, the trapping of any animal could only be carried out by a fully licensed trapper and was likely to be a long, drawn-out procedure, with no assurance that a big, photogenic leopard would be the one that walked into the trap. Doom and gloom was the order of the day, both on the location, which was just outside Arusha in Tanzania (as it had just been renamed) and our office in Nairobi. I called all the local trappers in both countries, as well as Uganda, to see if they could help, but they were all fully occupied.

Jack Bousfield, my brother-in-law, happened to be staying with us at the time after having come up to Nairobi for business. Fortuitously, Jack received a telephone call from a friend of his who asked if he could help him - a leopard was killing his sheep and goats around his house and the Game Department had just given him a permit to trap or kill the cat.

Jack, being a licensed trapper and hunter, and at a loose end, was just the man for the job. I dropped everything and together we jerry-rigged a trap, took it out to the man's farm and set it in some thick bush, not far from his sheep and goat pen. We baited the track with a young goat, in a safe compartment at the end of the trap, and retired back home to see if anything transpired.

The next morning, before even the sun was up, Jack's friend was on the phone - there was a whacking great Tom leopard in the trap, making such a fuss that the farmer was too scared to get near enough to have a shot at it.

'Will you come and get rid of it?' the farmer asked.

We were there in a flash, and sure enough, there was a huge male leopard in the trap and he was not happy. I personally had serious doubts that the trap would hold up, as we had only whacked it together with some chicken wire and staples, but Jack had no such qualms. He went straight to the trap with a big tarpaulin and before I really knew what was happening, he had the whole cage wrapped up and was cutting the bush to get it out of the thicket.

Once we were in the open, we made sure the trap was secure, then lifted it onto the Land Cruiser and drove off to the Game Department to try and pull some strings to expedite its removal to Arusha. It is times like this it is nice to have friends in authority. I got in to see Ian, then the Chief Game Warden, and told him the story. He was sympathetic and while it was really beyond his remit, he called the Chief Game Warden in Tanzania. They had a long chat, with Ian being at his most persuasive self. This resulted in us being give a special permit to move the animal on condition that once the scene was accepted, we would release it into a safe environment in Tanzania (the last was a condition far better than I personally had hoped for as I really didn't fancy a trip back up to Kenya with a less than happy leopard on board).

In the end, the shot was successful, and the film people were ecstatically happy. Jack got handsomely paid and the leopard was given a new home high up on the slopes of Mount Meru.

AFTER WORKING on *Born Free* I was sounded out about handling the animals for A *Ring of Bright Water*, the film adaptation of the book by Gavin Maxwell, about an Englishman who takes an otter from Iraq and raises it in the UK.

The film once again paired Bill Travers and Virginia McKenna, the stars of *Born Free*. Virginia was very easy to get on with, a very pragmatic, thoughtful person. Bill on the other hand, was a very different proposition altogether, so when I heard he was going to be the lead in the new film, I thought it might be simpler all round to let somebody else take the job.

My next project was *The Last Safari*, released in 1967, about a big game hunter, played by Stewart Granger, who is obsessed with hunting an elephant that had killed his friend. Working on it was a disaster, thanks to one of the second unit directors, who seemed to be cast in the same mould as the first man in charge of filming *Born Free*. He thought all animals could be trained to do anything, on command of someone whose only association with animals was probably a cat, and not many people have ever trained on of those.

'In Hollywood we have animals that will do whatever we want!' he railed, based on his experience filming Westerns in the 'green screen' world of the California film industry. He just couldn't understand why we couldn't get wild African elephants to do his bidding, even if it ultimately meant them committing 'hara-kiri'

As the 'lead' hunter I had the use of a helicopter to assist me to fulfil the director's dreams. There was to be a pivotal scene in which Stewart Granger's character finally confronts his nemesis, the killer elephant. According to the script and the film's director, Howard Hawks, it had to be a very large elephant with impressive tusks, standing under a tree. When the hunter sees it, across a wide-open plain, he approaches the animal, whereupon it charges him. This was all nice and straight forward – in theory.

The complications were, of course, innumerable. First, we needed to find a big bull elephant, with long ivory, as specified by the director. We were filming around the edges of the Tsavo National Park in Kenya, one of the few easily accessible areas in which such elephants could be found, but even there, in the 1960s, these big tuskers were already thin on the ground. I flew over our permitted hunting areas in the chopper for days and couldn't find anything that would even half-way meet the script requirements.

After one day ran into another and the chopper hours marched on with absolutely nothing to show for it, patience, and tempers were becoming a trifle frayed. One morning, after another fruitless two hours or so of flying, we landed to refuel. The second unit director, literally frothing at the mouth, came over to the aircraft and accused me of wasting money and time enjoying myself, declaring that he would go up himself and have no problem at all in finding a suitable elephant.

He took off and was back 20 minutes later. 'I knew it,' he triumphantly announced, 'there are plenty of elephants around.'

'Of course there are plenty of elephants, that's why we are here, and I probably saw all the ones you have just seen,' I said, knowing the pilot had taken him over the ground we had covered that morning. 'But none of them are suitable.'

'Nonsense, there's a suitable one just over there,' he said. pointing to some trees across the vlei. 'We'll set up and use it.'

As there was no point in arguing, I left him to it, hoping he would realise his mistake once we got the elephant he had pointed to out into the open. The crew and I, along with John Fletcher, the other hunter we had working with us, headed to where the director wanted the camera set up. Again, I pointed out that even at the distance we were away from the elephant, its ivory did not meet the requirements of the script. My comments were totally disregarded,

'Do your job,' he said. 'Get it to charge'.

We did. From 70 yards away, the elephant started its charge with all the necessary side effects - screaming and bellowing, ears out, and having a good old go at us. John and I ran either side of the camera's line of sight, where we stopped and turned to face the elephant. It kept on coming at us, right down the barrel of the lens.

It was all very tense and rapidly getting out of control. I stood there, waiting for the idiot in charge to realise his mistake and tell us to try and turn the elephant before it was too late.

Nothing happened. When the animal was no more than four metres from us, and still coming, I whacked it in the head. My shot turned the elephant, but my bullet must have been a bit high, missing the brain, as it didn't go down. Backing me up, John, cool as a cucumber, put a .475 bullet smack into its brain from side-on, and down it went. Four or five tonnes of elephant crumpled to the ground and slid forward in a cloud of dust, right into the camera.

When I turned around, heart pounding, ready to blow my stack at the director, he was nowhere to be seen. It seemed that the minute the elephant had first screamed the man had turned on his heels and legged it to a safer place.

I was shaking. Apart from the fact that I had been shit-scared, I was livid - so much so that I could hardly speak. I think that if the man responsible had been anywhere near I would not have been answerable for my actions. In fact, I never did speak to him again during the rest of my time working on the film. Luckily there was another second unit director with whom I had no trouble working, as he would listen to reason and adjust his needs to what we could produce

As dramatic as the footage was, with the charge, and the elephant falling and skidding to a halt, they couldn't use any of it in the film because, as I had pointed out, the ivory and indeed, the elephant itself, was deemed to be too small to make any impact. As a result of one man's arrogance and bone-headed idiocy, an animal had been killed for nothing. We had quite a few other close calls trying to get that particular shot, but in the end the scene had to be abandoned as unworkable.

. . .

IN 1966 A FILM crew came to Kenya to film the pilot for the television series, *Cowboy in Africa*, which was subsequently released on the big screen as a feature film, *Africa, Texas Style*.

The film starred Hugh O'Brian as an American cowboy who comes to Africa to teach the locals about catching wild animals by roping them from a horse, on a farm owned by a former RAF officer, Wing Commander Hayes, played by John Mills.

For want of a more convenient location, and as I was supplying most of the horses that were to be used, the producers chose my farm to film the bulk of the action. In a totally unexpected coincidence, it transpired that John's wife, Mary Hayley Bell, and I had been at school together, in Shanghai. Their daughter, Hayley Mills, who went on to become a famous actress in her own right, spent a lot of time with them on location and became quite friendly with my family, all of whom thought she was something quite special, as were her father and mother.

For the more definitive catching shots, the filmmakers brought some specialised horses from America that had been used for steer roping, team roping, and other rodeo activities. Although not stated, my impression was that their horses were no longer fit for competition work, probably due to injury, and were considered expendable as there were no arrangements to take them back to the States once filming had been completed.

This impression was reinforced once shooting started, as whenever they were used, they invariably appeared stiff and sore afterwards. That having been said, they were still good horses, just not up to the stresses and strains of full competition work. On the plus side, however, they were quiet and reasonably amenable. This was just as well, because neither of the two starring actors could do much more than just sit on a horse – even then, there would be someone hidden holding the horse.

In an effort to keep the horses working I made use of a small stream running in front of our house on the farm which supplied all our water requirements. Downstream from our take-off point I had a pit dug to form a sort of wading pool, around which I put a fence to which the horses could be tied. I rigged up a two-inch delivery, petrol-driven high-pressure pump next to the pool so that once the horses were in they would be deluged with water. Every day after work was over, those horses that had been used would get the treatment and it seemed to work very well. Throughout the whole time the film was being shot, we managed to keep the horses working without resorting to novocaine or other painkiller injections.

The whole company involved in making the film proved to be very friendly and informal, from actors to odd-job men. They used our house as a place to sneak off and relax for a while, despite the fact that there were full blown catering facilities available at all times.

As a result, we all became very friendly, with young Anne always getting special attention.

Me on the silver screen, playing a Somali 'shifta'.

I even had a bit part in the film playing a shifta, dressed up as a mounted Somali bandit, with my skin tinted. On watching the film, the fact that my horse had a European bit in its mouth was automatically a dead giveaway that I was not an African criminal, but details like that didn't seem to worry the production crew too much. The film was what it was - light, escapist entertainment.

While the film crew was on site, my bank account showed remarkable activity as much of the construction work and local business was done by me on their account. The buildings and stock-yards erected for use in the film, came in very handy later. The big problem was, however, that as soon as the money came into the account, it flowed out again. The production company funnelled funds to me to buy animals and build sets, but once I'd met all the outgoings my profit didn't equate with the money passing through the account, at least not as far as the tax man was concerned. I couldn't convince the tax people to look at my returns sensibly and, as a result, ended up with a ridiculous tax bill that I had no hope of ever paying.

IN AN EFFORT TO make ends meet I had to step up my professional hunting. I was what one might consider a second-class odd-job man in the profession, someone to call on when there was no-one else available, or when one of the big companies was short of a man. At odd times I was able to set up a safari for myself, contracting the outfitting to one of the companies

In early 1969 I had quite a good safari booked for the whole of the month of September. I'd made all the arrangements for hunting blocks and hotel accommodations, and sorted out the other details which I could handle myself. Then, in late August, my clients rang to tell me they had a problem and wouldn't be able to take up their booking.

Under normal circumstances and given sufficient time I could probably have found someone else to take up the bookings I'd made, which would have enabled me to return a large part of the clients' deposit, less some small expenses. However, as they had left it so late, I had to tell them that, as much as I hated to do so, I had to keep their deposit as there were staff to pay, deposits on bookings to be forfeited and other expenses. They were quite understanding, and rang off saying they hoped they would be able to set up another safari sometime in the future.

A week or so after the telephone call I was in Nairobi, tidying things up and staying with a friend, Bill, who was a well-connected local racing journalist.

'You know, I'd like to go over to Ireland to see the yearling sale,' I said, fancifully, over a drink. It was something I'd wanted to do for a long time but never expected to have the opportunity. 'Especially now I've got an idle month and a bit of unexpected spare cash.'

Without further ado, Bill picked up the telephone and called Liam Ward, the then champion jockey in Ireland, told him the story and asked if he could put me up during the sales if I could make the necessary travel arrangements. The next thing I knew I was on an aircraft flying to Dublin. Liam, whom I had met previously in Nairobi, greeted me at the airport and took me to his home where, I met his wife, Jackie, and was installed in the utmost comfort to attend the sales, which were due to begin the next day.

Having freshened up from the journey, I went downstairs to have tea and during the course of the conversation I casually asked Liam what he thought the chances might be of me getting some sort of a job in the racing industry in Ireland.

'I'm getting a bit tired of the uncertainty and increasing mismanagement in the hunting business in Kenya since independence,' I said to him. In addition, a co-operative of locals had combined together and applied for a loan to buy the farm I was renting; a deal that was due to be ratified shortly. On top of all that, Anne was approaching the age where I thought she would be better off being educated overseas. In short, I was ready to leave Kenya.

Liam and Jackie put their heads together and decided that the best person to approach for advice would be Captain Timmy Rodgers, the President of the TB (thoroughbred) Breeders' Association of Ireland and one of the biggest, most influential stud farmers in the country. Liam rang the Captain, who suggested we come over for a drink and to talk things over.

In the hour or so we were at Airlie, I was offered the most fabulous job imaginable - that of his assistant for the forthcoming covering season, providing I could get to Ireland by the middle of January. The rest of my time in Dublin passed in a whirl of going to the sales, meeting people and finding out what living in Ireland would be like. I had to consider not only my own point of view, which was very flexible as to where I lived, but also that of the rest of the family, whose whole life had been spent in the highlands of Central and East Africa, with all that entailed.

Back in Kenya, a change of some sort was inevitable, due to the tax bill hanging over my head. The family accepted the situation, so it was all hands and the cook flat out, disposing of our assets and preparing for the move, interspersed with going on safari. I had two short safaris, in October and November, then a long one for the whole of December. In addition, I had to sell off all the horses, find homes for the various wild animals that lived with us as pets, and wind up the farm.

All went as smoothly as anything done in such a rush could go. Best of all I even found a way to deal with my tax problem via a 2000-shilling payment to an accommodating Indian gentleman in the tax department. He took care of all the details and provided me with a tax clearance, allowing me to leave the country in a civilised manner, rather than doing a runner across the border into Somalia.

By the first of December I was in Arusha, as part of a three-hunter safari to take a very important French family out for the month. This would be my last safari in Africa. Initially, there was something of a hiccup. When I was running Ker & Downey, the matriarch of this same family had booked a safari with us which had turned out to be less than satisfactory. This had resulted in a somewhat caustic parting at settling time, with me, as the manager of the company, taking the brunt of her displeasure.

When being booked for the current safari, I hadn't bothered to ask who the clients were as one client was pretty much the same as another, and names did not become relevant until we met. It was only when I arrived at the hotel in Arusha, prior to going to the airport to meet them, that I found out who we were meeting.

On arrival at the airport to greet the clients, I made sure I remained out of sight during their arrival, busying myself with clearing their effects and getting everything into my car, while the other two hunters did the social honours and escorted the party to the hotel.

Meeting for drinks before going in to dinner, and not being able to put the moment of confrontation off any longer, I went over to the lady in question. She clearly recognised me, but was much too dignified to react.

'I accepted the safari without enquiring as to who the clients were,' I confessed to her, 'If you're unhappy with my presence I understand, and am quite prepared to make way for another hunter, if we can find one at such short notice.'

'Let us let bygones be bygones,' she said. 'And start afresh.' It was very gracious of her. She even went so far as to make arrangements with the senior man for me to be her hunter, in order that her future son-in-law could have his services.

The safari got off to a good start. The hunting was fair to good as we were finding some nice trophies and, most importantly, everyone appeared to be enjoying themselves and having a good time. Just before Christmas, my client and I had been gently tooling around looking for a good zebra, as she wanted a nice skin for a decorating job she had in mind. Not finding one that suited, and with the sun climbing high in the sky, we headed back to camp, arriving in time for a leisurely lunch and siesta. The afternoon would provide another opportunity.

The camp staff were just clearing away the coffee cups when Limongira, my gun-bearer, came to the front of the dining tent followed by a group of Masai moran, young warriors, all talking at once and gesticulating towards a big thornbush thicket about five hundred yards away.

It transpired that when the women from their manyatta had gone down to the waterhole at the edge of the thicket that morning to get water they had been chased away by a buffalo that had taken up residence there the previous night. The moran said they had tried all morning to dislodge it, with no success, and now wanted us to go and shoot it, so they could get some water.

At first I wasn't interested, but when they said it was a big old bull with a really good head, I thought: why not at least have a look? I knew that being on its own it was most likely an old animal or possibly one that had been previously wounded and neither followed up nor reported. This sometimes happens, even in the best of regulated circles, but whatever the reason, it was likely to be a fairly tricky situation and being so close to our camp and water supply, as well as that of the Masai, it had to be dealt with one way or another.

Although my client had told me earlier that she would like to get a buffalo with a good head, she now said she wasn't particularly keen, as she'd had a good lunch and was looking forward to a rest. Under pressure from me, however, she gave in and agreed to go along, if only to have a look.

We made our way to the thicket, where I got Limongira to organise the moran to go around the edges, throwing the odd stone into the bushes. I wanted them to establish exactly where the buffalo was, but not to make too much of a disturbance, as he might burst out and take off.

As the moran began throwing rocks, I heard a grunt and rustling in the bush, which gave me a pretty good idea of where he was. My plan was to creep in and try to get a look at his head, without alerting him. Before actually going into the thicket though, I arranged with my client to stand behind a large, gnarled old wild olive tree close by, which would provide some protection if the plan started to fall apart.

'Don't move a muscle until I see if we can do any business,' I told her.

I went to Limongira. 'Stay with her and make sure she comes to no harm if the worst happens,' I said to him.

I double checked my rifle. As this was my last safari and I was in the process of getting ready to leave for Ireland, I had sold all of my personal firearms the previous month. For this trip, I had hired a couple of rifles and a shotgun from the local gunsmiths in Nairobi. As there was no suitable double rifle available, I had opted for a Brno .458 magazine rifle as my heavy calibre weapon.

There is nothing wrong with the Czech-made Brno, but I had spent all my time in Africa using English, or to a lesser extent, American weapons, and had trained myself to flick the safety catch on to 'fire' as a reflex action when raising the weapon to my shoulder. Aware that the Brno safety catch operated in the opposite direction to that of the English and American weapons and bearing this in mind, when I put one up the spout, I carefully pulled the safety back to 'fire', before creeping into the thicket. I didn't want to be caught fiddling about, if I needed to react quickly.

It was quite dark, with sunlight filtering in here and there, mottling the surroundings and considerably reducing visibility. The underbrush was also very dry and brittle so I moved slowly, testing each step carefully before putting any weight down, at the same time keeping a very sharp look out to my front and each side.

Eventually, I got to a position where, peering through the tangle of bush, I just could see the rough outline of the buffalo. It was about thirty yards ahead, through what appeared to be an old game trail. I flattened myself against another substantial wild olive tree and tried to get a look at the animal's head, which was stuck into, or behind, a thick clump of underbrush. All I could see was the body, angling away into the gloom; the only way to get a better look was to move out into the game track, which was more like a tunnel running through the thicket.

With the utmost caution, I started to ease myself away from my friendly tree and slowly made for the tunnel. As soon as I was clear of the tree, there was a snort. Dried twigs, branches, leaves and dust exploded in front of me as the buffalo, which had obviously been waiting for me, burst out from the bush and headed straight for me. I brought the rifle up and saw I had a dead bead on his forehead, just below the boss. I squeezed the trigger.

Nothing happened.

In bringing the rifle up, I had instinctively flicked the safety catch forward, as I would have done had I been using my own weapon. I had forgotten completely that I had already pulled the Brno safety catch back, to 'fire' and by pushing it forward, had returned it to 'safety'!

The next thing, I was on my back with my legs wrapped round the buffalo's hairy neck. I hung on to one of his horns, in order to flatten myself against his head, but he was scrubbing me along the ground. In a reflex action, I tried to stick my thumb in his eye, to make him lift his head, although what good that would do I hadn't had time to work out.

Suddenly, there was a loud report and the buffalo collapsed on top of me. He was still very much alive and throwing his head about wildly, but his forward movement had stopped. Somehow, I managed to disengage myself from him and dive behind a convenient tree. Another shot rang out and the buffalo collapsed completely.

From what my client told me later, as soon as Limongira had heard the snort and the crashing in the bush, he realised things were not going to plan, indicating to her to stay where she was. Limongira had ducked into the thicket to see what was happening, arriving just in time to see me being bulldozed along the ground and in danger of being totally obliterated.

'I couldn't get a shot at anything vital on the buffalo, as your arms and legs were covering all the places I could aim for,' he told me, once our collective pulse rates had subsided. 'So, I shot him in the back to stop him going forward'

Limongira's first shot into the buffalo's back, just in front of its pelvis, had broken its spine immobilising it. Once he saw me disentangle myself, he finished it off with a brain shot.

After Limongira's second shot I'd heard the sound of more breaking bushes. Fortunately, it was not another buffalo but my client, who was as brave as she was gracious. She had left the safety of the olive tree and charged into the bush, rifle at the ready, prepared to take whatever action necessary. This was a response, I must say, that set her light years apart from quite a number of her male equivalents who, in similar circumstances in the past, had been quite happy to leave their hunters to sort things out themselves when things got unpleasant.

On checking myself over, once the dust settled, I counted myself pretty lucky to have escaped with only a broken arm. On the positive side, the whole exercise was not a total disaster. The head turned out to be a very creditable 44-inches, with a nice curve to the horn and full boss. My client was quite happy to take it on her license, as not only was it a very nice trophy, it also had an exciting story to go with it. The camp staff benefitted from plenty of good meat; the waterhole was freed up for communal use; and last but not least, I received a nice big fat cheque from the insurance company, when eventually declared fit by the medical pundits to hunt again.

All in all, this lucky escape was not a bad tail-ender to my career as a hunter.

Sometime before leaving Kenya for Ireland, I had been approached by a Belgian couple, who were interested in my horse, Kara Tepe.

They were refugees from the disturbances in the Congo, which were reaching a crescendo. They were obviously wealthy and both passionate horse people; she was a very competent dressage rider, and he was deep into racing, with a good, comprehensive knowledge of the studbook and of breeding theories. They had bought a property in Karen and were building stables, collecting horses and settling themselves down to become players in the Kenya equine world. Hearing that I had some horses that might be of interest, they came up to Nanyuki one weekend, for a visit to the Mount Kenya Safari Club, and to see what I had to offer.

Kara Tepe had by now proved himself in more ways than one. He had not only become tractable, he had also regained his fertility, and produced some very nice foals, one or two from registered mares, and their offspring had been duly registered with the Jockey Club. A couple were even being prepared for the race track. The old boy's pedigree and racing record interested the Belgians more than his history at stud in Kenya and they rather liked what they saw when introduced to the him in his paddock, where he was accompanied by his two hand maidens, the donkey and the zebra filly.

My farm was nothing like the one the Belgians were building, nor was it like any of the other better class Kenyan stud farms, but they were very complimentary about the condition and general status of my horses. They showed considerable interest in my approach to breaking in large numbers of horses at one time, and seemed to enjoy a couple of the little party tricks I liked to show off to interested visitors. These included letting a little grey Arab gelding, standing only about 14.2 hands high, jump over a 22-foot spread of cavalettis (small jumps) in the loose school. Another involved a chestnut polo pony performing a range of complicated manoeuvres on command, while working loose in the round yard.

On hearing I was selling-up to move to Ireland, they very generously took all my registered stock, including Kara Tepe and his friend Rominella the donkey. Sadly, the deal couldn't include the little zebra filly, as the wildlife people wouldn't permit it. She went to the National Parks' orphanage on the outskirts of the city.

The Belgian couple's property in Karen duly became a registered stud farm, with old Kara Tepe standing as the resident stallion. Rominella was retained as his faithful companion and I am sure the pair of them lived out the rest of their days in far greater luxury than I could ever have given them.

Honouring my deal with Captain Rodgers I duly turned up for work early in January, a couple of weeks before the start of the covering season. Although still bruised and a trifle bent, I was fit enough to do what was required, and went to work.

In March I received a totally unexpected invitation to meet the Countess Batthyány at one of the better class hotels in Dublin. It turned out she was a great friend of my last hunting client, who mentioned that I, her hunter, had just moved to Ireland to work for Captain Rodgers.

It transpired that the countess, who owned a very nice little stud in County Wicklow, was having trouble with her current manager and was looking for a replacement. She decided I would be a good candidate and asked if I was interested? Naturally, I was, as it sounded a super job, but before making any commitment, I had to explain the deal to Captain Rodgers. The countess agreed that I should discuss her offer with him and let her know as soon as I could.

Captain Rodgers couldn't have been more accommodating. I found out from him that the countess was quite a large and influential international breeder, with studs in France, and Germany as well as Ireland and that she also owned a training stable of her own in France, from which she produced a number of extremely good and influential horses. For all that, she kept a fairly low profile, not selling any of her horses at public auction or looking for publicity in any way. With an eye to the main chance, and ever the businessman, the Captain suggested I stay with him until the end of the covering season, before moving down to Bally Keane, the Countess's stud.

On arrival, I found that as the countess was precluded from staying in Ireland for any length of time, due to unreasonable tax impositions, she could to do little to keep a tight control on the stud. She had relied primarily on the probity of her manager, combined with a little superficial oversight by her lawyer and a high official of the bank that handled her affairs in the country.

In discussing the management of the farm, the countess told me that I should run it as though I owned it. She also told me she had a very competent, trusted administrator at her home in Lugano who was always available if I had any problems; to this end she installed the latest communicating system at that time, a teletype machine to connect me with her office and with her stud in Germany.

I worked very harmoniously for the countess for four years, but when she passed the farm on to her brother, things changed. The brother wasn't interested in the stud and gave it to his wife as a present; she in turn appointed a board of directors to supervise the whole operation as neither she nor her husband were particularly interested in it. I did not get on with the chairman of the board. As much as I had enjoyed the job, the quality of the replacement horses once the countess had moved her stock out, left a lot to be desired.

On the agricultural side the farm was developing into quite a successful little enterprise, showing a tidy annual profit, something I was quite proud of. Before I took the place over it had more or less been left to return to a bracken covered wilderness, apart from the few paddocks set aside for the stud stock.

It didn't take me long to realise I was now a square peg in a very round hole. At an acrimonious board meeting, I was asked by the chairman why I hadn't sought permission before selling some of the surplus heifers. I had sold them because this was a practice that had been in place, and was integral in the management plan since I had started upgrading the little beef herd. By that time, however, I'd had enough; I played right into the chairman's hands by telling him where to put the job.

22

As luck would have it, just before I was due to leave the stud I had a telephone call from an old Kenyan buddy, Cameron Chisholm, now a consultant/contractor to the World Bank and living in Washington.

Cameron offered me a job in a World Bank-funded operation that he was putting together in the Cameroons. The job entailed setting up a cattle breeding operation from scratch in the old German/British West Cameroons. If I was interested, he wanted me to start as soon as possible.

The offer couldn't have been more timely. I was able to arrange for my family to move to South Africa, where they would be more at home than if they stayed in Ireland, get all my own affairs in order and set off for the Cameroons within a month of leaving Bally Keane.

I had come across Cameron shortly after he arrived in Kenya, as a horseman and aspiring polo player. He was a real dinky-di Aussie who had spent some years as a jackeroo in the Territory and western Queensland. He was a typical chancer, always full of big ideas and grand plans. The last time I saw him, he was working on plans to open a car assembly business in Mozambique. It appeared he had now moved up a gear and started a business consultancy firm in America.

His company had been engaged by the World Bank to do a feasibility study on setting up an integrated - from paddock to plate - beef cattle industry in Francophone West Africa and he was looking for people to implement his findings, which had been favourably received and approved by the Bank.

Cameron explained that the job involved setting up one of two ranches the bank wanted to see established, and then providing the initial throughput of stock to the abattoirs. He further explained that there was absolutely nothing on site, which meant that there would be no accommodation for wives and families, at least for a couple of years and that initially it could even mean living in local huts or tents. To overcome such problems the conditions of service were fair to good and quite liberal.

Being to all intents and purposes out of work, I agreed to take on the job. As so often happens, a couple of weeks later the phone rang again. It was Liam Ward and he had heard that I had resigned my job at Bally Keane. He wondered if I would be interested in a job as stud manager for the owners of the Waterford Crystal business as well as the Irish Lottery. They were putting together a new stud and were looking for someone to run it. He knew them well and was sure he could fix it up for them to take me on. Again, it was a case of a bird in the hand being worth two in the bush - I had already agreed to the World Bank job while Liam had not even spoken to the Waterford Crystal people.

'I'm sorry, I can't take it Liam,' I said to him. 'I've committed myself to go to the Cameroons.'

'Don't be a bloody fool,' he said, 'tell those people in the Cameroons to get stuffed.'

However, I'd made up my mind and, besides, Lorna was really looking forward to going back to South Africa, where she still had family. I don't think she was ever particularly impressed with either Ireland or its weather – Africa was much more to her liking.

Liam was quite upset, but having committed to Cameron I felt I had to stick with him. The next thing I knew, I was on a plane to Yaounde and Lorna was Africa-bound. Shortly after my arrival, at a meeting in the agriculture department, one of the locals we would be working with rolled out a 1:250,000 map of the western part of the country, the old German/ British colony. He stuck his thumb on a patch of nothingness, indicating that would be the area of my operations. I was then issued with a brand-new Land Rover and was left to get on with the job.

'I'm not having that,' I said, pointing to the Land Rover.

'That's what you're going to get, sorry,' an official told me.

I drove from Yaounde to Nkambe, where I settled myself in the local rest house before going to meet the District Officer in charge of the area. During our introductory conversation I asked the DO if he could find me a cook and a servant. He agreed to try and do so, but wasn't very confident, as those occupations had more or less died out since Independence. In the meantime, I made preparations for my trek into the wilds.

SOME 25 KILOMETRES off the road linking Nkambe to Wum, a vague old dirt vehicle track disappeared north into the countryside, ultimately finishing up in a sad little village called Dumbo.

This was the jumping off point from 'civilisation' to the wilderness that I was to turn into a ranch. It was patently obvious that I was not going to get much of a 'feel' for the ground by bush bashing in what purportedly was uninhabited country. The only way to survey the land quickly was by air.

The nearest township of any relevance was Bamenda, but even there, the facilities were basic in the extreme - a couple of banks, a few Lebanese shops and an hotel that was there in name only. It was not a base from which one could get much done - that had to be Douala, on the coast, another 12 to 14 hours' drive south. However, there was an American mission station on the outskirts of the town which had a STOL (short take-off and landing) aircraft, complete with maintenance and service facilities which they would hire out if the cause was good. They agreed to fly me around for a very reasonable fee.

As we surveyed this supposedly empty corner of the province from the air, I was not a little surprised to see, below, a bloody great town. On arrival back at Bamenda I contacted the bureaucrats in the provincial head office who assured me no one was living in the area. I assured them that was not the case - there was a town, not just a village in there, and it was slap in the centre of where I was supposed to start setting up the ranch.

I was again assured that no village or town existed by which time I was beginning to get a bit excited, so I asked the man I was talking to if he had ever been to the area, or even knew of anyone who had.

'No,' he said.

'Well, I've just flown over the area and there bloody well is a town there.'

It didn't take a great deal of effort to work out that I had just discovered what appeared to be a den of iniquity, a hot bed of criminals from Nigeria and Ghana, who had established a discreet little spot from which they were rustling cattle from the nearby highlands. Amongst other illegal activities, the rustlers were slaughtering the beasts in the town and trucking the meat into Nigeria.

This was startling news to the authorities, although it beggars belief that the town could have sprung into being overnight. Some of the oh-so-innocent men in power must have been aware of it, and doubtless profiting from it into the bargain.

Now that I had blown the whistle, however, the army and the Gendarmerie swept in to chase them all away. I later heard that every man jack of them, about 1,000 illegals, were cleaned out.

On my first trip from Nkambe, where I had established my temporary headquarters, the gearstick of the Land Rover snapped off in my hand while I was changing gears. I managed to get it welded back into place by a man who had a welding machine by the side of the road, and limped on to Yaounde.

I handed the Land Rover's keys to my boss. 'I'm on the first plane home unless you get me something decent to drive.'

He agreed and this time I made sure I got a Land Cruiser. I never looked back. Having driven Land Rovers for too many years to be fooled by their hype, I was not interested in renewing my acquaintance with them - especially under the conditions we were going to be working. My antipathy towards Land Rovers was such that I actually bought the very first Land Cruiser to arrive in Nairobi, and subsequently have never regretted making the change.

The Cameroons gives the impression of being God's own country. My first thought was that it could be the bread basket of the world. If one threw some seeds in the soil it might be wise to take a step back, as the resulting plants grew so swiftly and prolifically. I often wondered why the potential had never been fully exploited.

The people were extremely nice. In the western part of the country, they had been ruled by the Germans and subsequently by the British, but had later voted in a referendum to join with French Cameroun, something I believe many came to regret. The authorities were trying to impose French as the national language, but many of the people in the old protectorate I met spoke very good English and were reluctant to change.

Another thing I noticed was that the Roman Catholic Church had a good grip on the country; the road from Nkambe to Bamenda and onto Douala was lined, virtually wall to wall, with catholic schools and churches. However, the area around Dumbu and onto Wum, having been a big German enclave, still held on to some Protestant ways.

Just getting anywhere was a major mission. Douala, on the coast, was the nearest big town and the only source of any building supplies, equipment or goods other than raw timber. The trip to Douala, however, entailed a 17-hour drive each way, mostly on pretty basic roads.

To get to my proposed ranch, I had to cross some 17 little streams and creeks, and a major river – The Alu. There was no accommodation of any sort available in the village of Dumbu, so I made do with an old stone hut, built by the British Colonial Public Works Department around the time the road from Nkambe to Wum was being constructed, in the 1920s. The hut was derelict, just the bare shell remaining as it had not been used for many years.

As a priority, I patched the hut up sufficiently to move in. I built an office and a workshop-cum-maintenance area on the cleared land surrounding it. There were no amenities whatsoever other than a small lean-to at the back that served as a kitchen and a concrete bath built onto one of the walls. All the water had to be fetched by hand from the stream nearby and stored in a couple of 44-gallon drums. Any light at night was from a kerosene lamp and the same fuel was used to power my Silent Knight second-hand refrigerator.

My accommodation was about 12 miles from the centre of the ranch property and to even get onto the eastern boundary I needed to cross the Alu River. In the dry season it ran at about 70 to 90 centimetres deep, but during the rainy season, I learned, the Alu could flow at a depth of 30 feet (10 metres) for weeks on end.

Not being prepared to strand my crew or myself for anything up to five months a year, I needed a bridge, urgently. I approached the Public Works Department, who took forever to eventually tell me that it would take up to three years for them to build a bridge, should they decide to take the project on. By that time my contract would be just about up!

Instead of wasting my time with the bureaucrats I found a young Swiss national working in the province as a water consultant for some aid project. He was a qualified road engineer and interested in the project from the design point of view. The next hurdle was to find someone with the necessary skills and experience to supervise the building of a bridge.

From the local DO I discovered there was an old West Indian man named Vigo living in the province, who had been brought into the country by the old British PWD as road construction foreman. Retired a long time, he lived with his local wife in a small village not far from Bamenda. I went to see him and managed to get him to agree to take on the job, provided I could supply him with a young assistant to do the necessary 'bossing up' with the labour.

Having lined up the two major players for my bridge, I set about getting labour. It was a lot easier than I expected. Once the call went out, they came in from all over the country. Within a week I had about 40 stonemasons and about 100 labourers. During the next six months, under the direction of old Vigo, and a very sensible bilingual young man whom I made his assistant, the bridge began to take shape.

There were three 12-metre pylons and an abutment at each end, all made out of shaped local stone. The timber work was done on site with wood from the German sawmill in Wum, and the steel work was prefabricated in Douala before being brought up in sections for assembly on site. Other than the stone and timber, everything else, including food for the labour, had to be brought up from Douala. A MAN four-wheel drive truck I had bought at the beginning of the project did sterling service, making the trip weekly for the whole six months with barely a hitch.

As part of my work developing the ranch, I had felt it necessary to identify the boundaries, so I walked all over the area with a compass identifying various crucial points by building little cairns of stones. The caldera was about 20 miles across and covered a total of roughly 300 square miles. When stocked to capacity the ranch would occupy about a third of the area.

Down in the bottom of the crater it was hot and steamy, but higher up, on the rim, it was much milder and more pleasant. The caldera looked like a huge park, with open grassland interspersed with streams draining towards the Alu River. Many of the waterways were lined by beautiful stands of hardwood trees; scattered throughout the basin, avocado trees of various quality grew like weeds. The birdlife was fantastic, encompassing a variety that would keep a serious ornithologist occupied for a lifetime, including, to my delight, hundreds of lovely blue touracos, a bird I had never seen before.

Right in the centre of the crater was a big rock that reminded me of Ayers Rock (now known as Uluru) in Australia. A stream bubbled up from under the rock and ran down a slope to a small hillock. It was such a picturesque spot that I decided it would be the ideal spot to build the ranch house.

Just below the crest of the hillock, I dug out a reservoir and diverted the stream to flow into it. The overflow re-joined the stream below the site for the house, which I levelled out with the little bulldozer and grader I had on site for clearing and road making. I planned the house's elevation to make maximum use of the fantastic views available, as I felt anyone living there would need something to compensate for the isolation.

The ranch took shape. It was to be open-range ranching for many years to come, as we had neither the budget, nor the time for any fencing to be put into place. The herds would be made up of about 110 animals each, and were looked after by two herdsmen to a herd. We built a cattle dip; made working yards; constructed a landing strip for light aircraft, complete with wind sock; laid out a useable road from Dumbo to the proposed headquarters site; and installed a number of culverts over the many streams.

Work progressed on the bridge over the Alu River. The steel components were delivered sequentially, so that the first to arrive would eventually fit into position on the far (west) side of the river. Each section was off-loaded from the truck by hand, laid on rollers on the ground, then bolted and welded to the section ahead. Using the winch on my Land Cruiser, parked on the western bank of the river, the bolted and welded sections were inched onto and over the pylons until eventually the river was spanned. After that we bolted the timber tracks that would fit the bridge's road surface into place.

From start to finish it took our rag-tag, improvised team just over six months to do what the PWD engineers had estimated would take them up to three years. The bridge over the Alu River was a major undertaking, but we managed to complete it in time to allow for all the other work to proceed at a rate that would have sufficient infrastructure in place when my contract was up.

. . .

NEARLY FOUR YEARS after taking up my appointment, I signed off the acceptance for the completion of the manager's house, as the last item in the developmental phase for the ranch. The property was now ready to function as a fully operational cattle ranch.

A week or so after winding up and finalising all the building and construction work, I was packing up everything in my little temporary accommodation on the outskirts of Dumbo prior to taking my leave.

Another wet season was building up. It was a good time for me to take a break - my contract would be up about the time I was due to return from leave. If my contract was not extended, then at least everything was new and pristine for whomsoever was appointed to take my place and my gear, such as it was, was all packed up, ready for overseas transport.

Overnight, there was a monumental storm. The thunder crashed like artillery; lightning lit up the sky and it seemed the whole world was shaking and lit-up by natural electricity. The storm raged on into the morning and there was nothing one could do but wait it out.

When it finally blew itself out and the rain stopped, I thought I had better go out and see how all my buildings and other infrastructure had fared. The road into the ranch was no worse than I anticipated and the administrative buildings and the staff accommodation looked as though they had survived without too much damage.

However, the manager's house, my pride and joy, was another matter altogether. It looked as if it had been hit by a bomb. It seemed the water reservoir at the top of the little hillock had taken a direct hit from a lightning bolt, with the resulting energy running down the inlet pipe into the house and into the lavatory. The throne had been blown into a million pieces. The toilet seat itself had flown out of the bathroom into the body of the house, while the whole building appeared to have been lifted off its slab and shifted six inches sideways. It was a complete write-off and would need to be totally rebuilt.

The storms I experienced on that ranch were amongst the worst I had ever seen, even though I made sure to take my leave during the wet season as nothing much could be done anyway. The weather events I did see were bad enough to make one respect their violence. Over my time there, if I remember correctly, we lost at least three herdsmen, all of whom were struck by lightning when out looking after their cattle. I am not sure the originators of the scheme had taken on board these risks when putting their plans together.

Towards the latter part of my tenure, the odd 'big man' and government fat cat would call in to inspect the project, but few of them bothered to venture across my new bridge into the heart of the operation. The people I worked with on the site were good, but trying to get those in positions of authority to do things was difficult. I thrashed about and made a nuisance of myself and although I enjoyed the work, I was not popular with the people who were supposed to be supporting me.

Some of the French nationals working behind the scenes were more difficult to deal with than their local counterparts, and they were bad enough. For example, once I started to acquire some cattle I obviously needed veterinary equipment and dips to be available when needed. From the initial, reasonably timed approach, it took some 15 stormy months of effort before the first consignment of the supplies I needed arrived.

On paper, Cameron's plan covered the whole of Francophone West Africa, however, as with so many schemes, the theory and concept did not equate with reality. In this case I subsequently discovered that the Dumbo Ranch, as my little effort was called, was the only one in the whole scheme that ever managed to get any infrastructure in place or cattle on site. If my experience with the planning, management and the local support was anything to go by, that was no surprise.

One of the other difficulties that I had to overcome during my time developing the ranch was related to the fact that, in the 1970s, South Africa was a pariah state, cut off from much of the world because of its apartheid policy.

Although I was a resident in Ireland at the time of engagement, I travelled on an Australian passport. Many countries, including the

Cameroons, had banned their people from visiting South Africa and it would not do for me to be seen to be coming and going from the bastion of apartheid. Lorna, however, was a South African citizen and now living there.

As with most of these problems, I found a way around them. By booking a flight to Australia via Johannesburg, I was able to disembark on arrival at Jan Smuts (as South Africa's largest airport was then known) and, with the co-operation of the South African Immigration service, avoid getting my passport stamped. A loose-leaf insertion, to be surrendered on departure, was placed in my passport allowing me to enter and leave the country with no lasting record that I had done so. I used the same gambit for all my leaves, with, as far as I know, no one in the Cameroons ever questioning it or apparently noticing there were no Australian arrival or departure stamps in my passport.

While on leave I was informed by letter that I would not be offered another contract; the reason given was that with everything necessary in place, the management and running of the ranch could be undertaken by the locals.

About a year after I finished, I received a letter from a man I had been grooming to take over the ranch. He told me he had not been considered for the job, even though he had worked with me from the very beginning and knew more about the project than anyone else in the country. His problem was that unlike three other Cameroonian men who had been sent to me for on the job training in my final year, he did not have the benefit of a three-year college degree in America, and a degree in land management and animal husbandry. Those chosen three, together with all their documented qualifications, had hot-footed it back to where they'd come from early on in their stay at the ranch, when I had told them that their first job would be to get themselves a few carriers and walk around the boundary of the property, as I had done in the beginning, to familiarise themselves with the place.

The man concluded his letter by telling me that, apart from the bridge over the Alu River, all the infrastructure and the cattle, had disappeared off the property which was, at the time of his writing, totally abandoned.

IN 1977 I found work in Botswana, as the General Manager for Tati Company, a big player in the north eastern section of the country. Tati owned large amounts of real estate in Francistown, together with five cattle ranches covering some 500,000 hectares along the border with Rhodesia (now Zimbabwe).

I had to familiarise myself with the responsibilities of the job, which included real estate development and urban land management; the company was deeply committed to the development and expansion of Francistown and was selling off commercial and domestic sections of land as part of their program.

I can't say I was particularly interested in that part of my duties, nor the running of their commercial businesses, including the largest African beer brewery in the country, which they owned and operated in Francistown. The various concerns were all being run by competent managers and, from my point of view, didn't need my supervision or interference.

The ranches, on the other hand, were a disaster. Four had managers on them and I made my headquarters on the fifth, Lady Mary, the ranch nearest to Francistown. It didn't take me very long to see that there was no organisation, and no plan. The four managers, as far as I could see, did nothing constructive from one month's end to the next, and nor did they show any interest when I tried to get them onto a more productive plane.

Inevitably, they and I parted company, with me staying. By rearranging the mating program; identifying the ranches as breeding, fattening and finishing units; and culling a lot of the old bulls and replacing them with breeds better suited to the conditions, I was able to run all five ranches with the aid of one other man. If nothing else, I saved cost of the wages of three managers.

During my time in Francistown, Lorna remained in South Africa, while Anne progressed from high school to university. Two or three times a year, I would drive the whole 1300 kilometres from Francistown to Pietermaritzburg in a day, stay a few nights and do the return journey in the same time. I was more than happy with this arrangement, as it meant Anne could live at home with her mother and continue to indulge and develop her rising equestrian skills

After about five years I left the Tati Company, if not improved on the commercial side, at least no worse than when I took over. On the ranching side I certainly left them with an effective and workable arrangement, which allowed for a much more efficient system of sending their off-take to the meat works in Lobatse.

I was enticed away by the offer of a major part in a proposed tourist venture covering large tracts of country on the eastern Botswana/South African border, being set up by a large farmer and cattle dealer in Gaborone named Dereck. The venture capital for the project came from some entrepreneurs in America.

In some ways, I was foolish to make a move without making sure everything was ready to go, but in others it was actually a godsend. After a couple of months doing nothing, waiting for the money to come from America, Dereck asked me if I knew anything about feeding cattle as his buying organisation bought cattle all over the country, many of which were too young or too low in condition to go straight to the meat works.

These cattle were spread out over all his ranch properties and tied up a huge amount of capital while they grew out to slaughter size. He quite rightly felt that if he could set up a feedlot, he could move them on in months instead of years, thereby freeing his capital for other ventures.

In my agricultural training I had tended to specialise in feeding, albeit in horses rather than cattle, but the principle was pretty much the same. Between us we set up a small trial operation to feed 500 head. It was very much a case of the blind leading the blind, but with the help of the University of Pretoria and one or two others well informed in the basics, we managed to send our first draft off in 120 days. They may not all have made triple A grades, but they were certainly better than most he sent off.

From that humble beginning, in three years we were moving between 15,000 and 20,000 head a year, mostly young animals, which we finished in about 90 days. It was a gold mine for Dereck as he negotiated most of our purchases on 90 days credit and also bought the main ingredient of our home-made ration, 'hominy chop' from the local maize mill in Lobatse very cheaply as they were not allowed to market it in South Africa for political reasons.

That, too, was on 90 days, so with careful handling we could process and feed a whole yard full of cattle from arrival to despatch without spending a penny. The meat works cheques after slaughter handsomely took care of all the outgoings, and left him with a tidy profit, as most of those we sent out were graded double or triple As, the top of the range.

A disagreement over how much I should earn, by way of a bonus, led me to receiving a note from his accountant saying my services were no longer required. It was quite a blow, but as one door closed another opened. The local manager of the Commonwealth Development Corporation ranch in Botswana, a 365,000-hectare property on the Molopo River in the south east of the country, offered me a job as his assistant.

My duties were mainly to sort out a breeding system for their herds of cattle as the previous manager had brought in over the years a conglomeration of breeding stock covering some 13 different breeds. Many of these were totally unsuited for the conditions found on the eastern limits of the Kalahari Desert. My remit was to weed out anything I thought unsuitable. It was also suggested that I try and do something about the virtually feral cattle that existed in a number of the paddocks, especially those in the further reaches of the property, as they made clean mustering well-nigh impossible.

These animals were impossible to yard, only coming in to drink water every second or third night, and so wary that even the slightest sound, or scent near the yard sent them back into the bush. There they would wait another two or three nights before venturing in again for a drink.

After trying out a number of ineffective ways to deal with them I came up with a plan which entailed digging a hole just outside the yard rails which surrounded the watering points, deep enough for me to sit in comfortably, while I waited for anything to come in. In the cool of the night my scent did not rise beyond the hole and I made sure I was suitably muffled up so as not to make any noise.

On a moonlit night I could clearly identify the feral animals and once a few of them were in the yard drinking I could open up, sometimes killing as many as three before they managed to escape. It was lonely, miserable work but it had to be done. By the time I left the property I had killed about 350.

THE CDC, being a huge international operation, had a one-size-fits-all mentality. Their cut-off date for employment was the age of 65, irrespective of whether the employment was local, temporary or international. So, after a few short years and a wonderful time, I was given my marching orders and sent back to the drawing board, with ever-dwindling options.

Once more unemployed, or retired as it was designated, Lorna and I moved to Howick in the Natal Midlands of South Africa. After a month of not knowing what to do and going out of my mind with boredom, fortune once again shone its sympathetic light on me.

Between us, we had decided I wasn't going to have anything more to do with horses. With no bright ideas in mind it looked as though we were just going to have to wait together until we both fell off the twig, either singularly or together. It was not much of a future to look forward to.

Amongst our goods and chattels, I had truckloads of horse gear that I'd made or bought over the years. It was too good to just throw away so I advertised it for sale in the local paper. I had one response, a young fellow, mad keen on horses, but like so many young footloose people, he had no money. That didn't stop him talking and from his conversation I gathered he was also very keen to start playing polo. However, without any funds the only way he could possibly get a start was to work in the stables of someone wealthy enough to play and maintain a fairly large string of ponies.

To that end, he had recently talked to a large sugar farmer from the coastal area just north of Durban, who had a small farm in the Midlands, not far away from where I was living. The farmer was looking for someone to take over the property as a spelling farm for his and his two sons' ponies. All three of them played fairly high goal polo; the two sons being both on the selection roster for the national Springbok polo team.

To me, it appeared the ideal opportunity for the young man I was talking to, to get a foot into the game but he seemed to think the job somewhat beneath his dignity and wasn't interested. From my point of view, it looked like something I could do, so I asked him if he would intercede on my behalf. He did and I was asked to go up to the farm for an interview.

The farmer's name was Murray Armstrong and he offered me the job. For the next 13 years, I had the pleasure of running the farm, and taking care of the resting ponies. While these were not the most adventurous years of my life, without any doubt they were amongst the most pleasant.

As the time passed my relationship with the family reached a level which I would grace with the term friendship, always bearing in mind I was an employee. As a measure of our association, whenever the family came up to stay at the farm Murray and his charming wife and I would go out to dinner at one of the very good restaurants dotted around the midlands. We took turns at meeting the cost - it was the only way I could show my appreciation for their kindness, and I believed they enjoyed our evenings out.

The name of the farm was Kwa Heri - Kiswahili for good bye. It was appropriate, as I knew it would almost certainly be my last job. Having settled into a workable routine at the farm, we gradually drifted into a system in which I bought possible recruits for their string of ponies from off the race tracks around Pietermaritzburg and Durban. On their arrival at the farm, I would try the horses out; if they showed any promise we started their training for polo. If they didn't, we'd sell them on as possible show jumpers, eventers or just hacks. At any one time we could have up to 70 horses being worked or spelled, enough to keep me, and the little team of grooms we employed, fully occupied.

At the beginning of my association with the Armstrong family Murray offered me a rent-free house on Kwa Heri, but by then we had more or less settled into our little house in Howick which was about 17 kilometres from the farm. I felt we'd had enough of living in isolated places and that Lorna was entitled to some comfort and civilised living after the peripatetic life she had put up with over the past 40 years or more, so I declined the offer.

I was quite happy to carry the cost of my commute, just as I did the use of my vehicle for the farm's work, in return for the pleasure of seeing Lorna settled and from having lucked onto such an interesting and delightful job.

LORNA SUCCUMBED to the ravages of cancer in 1995. I am sure it was a great relief to her, as it is a condition that even the strongest cannot take lightly.

She left a hole that could not be filled. She was certainly the only person I ever met who could possibly have put up with me and my irresponsible, selfish ways for so long. One doesn't want to have the word sentimental applied to oneself, but her passing did leave a huge void.

At the tender age of 83 I was mustering in a hillside paddock in the midst of a violent rainstorm, when my horse slipped and fell heavily. In the process, I broke my leg and tore some ligaments. It took quite a while to mend and was more uncomfortable than I remembered was the case with other breakages in the past. That was it, I thought, I'd had enough. I decided I was too old to be fooling around with bloody horses any more, even though it meant effectively ending my working life. The Armstrong family were doubtlessly very relieved at my decision as, in retrospect, I am sure I had outlived my usefulness to them by some years, but they were much too generous to do anything about it.

Living on my own in Howick with nothing to do but feel sorry for myself and watch my friends move on one by one, was not something I looked forward to with any enthusiasm. Attending funerals has never been one of my favourite occupations, so once again, following a life time's habit, I began to get itchy feet.

Anne had moved to New Zealand with her two children and was living virtually on her own as her husband, Miles, was still heavily committed to his oil and gas exploration work in Botswana. She suggested it might be an idea for me to join her and her family there. If I chose to do so, she said their house was of such a construction that they could easily build an extension onto it to accommodate me. At the time she made the offer, however, she hadn't experienced the bureaucratic red tape intrinsic in any building project in New Zealand.

I left a hot, humid Durban in mid-September and landed two days later in Christchurch, again to a bright sunny day, but in the wake of a heavy snow fall. The glare was something I had never encountered before, even in the Arabian Sands, and it was bitterly, bitterly cold.

The extension to the house, on a small holding was nowhere near finished, but at least the bedroom was habitable, which provided me with somewhere to sleep while the rest of the building work was completed. For the next two years I gardened, ran a couple of steers and a few sheep on the block, and generally tried to keep myself useful and busy while the family went about their various occupations.

Miles continued on with his work in Botswana but things were not going well, no doubt aggravated by his feeling it necessary to frequently hop between the two countries, trying to keep all his balls in the air at one time. His eventual decision to move from Botswana to New Zealand did not work out either. He and Anne decided to go their separate ways. Anne moved from Leeston to Moeraki, while Miles went back to his spiritual home, England.

The children, now young adults, had left the nest and were testing the outside world for something to focus on. Then, quite out of the blue, first one, then the other homed in on something I too had been interested in for years – fish and aquaculture and its relevance to the future.

Both signed up to read marine biology at the university of Tauranga. Now one is working for the West Australian Fisheries Protection Service while the other is working on her Doctorate in the discipline, at her alma mater.

Patterns are hard to break. Once again, I had to move. I imagine that at my age it will be for the last time. I now live, very comfortably, in a converted three-bay hayshed shed with living quarters on one end and a fairly comprehensive workshop at the other, in the coastal village of Hampden. I have a little blue heeler for company and to remind me of the good old days.

Up until quite recently, I have been able to put to use some of the self-taught skills acquired over the years, but now even that is being denied me, as my eyes no longer function as well as they did in the days of yore and my co-ordination is getting a bit shaky.

The writing of this book has provided me with a good deal more than just a means of occupying my time. It has taken me back, to relive the good times I have enjoyed over nearly 100 years and that in itself can't be a bad thing.

I am often asked by people, including the co-author of this book: 'what is the secret to a good life?'

While I can't answer that, I can definitely say that nobody could have enjoyed a better life than I, because I have done exactly what I wanted, wherever I wanted, and had the support of a wonderful woman.

Thinking back to that young child emigrant headed for Australia in 1938, I can still recall the tales of the outback as told by a couple of the more mature passengers returning from a trip 'home' to the U.K.

I remember, again, the seasoned old man who appeared to have been all over the country and tried his hand at just about everything, giving me that piece of advice which I have never forgotten. Indeed, it has served me very well.

Don't worry about money, or what will happen next. Something will always turn up. I have followed his advice over the years and rarely found it wanting.

The End

ACKNOWLEDGEMENTS FROM TONY PARK

I often get emails from people asking me to write, or help write their biography or the memoir of a relative or loved one. Inevitably, these people have had interesting lives, but it's fair to say that when I received an email from Peter Whitehead outlining his life, I was amazed.

I agreed to work with Peter on his autobiography not only because the breadth of his experience in Africa interested in me, but also because, like me, he is an Australian military veteran. I found his wartime service fascinating, encompassing as it did both the army and air force during the Second World War.

Unlike most of the other biographies I have written with (equally) interesting people, Peter had written a good deal of his story already. In fact, most of *Bwana, There's a Body in the Bath!* is Peter's work, edited and tweaked by me. What isn't, is based on interviews I conducted with Peter at his home, in New Zealand, and was then worked on by both of us.

I would like to thank Peter for contacting me (and for reading my novels), and for being an absolute joy to work with.

I must also give special thanks to some important family members. Peter's daughter, Anne Harrison, played a vital role in keeping both Peter and me organised when it came to emailing files back and forth, and to helping Peter navigate the world of Microsoft Word. Thank you, as well, to Peter's step-daughter, Deanie, who helped fill in some more family detail. I'd also like to thank my mother, Kathy, who helped a great deal with the editing and proofreading on my side. I am also grateful to Anita Harrington for her lovely foreword and for proofreading the manuscript. Thanks, also, to Peter Toschi for proofreading this edition.

Thank you, as well, to Brett Martin for supplying the Tiger Moth picture, to Laurie Whiddon for his excellent map of Africa, and to Charley Swynnerton for her illustrations.

Lastly, but most importantly, if you've made it this far, thank you for coming along on the journey of Peter's adventurous life.

www.tonypark.net

www.ingramcontent.com/pod-product-compliance
Lightning Source LLC
Chambersburg PA
CBHW030109240426
43661CB00031B/1345/J